D0712107

Ageing, Popular Culture and Contemporary Feminism

Ageing, Popular Culture and Contemporary Feminism

Harleys and Hormones

Edited by

Imelda Whelehan
University of Tasmania, Australia

and

Joel Gwynne
National Institute of Education,
Nanyang Technological University, Singapore

palgrave
macmillan

First published 2014 by
PALGRAVE MACMILLAN

Palgrave Macmillan in the UK is an imprint of Macmillan Publishers Limited, registered in England, company number 785998, of Houndmills, Basingstoke, Hampshire RG21 6XS.

Palgrave Macmillan in the US is a division of St Martin's Press LLC, 175 Fifth Avenue, New York, NY 10010.

Palgrave Macmillan is the global academic imprint of the above companies and has companies and representatives throughout the world.

Palgrave® and Macmillan® are registered trademarks in the United States, the United Kingdom, Europe and other countries

ISBN: 978–1–137–37652–7

This book is printed on paper suitable for recycling and made from fully managed and sustained forest sources. Logging, pulping and manufacturing processes are expected to conform to the environmental regulations of the country of origin.

A catalogue record for this book is available from the British Library.

Library of Congress Cataloging-in-Publication Data

Ageing, popular culture and contemporary feminism : Harleys and hormones / edited by Imelda Whelehan, University of Tasmania, Australia ; Joel Gwynne, Nanyang Technological University, Singapore.
     pages cm
     ISBN 978-1-137-37652-7 (hardback)
     1. Mass media and older people. 2. Older people in popular culture.
3. Feminism. 4. Ageism. I. Whelehan, Imelda, 1960– editor. II. Gwynne, Joel, editor.

P94.5.A38A34 2014
305.26—dc23   2014028985

Contents

Notes on Contributors

Liz Byrski is Senior Lecturer in the School of Media, Culture and Creative Arts at Curtin University, and the co-ordinator of the Curtin Writing Network. She is the author of a dozen nonfiction books and eight novels. She is a former print and radio journalist and columnist with more than 30 years' experience in the British and Australian media. She was a broadcaster and executive producer with the Australian Broadcasting Corporation in Perth and has worked as an advisor to a minister in the WA Government.

Penelope Eate is Lecturer and Research Assistant in the Gender Studies and Social Analysis (formerly Gender, Work and Social Inquiry) and Asian Studies faculty at the University of Adelaide, South Australia. She lectures and tutors in courses on gender, race, postcolonial theory and media studies. She has research interests in the area of masculinities, particularly in film and hip hop. Journals in which her work has appeared include *Outskirts*, *The Journal of African American Studies* and *Social Identities: Journal for the Study of Race, Nation and Culture*.

Kirsty Fairclough-Isaacs is Lecturer in Media and Performance in the School of Arts and Media at the University of Salford, UK, where she teaches courses on feminism, celebrity, comedy and film studies. She is the co-editor of *The Music Documentary* and co-editor of *The Arena Concert: Music, Mediation and Mass Entertainment*. Journals in which her work has appeared include *Celebrity Studies* and *Genders*.

Sarah Falcus is Senior Lecturer in English Literature at the University of Huddersfield, UK. Her teaching specialisms are in contemporary women's writing and writing the twenty-first century. She is the author of *Michèle Roberts: Myths, Mothers and Memories*. Her work has appeared in a number of edited collections and in journals such as *Critique: Studies in Contemporary Fiction*, *Contemporary Women's Writing*, *Ageing and Society*, and *Journal of Gender Studies*.

Joel Gwynne is Assistant Professor of English at the National Institute of Education, Singapore, where he teaches courses on contemporary literature and feminism. He is the author of *Erotic Memoirs and Postfeminism: The Politics of Pleasure*, and co-editor of two books: *Sexuality and Contemporary Literature* and *Postfeminism and Contemporary*

Hollywood Cinema. His essays have appeared in the *Journal of Literary Studies, Women's Studies International Forum, Journal of Gender Studies,* the *Journal of Contemporary Asia, Feminist Theory* and *Film, Fashion and Consumption.*

Hannah Hamad is Lecturer in Film Studies at King's College London, where she teaches in the areas of film history, Hollywood cinema, and fathers in film, among others. She is the author of *Postfeminism and Paternity in Contemporary U.S. Film* (2014), as well as numerous chapters and articles on Hollywood stardom, contemporary Hollywood cinema, postfeminist media culture, contemporary celebrity culture and UK reality TV. Her work has appeared in the journals *Celebrity Studies* and *Continuum: Journal of Media and Cultural Studies* as well as in a range of edited collections.

Lynne Hibberd is Senior Lecturer in Media and Cultural Studies at Leeds Metropolitan University, UK, where she teaches courses on popular film and television. She has written chapters in *Reframing Disability? Media, (Dis)empowerment and Voice in the London Paralympics* (ed. Richard Scullion et al.) and *The Handbook of Gender, Sex, and Media* (ed. Karen Ross). Journals in which her work has appeared include *Feminist Media Studies* and *Critical Studies in Television.*

Georgina Ellen O'Brien Hill is Visiting Lecturer at the University of Chester, where she teaches courses on Victorian literature and literary theory. She has published chapters in *Women and the Victorian Occult* and *Acts of Memory: The Victorians and Beyond* and articles on the work of Florence Marryat, Charlotte M. Yonge and Charles Reade. Georgina has co-edited a special issue of *Women's Writing* journal on the work of Ella Hepworth Dixon and has reviewed for *Journal of Victorian Culture* and *Victorian Studies.*

Sharron Hinchliff is Lecturer at the School of Nursing and Midwifery, University of Sheffield, UK, where she teaches courses on sexuality and sexual health, critical health psychology, health promotion, and qualitative research methods. Sharron is a critical social/health psychologist. For over 15 years she has carried out research and published widely in the overlapping areas of sexuality, sexual health, gender and aging. Her work has been published in the *Journal of Women and Aging, Culture, Health and Sexuality,* the *Journal of Sex Research, Archives of Sexual Behavior* and the *Journal of Health Psychology.* She also writes about women's sexuality, ageing, and body image on her website (www.sharronhinchliff.com) where she aims to produce a counter-discourse by challenging negative representations of older women as unattractive and asexual.

Deborah Jermyn is Reader in Film and Television at the University of Roehampton where she teaches Hollywood cinemas, feminism, and visual aesthetics. She is the author of several books including *Sex and the City* (2009) and *Prime Suspect* (2010) and co-editor of several collections including *Falling in Love Again: Romantic Comedy in Contemporary Cinema* (2009). Much of her recent research has focussed on representations of ageing and older women in the media, including articles in *Critical Studies in Television, Celebrity Studies* and *CineAction*, and she is the editor of *Female Celebrity and Ageing: Back in the Spotlight* (2013). She is currently working on a book about the director Nancy Meyers.

Dominic Lennard is Associate Lecturer in the Centre for University Pathways and Partnerships at the University of Tasmania, Australia, where he teaches academic writing, research, and study skills. He is the author of *Bad Seeds and Holy Terrors: The Child Villains of Horror Film* (2014) as well as book chapters and articles on topics including film stars, Tim Burton, the 'bromance' phenomenon, Batman on film, and representations of children's culture in horror cinema.

Dee Michell is Senior Lecturer in Gender Studies & Social Analysis (GSSA) at the University of Adelaide, South Australia where she teaches courses on Social Research. Dee is the author of *Christian Science: Women, Healing & the Church* and *Ways of the Wicked Witch*, and co-editor of *Universities in Transition: Foregrounding Social Contexts of Knowledge in the First Year Experience, Recipes for Survival: Stories of Hope & Healing by Survivors of the State 'Care' System in Australia* and *Women Journeying with Spirit*. Journals in which Dee's work appears include *Feminist Theology, Ergo: The Journal of the Higher Education Research Group of Adelaide, Journal of Higher Education Policy and Management, Developing Practice, Australian Universities Review, Australian Social Work* and *Women-Church: An Australian Journal of Feminist Studies*.

Elizabeth Rawitsch received her PhD in Film, Television and Media Studies from the University of East Anglia. Her research on American popular culture and national identity has appeared in *The Journal of Popular Film and Television* and *In Media Res*. She is the author of *Frank Capra's Eastern Horizons: National Identity and the Cinema of International Relations, 1922–1961* (I.B. Tauris, forthcoming) and is preparing a book on cinematic representations of Territorial Hawaii.

Rebecca-Anne C. Do Rozario is Lecturer at Monash University. She teaches fairy tale, fantasy and children's literature and has published in a variety of journals, including *Children's Literature, Musicology Australia* and *Marvels and Tales,* and edited collections including *The Gothic in Children's Literature: Haunting the Border.*

Katsura Sako is Associate Professor of English at Keio University, Japan, where she teaches academic English. Her main field of research is in postwar and contemporary British fiction. She has published articles on the works of A.S. Byatt and Margaret Drabble, one of which is collected in *Realism's Others.*

Casey Tonkin is an undergraduate student in the Bachelor of Media program at the University of Adelaide, South Australia.

Deb Waterhouse-Watson is Lecturer in the School of Communication and Creative Arts at Deakin University, Australia, where she teaches Media Studies and Children's Literature. Her research centres on questions of representation and gender in popular media, including children's fantasy, social media and the news, and she is the author of *Athletes, Sexual Assault and 'Trials by Media': Narrative Immunity* (2013).

Imelda Whelehan is Professor of English and Gender Studies and Pro Vice Chancellor (Research Training) at the University of Tasmania, Australia. Her research focuses on feminist thought, popular fiction and film, and adaptation studies. Recent books include *Screen Adaptation* (with D. Cartmell, 2010), *The Cambridge Companion to Literature on Screen* (ed. with D. Cartmell, 2007) and *The Feminist Bestseller* (2005). She is also co-editor of the journal *Adaptation* and Associate Editor for *Contemporary Women's Writing.* She is currently writing on bras and postwar Hollywood.

Rosie White is Senior Lecturer in Contemporary Literature, Theory and Popular Culture at Northumbria University, UK, where she teaches courses on popular literature, media and gender. She is the author of *Violent Femmes: Women as Spies in Popular Culture* (2008); her forthcoming monograph will focus on women and television comedy. She contributed to *The Femme Fatale: Images, Histories, Contexts* (ed. Helen Hanson and Catherine O'Rawe, 2010), and *Femininities On Screen* (ed. Melanie Waters, 2010). Journals in which her work has appeared include *Feminist Media Studies, Women: A Cultural Review* and *Paradoxa.*

Introduction: Popular Culture's 'Silver Tsunami'

Imelda Whelehan and Joel Gwynne

For some years now, a 'silver tsunami' in western societies has been forecast and its impact on business, healthcare and public policy is constantly interpreted and reinterpreted. A casual Internet trawl through such trend-watching shows a preponderance of dire warnings about the 'burden' of an ageing population who present a horrifying drain on resources, as if they are in essence vampirically drawing the lifeblood from the young. The old, like the undead, it is implied, prey on youth as if they are a different species. The most predictable stereotypes about ageing are deployed to 'prove' this idea that the older section of the population is purely a drain: older employees are technologically inept, and their decline in efficiency needs to be managed as they are ushered out of the office. The inverse of this argument is that today's baby boomers are yesterday's revolutionaries and radicals; theirs is a history of social change, political protests and questioning tradition; they are used to making demands and having them met. The old and ageing saturate the news in some ways, but they remain largely out of focus in popular culture. Unattractive portraits of the old affect the middle aged so that fear of ageing and the search for means to manage it 'successfully' inform its depiction in popular discourse and advertising. Clearly representational tropes depicting the old lag behind the realities of long-lived baby boomers, and some prominent elders in popular entertainment are bucking trends and remaining very visible in their fields – one need only think of Meryl Streep in film or Betty White in both television and film. Such stars are box-office gold – broadly popular yet speaking to their own age demographic, recognising the emergent power of the grey economy to shape new trends in entertainment. The success of recent films such as *The Best Exotic Marigold Hotel* (2011), *Cloudburst* (2011), *Song for Marion* (2012), *Quartet* (2012) and *Le Week-End* (2013) confirm an appetite for more diverse and positive images of ageing. In the realms of popular fiction, definitive 'chick' Bridget Jones has grown up: with the publication of a third novel, *Bridget Jones: Mad about the Boy* (2013), she officially passed 50. Older men mourning their macho past are more visible in film, portrayed by the likes of Bruce Willis, Sylvester Stallone and (behind the scenes) Clint Eastwood.

While popular cultural productions seem to be relishing the opportunity to develop some convincing portrayals of middle aged to old age characters, there has been a muted response from feminist criticism. Since the late 1960s and the emergent women's movement, older women have earned patchy attention in feminist writings (aside from the important contributions of Margaret Morganroth Gullette and others in the field of age studies), and a core feature of postfeminism is its persistent obsession with youth. Given the powerful impact of feminist discourse over 40 years and more, it is extraordinary that feminism itself has not 'grown up' and been able to consider women's experiences through the entire life-course. Of course, a few influential writers such as Simone de Beauvoir, Betty Friedan, Germaine Greer and, very recently, Lynne Segal have written evocatively about ageing; but these perspectives have generated the least feminist discussion, as if this area has been more than dealt with in such writings and thus requires little further comment. In the domain of popular culture, one explanation is that the focus on gender and representation – which looks to deconstruct classic ascriptions of masculinity and femininity and explore how new inflections of gender are performed or how 'old' ones are rebooted and refreshed – loses some of its essential meaning for women post-child-birth and postmenopause. For if menarche and the capacity to reproduce in many ways define femininity and sexuality, what *do* women become after this phase of their lives? And if menopause is not only a physiological fact for women, but also a metaphorical life stage applied to men, what happens to our gender when we age? Postmenopause, a woman is practically a social pariah: with the loss of reproductive function her sexual attraction is also in question. Dr Robert A. Wilson, a hormone therapy pioneer during the 1960s, suggests that the 'unpalatable truth must be faced that all postmenopausal women are castrates.'[1] The reference to the female eunuch takes us back through the writings of Freud, De Beauvoir and to Germaine Greer and essentially to a the problem of the feminine generally, chiming with many women's unexpressed fears that this is among the chief losses associated with menopause. Menopause takes on various cultural references so that, as Jacquelyn Zita notes, it is 'a biological event occurring inside the body and coinciding with various meanings and interpretations originating outside the body.'[2] In this volume that fact of the ageing body and what that body comes to mean discursively is central to much of the analysis presented.

The idea for this collection sprang from a chance meeting between the editors at a conference. Although Imelda had contributed a chapter to a collection edited by Joel,[3] we had not met and we work in different continents. Prompted by our shared interests in feminism and postfeminism, we were keen to explore how narratives of ageing are embedded in popular culture, as well as how feminist critiques might respond to them. A call for papers for an edited collection followed; the response we had was huge and confirmed our sense that more scholarship was required in this field. Since we started this project, more publications have emerged,[4] ranging from scholarly collections to memoir to further cultural products foregrounding the ageing and the old. The subtitle – 'Harleys and Hormones' – is partly flippant, partly an acknowledgement of key stereotypes that accompany images of ageing men and women: men trying to recapture a lost and reckless youth through the hankering after high-performance vehicles; women at the mercy of bodies in transition. These quite different associations are just two that shape the meanings behind representations of ageing in popular culture and show the ways in which they become fixed and 'true' in the popular consciousness.

Portrayals of a woman having hot flushes or a middle-aged man astride his motorcycle often evoke laughter, and laughter is a good strategy to deflect fear or prevent further analysis of the preponderance of such representations. The twentieth century saw the highest leap in age expectancy ever, yet images of the ageing have not changed significantly. Grannies in cardigans and men shuffling about their gardens remain dominant depictions; and yet each successive older generation seems to be getting younger by comparison to the previous one. Over 50s stay healthier longer and have broader aspirations for their own futures; those who have money are able to demand to see themselves represented in the world and have contributed to the recognition of the problem of ageism in the workplace and wider society. Yet while ageing remains the 'problem' and younger generations are encouraged to share that view, we are confronted with a social reality disguised as some kind of perverse 'choice': the lack of acceptance of the fact that we all age forestalls fuller discussion of the problem of the ageing population, almost suggesting that the old arrive, surreptitiously, from some mysterious invisible place.

While the resources interrogating the meanings of old age often come from philosophy, social gerontology, feminism and literature, this volume focuses on popular culture in order to explore what images of the ageing and the old engage and entertain us and what truths and lies they may be perpetuating. In visual media, ageing takes centre stage when a lead character or popular actor's performance is being evaluated. In popular fiction and music, especially in the case of the latter, it is difficult to avoid the harsher glare of publicity as the creator's identity is used to sell products. In mass-market fiction, author photographs usually accompany a book jacket and website; in popular music – officially the preserve of the very young – elder states*men* in the field fare better than women. Popular culture is entirely responsive to the vicissitudes of trend and taste, and whilst often cast as conservative, reactive and shoring up 'traditional' norms and values, the very business of tapping into winning formulae and representational tropes exposes the cracks and fissures in our comfortable assurances that we know what ageing means and is. Public policy in several countries has dictated the rise of pensionable age due to the financial pressures of an ageing population; greater health and concern with wellbeing allows individuals to hope for better functioning as well as longer lives. Those older segments of the population cannot be obscured from popular view forever and more and more examples of this demographic are peeping through. There is no tidal wave of age-positive images tracking against the fact of this silver tsunami: and in this collection recurring themes include questions about whether they are exceptions that prove a rule rather than the tip of an emerging iceberg.

Postfeminist identity formation, as has often been asserted, relies on the realities of consumption from which to make rhetorical claims about choice and freedom, and many of the images of positive ageing are tied to products and services in a market where 'leisure' is increasingly costly. There might be much in postfeminist thinking to occupy the ageing western individual with its discursive emphasis on individual responsibility and empowerment suggesting the freedom to navigate identities and celebrate age with a new face. More recently, postfeminism's apolitical optimism is held up for critical scrutiny exposing how it is more convenient to forget or obscure the fact of ageing, unpalatable as the prospect remains to the young and the youthful. As Penelope Lively implies, death and the domain of the old become increasingly mystified in a culture that emphasises youth – and products and lifestyle choices – as 'age-defying'. It suggests that those who don't retain their youthful exterior have failed, rather than the more obvious interpretation that they have succeeded in evading the ageing industry itself. Whether negative and predictable or hopelessly positive, depictions of ageing manage to seem prescriptive: the no-longer-young (anyone over 45) dress too young or too old, have given up on a 'healthy' sex life or are still sexually active and acting disgracefully. The only measurement used to gauge ageing is lack of youth, and the only way to deal with it is to 'defy' it and remain provisionally, improbably young.

Much recent research on ageing and society focusses on women; this focus is true too of the less substantial body of work on ageing in culture. Since sexuality, desirability and reproductive age have tended to go hand and hand, women are on the 'scrap heap' once their hormonal levels start to shift. For men, generally, the time at which one is 'past it' may be more variable. Western culture has space for the 'distinguished' mature male, and respect for older men acknowledges the dynamics of patriarchal power. As the average lifespan of a western woman has all but doubled over the past century, menopause is less of an endpoint and more of a transitional stage; so while it may signal the end of women's reproductive life, the traditional association with the end of *productive* life is out of kilter with contemporary experience. The chapters in this collection reflect in new ways on the representation of ageing in popular culture. While each contribution adds its own critical slant to contemporary debates on gender and ageing, there is general agreement that popular culture operates in two seeming mutually exclusive ways – in fixing ageing as beyond the pale (particularly in visual cultures) and yet showing the exceptional ageing person as worthy of our audience engagement or sympathy. In common with other forms of stereotypes, those which depict the old have a certain fluidity and contain within them the germs of their own destruction, not least when seniors are seen behaving 'badly'. Central to this collection is a consciousness that there are less clear ascriptions applied to ageing masculinity than to femininity, but while journeys and forward momentum seem to characterise the life stories of midlife and older women, men are portrayed to a greater extent as always looking backward, capturing something which previously eluded them or they sense they have lost. Whether it is the physical prowess that has defined their superior masculinity or the late flowering of paternal instincts (perhaps only manifested in grandfatherhood), these symbols of strength (tempered often with a kind of wisdom or emotional intelligence) suggest the confusion around what contemporary masculinity means, laying claim to family-based, domesticised identities. The chapters that focus specifically on masculinity are fewer in number, and this imbalance is one that we hope future scholarship will address. Part of the problem, it seems, is that critical approaches to masculinity and representation are themselves in the minority in gender studies-related scholarship, and when it comes to the ageing male critical language remains at a developmental stage. Grey hairs, a widening girth and slower reflexes do not necessarily disqualify the older man from screen presence, and certainly characteristics such as wisdom, experience and understanding play to the strengths of the older man, as witnessed by Bruce Willis's performance in *A Good Day to Die Hard* (Moore, 2013).

Our contributors concentrate on the representations of ageing in fiction and memoir, TV and film, but not in the new media. This decision was not a policy decision but rather an interesting omission in the final responses to the call for papers. Again, future scholarship will undoubtedly address this area, fast developing for the older Internet and new media user, as older people continue to defy the assumptions around their technological incapacities. It would be fascinating to know whether the Internet and increased computer literacy among baby boomers, make them more 'connected' with the concerns of virtual life and if ageing is less relevant in this sphere.

Whether it is harder to age as a man or a woman may be impossible to answer, even though Marilyn Pearsall asserts, 'as hard as it is to become a woman, it is even harder to become an old woman in patriarchal society.'[5] Penelope Lively, writing her memoir at 80, asserts that 'old age is forever stereotyped.'[6] Other writers on ageing, like Germaine Greer and Betty Friedan, emphasise the need to find new models of being and the strength to resist those which constrain, being prepared to 'risk a new stage in life, where there are no prescribed role models to follow, no guideposts, no rigid rules or visible rewards, to step out into the true existential unknown of these new years of life now open to us, and to find our own terms of living it.'[7]

Liz Byrski, author of seven bestselling novels that feature older women as central characters, reflects on her creative process in the first chapter of this volume. In discussing her approach to fiction, Byrski explores both her creative and political aspirations, arguing that the 'war on ageing' is predominantly a war on women, in which popular fiction has the potential to become a form of counterintelligence. In a society that measures women's worth by standards of youthful beauty and sexuality, the author considers the following question: Is it possible to influence negative attitudes to older women through the products of popular culture, and in particular through women's popular fiction? Byrski explores this question by demonstrating the ways in which feminist fiction may be able to counter older women's invisibility and by doing so encourage different kinds of dialogue surrounding women and ageing.

Imelda Whelehan further interrogates some of these concerns, positioning Byrski's explicitly feminist fiction alongside contemporary novelists such as Elizabeth Buchan, Fanny Blake and Helen Fielding, whose feminist fictional sensibilities remain present though comparatively obscured. Whelehan argues that while Buchan's *Revenge of the Middle-Aged Woman* (2002) and Blake's *Women of a Dangerous Age* (2012) may not entirely share Byrski's life-enhancing portrayals of older women, they nevertheless retain radical feminist potential by suggesting that divorce and separation may be central to the female protagonists' journey to liberation and rejuvenation. Such depictions of positively ageing women – which focus on the possibilities of independence beyond the heterosexual romance narrative – are especially progressive, Whelehan argues, when placed alongside texts such as Fielding's *Bridget Jones: Mad about the Boy* (2013). But Bridget, at 51, can no longer follow the chick lit script, and Fielding's latest contribution holds the classic romance narrative up to ironic scrutiny with an affectionate nod to her own imitators.

Recognising the obstacles that older women face when attempting to assert their sexual selves, Joel Gwynne's chapter on the memoirs of Wendy Salisbury focusses on the problematic narrative oscillation between feminist politics and postfeminist disavowal. By exploring Salisbury's celebration of her sexual relationships with younger men, Gwynne argues that these memoirs not only affirm the individualised trajectory of postfeminist discourse, but also illustrate the problems inherent in attempting to position sexual empowerment as a form of political agency. While demonstrating the manner in which Salisbury's memoirs fully capitulate to popular culture's prevailing message that female sexual desirability is inevitably bound up in discourses of youth, Gwynne juxtaposes Salisbury's first and second memoirs and suggests that the texts can nevertheless be positioned as what Margaret Morganroth Gullette has termed a 'midlife progress narrative'.[8] The second memoir in particular, Gwynne argues, reveals Salisbury's abrogation of her formerly sexual self by seeking more meaningful forms of pleasure and agency, and in doing so it charts the narrator's transition from postfeminist girl to mature older woman, potentially undermining the perceived postfeminist power of the sexual confession as an expression of liberated life choices.

While Gwynne explores older women's experience of sexuality in ageing, Sharron Hinchliff explores the impact of ageing on women against the background of a sexualised western culture whose discourses shape women's sexual subjectivities in ways that fit the postfeminist imperative that women retain their beauty and sexual activity as they age. Arguing that the attention paid to the sexual agency and expression of midlife women is an extension of the sexualisation of younger women – one that has simply moved further along the life-course – Hinchliff asserts that while advancing age was once understood as an experience of freedom from societal pressures of physical desirability and a relaxation of body anxieties, postfeminism and neoliberalism has ensured that these concerns remain in sharp focus for women in midlife and even beyond. Through a constant feeding into women's subjectivities that their value comes predominantly from how they look, Hinchliff concludes that an analysis of current media representations suggests that women will never be set free from the constraints that are closely tied to idealised visions of femininity.

Examining the representation of older male characters in films such as *Robot & Frank* (2012), *Extremely Loud & Incredibly Close* (2011), *Beginners* (2010), *Up* (2009) and *An Unfinished Life* (2005), Hannah Hamad argues that paternity (sometimes experienced by proxy or as a grandparent) becomes the means by which men are able to recuperate masculinities undermined by the ageing process. In the case of all the aged male leads under discussion in this chapter, earlier failures to adhere to the requisite cultural script for successful masculine ageing – fatherhood – are recuperated, as each, towards the end of his life, is afforded the opportunity to redeem his troubled masculinity and to enhance the quality of the lived experience of ageing manhood. Hamad suggests that this recuperability of deficient, problematic or culturally obsolescent masculinities through fatherhood is symptomatic of a much broader tendency of a postfeminist culture which declines to configure struggles for gender equity in the labour share of parenting as a feminist issue and rather one that can be solved by the practices of individual men. Further mining the under-researched territory of ageing masculinities, Dominic Lennard's chapter charts the resurgence of a number of older male action stars, focussing particularly on the heroes of *Rocky Balboa* (2006), *Live Free or Die Hard* (2007), *Rambo* (2008), *The Expendables* (2010), and *A Good Day to Die Hard* (2013). Situating these filmic representations of heroic masculinity in the context of post-9/11 America, Lennard suggests that the repopularisation of the tough-guy figure in contemporary cinema represents a discursive shift towards conventional gender roles in the wake of a backlash against the perceived feminisation of the American man. The chapter suggests that within these films, older heroes are often positioned alongside younger, less violent embodiments of the 'new man', and the violence enacted by the older protagonist serves to shore up masculinities perceived to be under threat from the process of ageing and by the gender politics that characterise the political flavour of the period of these stars' youth.

Recognising that it has long been received wisdom that studio executives have little interest in films about women, and even less about older ones, Deborah Jermyn's chapter interrogates the career renaissance of Meryl Streep, whose reinvention and 'blockbuster' success has been widely received as remarkable and indicative of a sea-change in the industry. Focussing on *Mamma Mia!* (2008) and *It's Complicated* (2010), with reference also to *Hope Springs* (2012), this chapter examines how Streep has evolved as a key star in the perceived 'greying' of contemporary Hollywood, particularly within a series of films which celebrate older women rediscovering romance. Jermyn concludes by suggesting that the 'feel-good' motifs uniting these films and their appeal to mature female audiences lie in their shared narratives of what Imelda Whelehan has termed the 'triumph of the older woman'.[9] These narratives bestow the sense of a future on their ageing female protagonists.

Examining newspaper reviews of the live performances of key pop artists who grew to prominence in the late twentieth and early twenty-first century respectively, Lynne Hibberd's chapter asserts that the contemporary fascination with celebrity culture ensures that even stars such as Madonna, Kylie Minogue, The Spice Girls and Girls Aloud do not evade public scrutiny in terms of 'successful ageing'. Identifying differing responses across online media forums and the mainstream news press, Hibberd suggests that social networking sites such as Twitter demonstrate vitriolic attacks on older women, while newspaper reviews reveal a more 'casual misogyny'. Hibberd argues that the performance of 'not-ageing' is merely one of the ways in which the performance of gender is still most closely controlled and monitored and that successful ageing is understood as organic and effortless while unsuccessful ageing is marked by extreme attempts to modify appearance through fitness regimes and cosmetic intervention. These elements are also influenced by the age of the material being performed, with greater tolerance given, arguably, to the faithful rendition of older favourites. Material which is revised and refreshed, or which suggests the desire to speak to a new generation of music consumers can be interpreted negatively to suggest some cougarish intentions on the part of artists like Madonna or Kylie. Perhaps film stars of long standing get an easier ride than pop stars who are in many ways revisiting their youth in every reprise of their old hits.

Kirsty Fairclough-Isaacs locates Meryl Streep and Helen Mirren as unusual examples of successful ageing in Hollywood while demonstrating that the maturing female star is only accepted within certain normative boundaries. In the context of postfeminist and neoliberal culture, where renovation of the self through cosmetic surgery and body modification has become an industry imperative, the chapter underscores how Streep and Mirren's resistance to these forms of intervention is possible only on account of their talent. Fairclough-Isaacs examines how successful ageing is implicitly linked to the legitimacy of the 'craft' of acting, with Streep and Mirren spared from the media's unremitting scrutiny of ageing bodies and allowed to mature on screen as 'authentic' talents. The chapter argues that while Streep and Mirren are in certain respects binary figures – Streep is revered for her refusal to display her body, whereas Mirren is revered for displaying it – positive reception to both is predicated on their ability to consistently deliver skilled performances. In this way, the chapter argues, both women differ from less critically and corporeally successful Hollywood actresses whose inability to secure critical acclaim for their performances has a dramatic impact on the way their ageing bodies are perceived.

Analysing representations of older women in television comedy, Rosie White's chapter argues that sitcoms and sketch shows provide a space in which ageing femininity can literally embody its contradictions. Exploring productions such as *Harry Enfield and Chums* (1994–1997), *The Catherine Tate Show* (2004–2009), and *Mrs Brown's Boys* (2011–), White illustrates how the shows' examples of unruly older women work to confirm and disrupt stereotypes about age, gender and sexuality. While arguing that the British comedy tradition in which younger men and women cross dress as older women opens up a range of queer depictions, the chapter concludes that characters such as Agnes Brown are anchored to the conventions of propriety and family, returning the representation of ageing femininity back to the misogynies of the pantomime dame of nineteenth-century music hall – a peculiarly anachronistic construction for twenty-first century television – and returning us to the notion that postmenopausal women are essentially 'male'. Cross dressing and the 'queered' performance which results creates its own deconstruction of gendered binaries, and comedy, especially, allows for more anarchic and unresolved tensions in the representation of the ageing body and behaviours. As one of the many chapters in this book that deal with age-appropriate behaviour, Elizabeth Rawitsch's analyses the resurgence in popularity experienced by Betty White since 2010. Exploring Betty White's popularity in the context of the 2008 economic recession, nostalgia for *The Golden Girls* (1985–1992), and the changing role of the grandparent in American culture, Rawitsch considers White's comedic performances in, and publicity for, a number of film and television productions, including *The Proposal* (2009), *Saturday Night Live* (1975–), and *Hot in Cleveland* (2010–). As an affable grandmother figure unexpectedly conversant in current slang and tween culture, Betty White's late-career star persona signals a cross-generational veneration of the eternally young older person, Rawitsch argues, which functions as a safe outlet for experimenting with the transgression of age-appropriate behaviour. By participating in cross-generational conversation that defies age-appropriate discursive markers, Betty White's late-career star persona offers, Rawitsch suggests, the hope that all ages may be perceived as golden.

Reality TV is one site where anxieties about ageing blend into studies in the abject. In a chapter exploring the neglect of the older mother and her lived experiences of labour and childbirth, Georgina O'Brien Hill examines the popular television programme *One Born Every Minute*, with particular regard to the classed implications of the 'good mother' mythology. While the author observes that the concept of remaining in control by 'coping' or 'working with' pain affects women of all social classes, she argues that older middle-class women are more literate in the discourse of childbirth and are therefore heavily invested in 'good mother' mythologies. The chapter suggests that even though factual television polices women's birth experience within the parameters of postfeminism and neoliberalism – with older middle-class pregnant women encouraged to invest in the illusion of choice over pain management – *One Born Every Minute* remains unique on British terrestrial television in representing older women's advancing age as a positive advantage which affords them the confidence and experience to assert their desires within a setting which does not, at times, respect their right to assert their will.

The following chapter echoes some of the themes found in the fiction discussed in the first two chapters, and the prominence of the journey and quest motif, to produce narratives of 'ripening' rather than decline.[10] Sarah Falcus and Katsura Sako analyse *Sex and the City 2* (2010), *Under the Tuscan Sun* (2003), *Eat, Pray, Love* (2010), *Letters to Juliet* (2010) and *The Best Exotic Marigold Hotel* (2011), taking as their starting point Meryl Streep's personal reflection on the increasing visibility of older women in Hollywood, only to reveal the complexity and often problematic nature of this new cultural visibility. While the authors acknowledge that these five films not only challenge romance and the idealised form of marriage and family, but also seek to present alternatives – from childless marriage to the affirmation of space for female independence outside of marriage – they conclude that new ageing and postfeminist cultures ultimately make it difficult to imagine ageing 'successfully' without recourse to youthing and consumption. As such, Falcus and Sako demonstrate how these popular films depoliticise ageing in order to produce a narrowly optimistic vision of it.

By juxtaposing two classic and contemporary Hollywood films in order to illustrate the obduracy of mother-blaming and ageism, Dee Michell, Casey Tonkin and Penelope Eate argue that both *Citizen Kane* (1941) and the more recent biopic *J Edgar* (2011) offer critiques of powerful men – William Randolph Hearst and J Edgar Hoover. The authors argue that at the heart of these stories are mothers who are presented as ultimately to blame for the dysfunctional personalities of their sons. Suggesting also that ageism has shaped the production of these films by prompting the uneven use and non-use of ageing technology, the chapter asserts that both films convey profound anxieties about the fluidity of gender in the process of ageing. While the central figures in both films are seen to age through the performance of younger actors at the height of their powers, other older men played by actors of the same age demonstrate that old men – even once powerful men – can become vulnerable, dependent and 'feminine'. These representations refuse to critique essentialist notions of gender and instead show how fear about age disrupting gendered distinctions between men and women becomes the basis for an ageism which remains surprisingly current in films made over sixty years apart.

Turning our attention to the genre of children's fantasy, Rebecca-Anne C. Do Rozario and Deb Waterhouse-Watson suggest that a range of diverse texts showcase women's ageing in a positive light. While the genre is more commonly associated with the empowerment of children, the chapter argues that it also provides an imaginative context where representations of elderly embodiment challenge conventional norms that situate ageing bodies within discourses of decline and degeneration. Focussing in particular on the short film *Granny O'Grimm's Sleeping Beauty* (2008), the television series *Once Upon a Time* (2011–) and the animated feature *Up* (2009), the chapter concludes that even though mainstream visual culture continues to reimagine fairy tales in ways which (re)produce anxieties about ageing, a space is beginning to open in which ideals of feminine beauty and masculine dominance are being destabilised from their position of privilege. In this way, the chapter argues for an interpretation of children's fantasy as agentic for the elderly, whereby kinship between the young and the old who both seek – and often succeed in obtaining – independence despite their undeveloped or disintegrating bodies.

Notes

1. Quoted by Anne Fausto-Sterling. 'Menopause: The Storm before the Calm,' in *Feminist Theory and the Body: A Reader*, ed. Janet Price and Margrit Shildrick (Edinburgh: Edinburgh University Press, 1999), pp. 169–178, p. 170. His writings and his Oestrogen Replacement Therapy led his book *Feminine Forever* (1966) to be a popular bestseller.
2. Jacquelyn N. Zita, 'Heresy in the Female Body: The Rhetorics of Menopause,' in *The Other within Us: Feminist Explorations of Women and Aging*, ed. Marilyn Pearsall (Boulder, Colorado: Westview Press, 1997), pp. 95–112, p.106.
3. Joel Gwynne and Nadine Muller, eds, *Postfeminism and Contemporary Hollywood Cinema* (Basingstoke: Palgrave Macmillan, 2013).
4. These include, Josephine Dolan and Estella Tincknell, eds, *Aging Femininities: Troubling Representations* (Newcastle upon Tyne: Cambridge Scholars, 2012); Jeannette King, *Discourses of Ageing in Fiction and Feminism: The Invisible Woman* (Basingstoke: Palgrave Macmillan, 2013); and Lynne Segal, *Out of Time: The Pleasures and Perils of Ageing* (London: Verso, 2013).
5. Marilyn Pearsall, ed., 'Introduction,' in *The Other within Us: Feminist Explorations of Women and Aging* (Boulder, Colorado: Westview Press, 1997), p. 1.
6. Penelope Lively, *Ammonites and Leaping Fish: A Life in Time* (London: Fig Tree, 2013), p. 20.
7. Betty Friedan, *The Fountain of Age* (London: Jonathan Cape, 1993), p. 33.
8. Margaret Morganroth Gullette, *Declining to Decline: Cultural Combat and the Politics of the Midlife* (Virginia: University of Virginia Press, 1997), p. 12.
9. Imelda Whelehan, 'Ageing Appropriately: Postfeminist Discourses of Ageing in Contemporary Hollywood,' in *Postfeminism and Contemporary Hollywood Cinema*, ed. by Joel Gwynne and Nadine Muller (Basingstoke: Palgrave, 2013), p. 87.
10. See, Barbara Frey Waxman, *From the Hearth to the Open Road: A Feminist Study of Aging in Contemporary Literature* (New York: Greenwood Press, 1990), pp. 1–22.

1
Conscientious Objections: Feminism, Fiction and the Phoney War on Ageing

Liz Byrski

It was my mother who made me a reader. She was of the generation of women who had devoured the restless, questioning women's novels of the thirties, moved onto 'the resistance writing' of wartime[1] and then the novels that juggled women's changing post-war roles and expectations in the fifties. All her life she devoured books, and many years later I came to understand that those novels were compensation for our comparative isolation, buried in the Sussex countryside, three miles from the nearest village and five from the town. She lacked the company of women friends or neighbours but found it in the books that have come to be known as 'the feminine middlebrow'. The middlebrow, according to Nicola Humble is:

> ...a product of the interwar years, its form, themes and successes were not immediately disrupted by the Second World War. [... It] is a hybrid form, comprising a number of forms from the romance and country-house novel, through domestic and family narratives.[2]

My earliest childhood memories from the late forties into the fifties are punctuated by the weekly visit to Boots Library and later, back home, Mum flicking through the pages of each new book deciding which to read first. I was thirteen when she began to share those books with me, introducing me to Monica Dickens, Winifred Peck, E.M. Delafield, Jocelyn Playfair, Elizabeth Taylor, Dorothy Whipple, and many more.

Once captured by the middlebrow I was riveted and there was no looking back to teenage fiction. I was reading purely for pleasure, and it was a very long time before I understood that I was reading politics of the sort that Grace Paley's words suggest: 'people will sometimes say,

"Why don't you write more politics?" And I have to explain to them that writing the lives of women is politics'.[3]

To write about women's everyday lives is to write about the tangled webs of marriage and families, of work and money or the lack of it, sexual politics, and the political reality of women living in a world defined by men, for men and to accommodate their preferences. The novels of the middlebrow teem with the politics of adjustment to changes in women's status in marriage, home and workplace, their class, their expectations and their aspirations in a rapidly changing world, as well as the realities of ageing.

Nicola Humble notes that the 'feminine middlebrow' novels were, and still are, overlooked as mere reflections on the middle class, domestic status quo, largely because they were written by women and because they constitute a feminine literature which concentrated on women's everyday experience, 'paying meticulous attention to their shifting desires and self-images, mapping their swings of fortune'.[4] Humble suggests that female authorship and the concentration on women's lives combined to deprive these novels and their authors of serious critical attention and credit for any literary value. Today, many of those novels are being republished and recognised for their value as 'a powerful force in establishing and consolidating, but also resisting, new class and gender identities'.[5] The middlebrow also made women feel that they were not alone because, as Nicola Beauman writes, 'the woman's novel at this period was permeated through and through with the certainty of like speaking to like.'[6]

In the late sixties through to the eighties, feminist consciousness-raising fiction politicised the lives of millions of women, drawing them into the women's movement as activists or fellow travellers or simply inspiring them to consider the politics at work in their own lives. Raised on the middlebrow and its restless tussles with everyday politics I, like so many others, was the perfect audience for those powerful feminist novels. I continued to read and enjoy contemporary women's fiction until, in my late fifties, I grew irritable and frustrated. I wanted to read fiction about the lives of women who had aged with me and were also a little ahead of me. The shelves of bookshops and libraries were packed with novels about younger women living lives which I had outgrown. As I returned, for consolation, to the feminist novels of the seventies I was shocked to realise that these, unlike the middlebrow, had failed to pay attention to the situation of ageing and old women, and more recent trends in popular fiction seemed even more youth focussed. Fortunately, my irritation and frustration as a reader proved motivational for me as a writer.

In the last twelve years I have written and published seven novels in which ageing and old women are the central characters. All have become Australian bestsellers, some have been published in England, France and Germany, and two are currently optioned for films.[7] Believing in the power of stories to show rather than tell, I began constructing narratives that would demonstrate the realities, the challenges and the rewards of older women's lives. I had been a journalist and nonfiction writer for most of my adult life and always wanted to find my niche in fiction, so the initial imperative was creative and personal, but it is fair to say that my writing also had a pro-social purpose. I wanted to contribute to a change in the conversation about women and ageing, and I had been writing and publishing magazine articles and broadcasting on the topic for several years. Now I hoped fiction might work as a form of viral marketing of age acceptance and of the feminist values of collectivity, sisterhood, friendship, equal rights and social justice. I wanted to speak to women in the same way that the middlebrow fiction and then consciousness-raising fiction had spoken to me, and I wanted to do so in a popular genre where age was underrepresented. Some feminist literary fiction has examined the lives and politics of ageing women: Doris Lessing's *The Summer Before the Dark* (1995), *Love Again* (1996) and *The Grandmothers* (2003) and Margaret Drabble's more recent work, as examples. But in women's popular fiction the over-fifties as a focus were, and still are, very hard to find, and representations of peripheral characters are often negative stereotypes, designed to create conflict for the main characters who are younger women, men and children.

Older women's dominance in the book buying market sits in uneasy contrast to their representation as subject material, because as a society we seem to find old age distasteful, particularly in relation to women. An obsession with sexualised youth and beauty in popular culture generally makes up the wallpaper of our lives and engenders a fear of growing old. Younger women, who feel the hot breath of age on their necks, are deprived of images of their elders living fulfilling, active and enjoyable lives and grow desperate to cling to youth. Alongside this deprivation the reality of an ageing population – which is a triumph of a civilised society – is viewed as only a burden for future generations. And so war has been declared. But the 'war on ageing' is a phoney war, one which most ageing and old people find offensive and frankly ridiculous. It is phoney because it creates a common enemy of which we will all eventually become a part and because ageing is as precious a part of life as childhood. In this chapter I will argue that because women live longer than men – and ageing and old women are subject to greater distaste, dislike, hostility and abuse – the 'war on ageing' is predominantly a war on women. I will consider how the products of popular culture, and specifically women's popular fiction, can constitute counter intelligence in that war and how writing about ageing and old women, making them visible in popular fiction, has been my own antiwar propaganda.

Scoping the Battleground

Despite the fact that women live to greater ages than in the past, live longer than men, stay longer in the workforce, and return to work at an age when many men are seeking early retirement, they have been airbrushed from the images of popular culture. As Imelda Whelehan writes:

> Post-menopausal women are assumed to disappear into a dismal neutered future or else the kind of femininity available with age remains unutterable in contemporary popular culture.[8]

Four decades ago Susan Sontag, then just 39-years-old, suggested that 'ageing is largely a trial of the imagination [...] much more a social judgment than a biological eventuality.' She pointed to the link between ageism and sexism, identifying the double standard of ageing for women as 'part of recurrent state of "possession" of her imagination, ordained by society – that is, ordained by the way this society limits how women feel free to imagine themselves.'[9] That freedom of imagination is crucial; the way we hear ourselves discussed, and see ourselves represented in the culture, influences the ways women can imagine, observe and experience their own ageing. Nothing much has changed. Sontag's 'double standard of ageing' is as relevant today as it was in the seventies. A war on ageing is a bizarre concept in societies in which people aspire to live longer and live well. Do we think we can live longer without getting old? '[Y]ou are not only as old as you feel, you are also as old as you are,' writes Molly Andrews, whose work on ageing and ageism contributes to a wide body of research that shows that old people frequently claim that they do not feel old; they feel, in fact, like the same person they have always been.[10] This acknowledgement of the original youthful spirit within exists alongside the knowledge that they are actually old, and (hopefully) proud of it. Concepts such as 'stretched middle-age' and 'successful ageing', which use youth as the model of 'success', disrupt the emotional congruence of older people and set some up for failure.

In this battlefield women are bombarded with images of youthful, often adolescent, beauty – airbrushed and eroticised in ways more in keeping with the sex industry than with beauty and fashion. While shopping centres thrive on the custom of older women, the wallpaper within them is tediously youthful and excludes old and ageing women as consumers. There are no billboards of feisty, wrinkled old women choosing an outfit for a special occasion, a bathing suits, or a track suit for their morning walks. Ageing and old women are cast as outsiders, unacceptable or wrong, fragile, dependent, or as the carers of other old people. There is an interesting dynamic at work here as, according to the Australian Bureau of Statistics, women over 55 have greater disposable income, have more free time than women in the younger age group (25–55), and make up 67 per cent of users of shopping malls between 10 a.m. and 4 p.m. on weekdays.[11]

As Simone de Beauvoir pointed out in the seventies, an absence of representations of ageing limits the ability to live as fully rounded human beings.

> If we do not know what we are going to be we cannot know what we are: let us recognise ourselves in that old man or that old woman. It must be done if we are to take upon ourselves the entirety of our human state. [12]

With notable exceptions in the areas of health and housing, feminist research has continued to sideline the issues of women's ageing, particularly in relation to representation. This absence has been noted by, among others, Marilyn Poole and Susan Feldman in 1999[13] and Toni Calasanti and Kathleen Slevin who, in their 2006 publication *Age Matters*, noted that feminists still 'exclude old people both in their choice of research questions and in their theoretical approaches'.[14] In view of the widespread anxiety about the ageing population, it is surprising that feminist attention is not focussed to a greater extent on the future situations of the millions of old women who will dominate that demographic.

In an era that has been defined as post-feminist it is heartening to see the recent resurgence of interest in feminism, currently most evident in the proliferation of new feminist online publications and lobbying movements organised through social media. Much of this resurgence has been triggered by the blatant misogyny and sexism of politicians, radio shock jocks, and celebrity sportsmen and by the vicious and hateful sexism directed at prominent women in positions of power. Even so, this revival is demonstrably ageist in its focus on young women.

Female singers argue about the pimping of young women by the music industry, and feminist commentators grapple with the abuse of young female celebrities on social media sites and many similar issues, all of them important. But a cone of silence still prevails around the enduring double standard of ageing and the woman-centred nature of the phoney war on ageing. Perhaps I am naïve, but I remain hopeful that the creative industries can contribute to recognition of ageism and change in this respect.

The promotion of social and attitudinal change through a systematic use of popular culture is not new, the most obvious examples of this promotion being the use of film by Britain, the United States, Germany and Japan in support of their military objectives in World War II. Popular music also has a long history of influence on social change – and never more so than during the social protest and anti–Vietnam War movements of the late 1960s and 1970s. In the 1970s there were arguments about the importance of ethical standards in the use of prosocial messaging in entertainment, but in 1993 William Brown and Arvind Singhal, among others, concluded that:

> Persuasion is a necessary part of a free and democratic society [...] Therefore we consider it is ethical to use popular media to persuade audiences to adopt prosocial beliefs and behaviours or to change beliefs that are destructive to people and society. [15]

As far as ageing is concerned ethical concerns should, I suggest, be directed to the way that narratives of 'successful ageing' are so often based on looking and staying young, rather than on accepting, adjusting to, and enjoying the rewards, the challenges and the inevitability of age.

Twenty years ago a television soap opera called *Soul City* went to air in South Africa and has had remarkable and continuing success in changing both attitudes and behaviour in relation to public health issues, including HIV prevention and the prevention of violence against women. It has become one of the most popular programs on South African television, regularly rating in the top three shows and is broadcast in ten countries to more than 25 million viewers. [16] The drama is direct, gritty and confrontational, and on a visit to Australia in 2010 its creator, Dr Garth Japhet, reported that viewing *Soul City* had resulted in the prevention of an estimated half-a-million new cases of HIV. [17] *Soul City* is perhaps the most successful example of the use of prosocial messages in soap opera, but it is certainly not the only one, nor was it the first. The series was inspired by the success of *telenovelas* designed to promote adult literacy, family planning and gender equality in Mexico between 1975 and 1981.[18] In Turkey soap opera has opened up the conversation on the status of women in the Middle East. In Rwanda radio soap opera has been effective in reducing ethnic tension, and in Brazil television plays have contributed to an urgently needed lowering of the birthrate. These programs succeeded because they followed the recipe for success defined by Brown and Singhal: the marriage of popular entertainment media and prosocial messages relies on the product first and foremost meeting the entertainment criteria.[19]

In the last two years mainstream cinema has begun to recognise that older moviegoers have turned their backs on many of its products. In 2012 *The Best Exotic Marigold Hotel* brought these audiences back, as did *Quartet, Cloudburst* and *A Song for Marion*, all released in 2013, and two French films, Michael Haneke's *Amour* (2012) and Stephane Robelin's *And If We All Lived Together* (2011). Television finally joined the party in 2012 with the BBC series *Last Tango in Halifax*. Irrespective of the various strengths and weaknesses of these recent productions, they indicate the industry's recognition of the changing audience demographic. They are not deliberately pro-social in concept, being driven by box office appeal and a growing recognition of the power of the 'grey dollar', but they are proof that entertaining explorations of old age can succeed in a competitive market.

As a writer, however, I am particularly concerned with the way that popular fiction can create awareness and contribute to social and attitudinal change. When I first began writing fiction, I assumed that the vast majority of my readers would be women over 45, but I have been pleasantly surprised by the number of younger women who turn up to hear me speak and who write to me about my books. It seems from this turn out that roughly 80 per cent of my readers are female and 20 per cent male. Of the female readers about 60 per cent are over fifty; the other 40 per cent are younger women, including a small percentage of teenagers. The younger women speak of the sense of relief they feel in reading books that show ageing as enjoyable and interesting. The sense of a different vision of the future is very important to them, and many tell me that they also understand their mothers better as a result of reading the books.

Counter intelligence in the war on ageing

Women's long and affectionate relationship with the novel continues into the twenty-first century; 64 per cent of book purchases in Australia are to women, and Australian women over the age of 45 constitute the largest demographic among book buyers.[20] So it is worth considering the potential influence that fiction, and specifically 'women's fiction', might exercise in the war on ageing. One of the most influential books of World War II was in the form of popular fiction written for women by a woman. Jan Struther's *Mrs Miniver,* published in 1939, is about the life of a middle-class woman and her family. It is a collection of short fictional columns originally published on the Court page of *The Times.* Struther's brief for those columns was to write for women about 'an ordinary sort of woman who leads an ordinary sort of life – rather like yourself'.[21] Like E.M. Delafield before her with *The Diary of a Provincial Lady* (1931) and subsequent titles, Struther wrote in the language of the middlebrow, creating a compelling narrative of the ordinary, middle-class, peacetime life, which reminded readers on both sides of the Atlantic of what was at stake. President Roosevelt told Jan Struther that *Mrs Miniver* had hastened America's entry into the war, and Winston Churchill reportedly said that the book had done more for the Allies than a flotilla of battleships.[22] Struther and Delafield captured the everyday politics of women's lives and have that middlebrow quality of like speaking to like. The feminist consciousness-raising fiction of the late sixties and seventies similarly changed lives. Dorothy Bryant's *Ella Price's Journal* (1972), Sue Kauffman's *Diary of a Mad Housewife* (1967), Erica Jong's *Fear of Flying* (1975), Marilyn French's *The Women's Room* (1978), and many others showed women the politics at work in their own lives and made them restless for change.

I began writing my first novel in a climate in which old women were considered uninteresting and feminism deemed unnecessary, troublesome, outdated. The challenge was to create the entertainment factor, which Brown and Singhal cite as the primary element of the novel, the film or the soap opera that is going to be able to hold its ground in the commercial market.[23] But older women do live dynamic, chaotic, vibrant and interesting lives, so my problem was not with the subject matter but with my own writing. After more than thirty years of journalism and non-fiction, my greatest challenge was to work my way through politics and polemic; to be entertaining rather than didactic. In *East Coker* T.S. Eliot writes of the struggle with representation despite twenty years of working with words: 'And so each venture is a new beginning, a raid on the inarticulate/With shabby equipment always deteriorating.'[24] My initial raids on the inarticulate were dismal and discouraging. There was a long and tedious period of grim attempts to break the didactic patterns of journalism and non-fiction and to dismantle the rhetoric, which somehow made its way onto every page. The hardest task was to cede control of the narrative to the characters and let them drive the story, even when they seemed to be taking it in a direction I had not chosen. I was writing character-driven fiction but kept pushing the characters out of the driving seat. I have since heard several writers say that writing fiction is like driving in the dark without headlights, and this perfectly describes my initial and continuing experience.

My novels are contemporary Australian versions of the society/friendship novels of the late sixties and early seventies. They are character driven and the central characters are older and often aged women who are dealing with the many and varied challenges, changes, opportunities and possibilities of this time of life. So, while my characters may enjoy travel, return to study, start a new hobby or business, or change of location, and rediscover romance, they also deal with family responsibilities, caring for grandchildren and aged parents, sometimes with dementia, loneliness, ill health, hiccups in or at the end of long relationships and uncertainty about income and living arrangements. I kept returning to Monica Dickens's novel, *The Winds of Change*, published in 1955, in which the ageing widow, Louise, is treated as an irritation and a burden by her adult children who, while wanting her out of the way, manage to restrain her attempts at independence. Louise is constrained by her late husband's profligacy, which has left her in dire financial straits and without a home of her own. She struggles to balance her own needs without intruding on her family, but she is profoundly diminished by her dependence on their grudging support. Louise eventually finds love and a home with a man whom her family considers unsuitable. There is a note of triumph in the happy ending, and the book stands as a reminder of the differences in women's lives between the fifties and the present, when finding love is only one possibility for independence and satisfaction in later life.

The central characters in my first novel, *Gang of Four* (2004), were all in their mid-fifties, and as I have aged so too have my characters, most of whom are now in their sixties and seventies, and occasionally in their eighties. Feminist values are inherent in the characterisations, but most characters are not identified as feminist and have never been politically active, while others are or reveal some past activism as their backstories unfold. In two novels I included characters who were and still are active feminists, and I set them alongside others who do not identify as feminist. For example in *Bad Behaviour*,[25] Julia, a lifelong feminist and a peace activist at Greenham Common, is reunited with her non-feminist and oldest friend, Zoe, a traditional wife and mother who is somewhat conservative in her thinking. And in *Last Chance Café*[26] two old friends from the seventies women's movement, Dot and Margot, embark on a campaign against the sexualisation of children and young girls, co-opting Margot's very conservative sister and her younger daughter as they go. Friendship between women was an important feature of consciousness-raising fiction; it was significant both in the pleasure of its presence and in the bleakness of its absence. Today many women cite the company and support of their women friends as vital to their enjoyment of and wellbeing in ageing and so friendship is a recurring theme in my work.

I examine social constructions of gender through the challenges of mid- and later life and critique them through the inner lives and actions of the characters. The theme of change, the challenges it represents and the decisions women make in response to it is always part of the story. Women in the novels face issues of identity, independence, family responsibilities, loneliness and love (or the lack of it), and the power of coming to terms with the past in order to build a future. The incorporation of social issues, which have included, for example, the sexualisation of children and teenagers in *Last Chance Café* and the effects of the British/Australian forced migration scheme on women who came here as children in the 1940s and 1950s in *In the Company of Strangers*,[27] has also proved very popular with readers.

In an effort to develop diverse and authentic situations, I have tried to avoid representing women as victims, even in situations where they are being victimised. These situations are rarely straightforward, and fear and a sense of powerlessness can create a state of inertia. In *Belly Dancing for Beginners*,[28] university librarian Gayle is married to a bullying and insensitive husband whose behaviour frequently borders on violence. By the use of a plot device around her gay son who has been banished from the family by her husband, Gayle's decision to stay in the relationship seems (I hope) like strength rather than weakness. It is through her developing friendships with other women and a new sense of self achieved through belly dancing that Gayle moves towards the congruence and confidence which enable her to end her marriage.

While romance is seemingly a non-negotiable feature of novels about younger women it is, for me, less significant in stories of older women, who so often seem happy with the single life. Romantic love does feature in the lives of some of my characters, but it is neither the driving force nor the motivational factor in any of them. The overwhelming response of readers to this seems to be one of relief that the characters are not motivated by longing for romance and the search for a man. If a character ends up falling in love with a man or another woman, the readers are happy for them, but their letters and emails certainly indicate satisfaction that the storyline does not propel the women towards men as solutions. Love is important to the readers but in much broader terms than to the readers of romance or chick lit. Romantic love as the answer to a character's search for meaning in later life is not appreciated; it can be only ever a part of the answer, with the resolution of other life issues being more important. And so my characters fall in love only sometimes, sometimes with the wrong people, as in *Belly Dancing for Beginners* and *Trip of a Lifetime*,[29] and sometimes with the right ones, as in *Belly Dancing for Beginners* (again), *Gang of Four* and *Bad Behaviour*. In *Food, Sex and Money*[30] long-divorced Fran finds love in her fifties with another woman, and in *Last Chance Café*, Margot's ex-husband, Laurence, is in a relationship with another man with whom he has lived since coming out in the early years of his marriage to Margot. The gay couple is an accepted part of the family. The inclusion of gay and lesbian characters and same-sex relationships seems important as they are a feature of so many families, but they are too frequently consigned to the ghetto of gay or lesbian fiction.

Men and marriage are, of course, a reality in the lives of many older women and so must be a part of the realistic representations of that demographic. I have attempted to avoid the demonisation of men, which was a factor in much seventies feminist fiction, and attempt instead to represent them as sympathetic as well as flawed as are the women. However, I must admit to succumbing to temptation with the creation of Brian, Gayle's husband, in *Belly Dancing for Beginners*, and Ellis, the arrogant and opinionated former lover in *Trip of a Lifetime*. Marriages, both good and bad, are explored through domestic scenes that will be familiar to most married women and which reflect the changing of expectations of women who married just prior to or during the days of the women's movement. *Gang of Four*, for example, begins on Christmas morning when Isabel is preparing Christmas dinner for her husband, adult children and grandchildren and is reflecting on the fact that this is the thirty-fourth year she has done this in the same number of years of marriage. Over dinner the domestic politics play out when Isabel mentions that it might be nice to do something different next year. Tension mounts later when she decides to take time out to travel alone in Europe in search of her late mother's history as a dancer. Her relationship with her husband, Doug, is tested by her desire to do this alone and, much later, when Doug turns up in Germany, the relationship is put at risk. From the moment of his arrival, Doug attempts to take control and imposes his own agenda, anticipating that Isabel will drop back in to the old habits of domesticity and acquiescence and will change any plans she has made for herself, in order to accommodate him. Tension builds and finally erupts in an argument that is pivotal to Isabel's determination that things will have to change when she gets back home. These sections of *Gang of Four* are currently used as exercises in textual analysis for Year 12 exams in four Australian States, as are some scenes in *Bad Behaviour* that demonstrate the shift in relationships between men and women.

My love of the middlebrow has lead me to strive for that sense of like speaking to like, in which it is possible to explore the inner life of and introduce possibilities through conversations between the characters. Women's conversations, so often dismissed as trivial or gossipy, are in fact frequently meaningful, reassuring and challenging – and, as Adrienne Rich suggests, important and empowering:

> The most notable fact our culture imprints on women is the sense of our limits. The most important thing one woman can do for another is to illuminate and expand her sense of actual possibilities.[31]

So, does all this add up to my claim to be writing feminist fiction? In the 1970s there was some tension among feminists about what constituted feminist fiction with one school of thought adopting Rosalind Coward's position:

> Feminism can never be the product of the identity of women's experiences and interests – there is no such unity. Feminism must always be the alignment of women in a political movement with particular political aims and objectives. It is a grouping unified by its political interests, not its common experiences.[32]

While Coward's definition may have pleased the political activists of the Women's Liberation Movement her broader application of it to feminism implies a separatism that disenfranchises many women and many texts, and it stands in judgement over feminist reading and writing. Coward's censure comes from a legitimate discomfort around the posing of a universal notion of 'woman' and a normative female experience around which to theorise the basis of feminist politics. As a feminist who learned feminism from fiction I was, and still am, politically aligned with the aims of second-wave feminism. As Gayle Greene writes:

> [...] whatever a writer's relation to the women's movement, we may term a novel feminist for its analysis of gender as socially constructed

and its sense that what has been constructed may be reconstructed – for its understanding that change is possible and narrative can play a part in it.[33]

I chose to write popular fiction because I enjoy reading it, because it engages a large and broad readership and because it can effectively create the intimacy of the inner life between writer and reader, which is such a powerful force for introspection and change. As a reader and a writer I am alienated by what Leslie Heywood has described as the 'anorexic logic' of the assumptions of modernism that favour 'masculine over feminine, control over emotion, mind over body and a realm of transcendence over the haphazardness of daily life.'[34] In reading and writing I seek a strong story line, credible, engaging characters and writing that makes readers an eyewitness to characters' lives. Entertainment value is vital and through that it is also possible to provide the sort of intellectual engagement that leaves readers with something to think about.

Scott McCracken argues that 'popular narratives can tell us much about who we are and the society in which we live.'[35] He cites Walter Benjamin who, in an essay entitled *'Detective Novels, Read on Journeys'* written just before the outbreak of World War II is caught up 'in the anonymity of the railway system,' where 'the self threatens to fragment into warring factions, and it is into this gap created by the fragmented self that the popular text enters'.[36] In that essay Benjamin describes the ways that different types of popular narratives provide the opportunity to project or fantasise different kinds of potential selves. McCracken goes on to examine 'the connections that relate to *the self who reads* to the *self of everyday life'*, (emphasis in original) and suggests that popular fiction 'mediates social conflict [...] it acts as a medium between reader and world through which the social contradictions of modernity can be played out'.[37] This potential for transgression is, I believe, at the heart of women's relationships with fiction and is a vital element of narratives of ageing. Women living in a man-made and male-dominated society accommodate some level of dissonance between that reality and their own reality, and in doing so the sense of self frequently threatens 'to fragment into warring factions'.[38] I would suggest that, as women age in a youth-obsessed world, dissonance is more acute. Popular fiction can provide validation through visibility, the chance to mediate one's surroundings and experiment with other selves. This chance, I suggest, makes popular fiction a particularly valuable vehicle for the deployment of prosocial messages that can make old women visible and counter negative representations. Without consciously prosocial creative production in cultural industries, there is little hope of an amnesty in this phoney war. In an environment dominated by the products of popular culture the conversation on ageing could be changed by encouraging creative writers in all forms, as well as publishers, producers and directors, to recognise the entertainment value and consequent financial benefits of bringing the stories of age to readers and viewers. Without this young people will be deprived of the stories and images of growing old with all its rewards and challenges, its joys and heartbreaks.

As a writer and a feminist, writing popular fiction has been a way for me to make sense of and maintain the value of ageing in the face of so much negativity; a way to hold onto the values of seventies feminism and start a new conversation about women and ageing. It is a way to recapture the pleasure of my first experiences of reading women's fiction and, at the most profound level, it was, and still is, my own conscientious objection to the phoney social and cultural war on ageing.

Notes

1. Elizabeth Bowen, 'Preface,' in Elizabeth Bowen (ed.) *The Demon Lover* (New York: Longmans, Green & Co., 1950), p. 3.
2. Nicola Humble, *The Feminine Middlebrow Novel 1920s to 1950s* (Oxford: Oxford University Press, 2001), p. 3.
3. Grace Paley, 'The Art of Fiction,' *The Paris Review* 131:124 (1992).
4. Ibid.
5. Ibid.
6. Nicola Beauman, *A Very Great Profession: The Woman's Novel 1914–39* (London: Virago 1983), p. 4.
7. *Belly Dancing for Beginners* (2006), *In the Company of Strangers* (2012).
8. Imelda Whelehan, 'Not to be Looked At: Older Women in Recent British Cinema', in *British Women's Cinema*, ed. by Melanie Williams and Melanie Bell (Abingdon: Routledge, 2010), p. 182.
9. Susan Sontag, 'The Double Standard of Ageing', *Saturday Review* 55 (1972), pp. 29–38. Reprinted in Marilyn Pearsall (ed.) *The Other Within Us: Feminist Explorations of Women and Aging* (Colorado: West View Press, 1997).
10. Molly Andrews, 'The Seductiveness of Agelessness,' *Ageing and Society* 19 (1999), pp. 301–308.
11. http://www.abs.gov.au/ausstats/abs@.nsf/Latestproducts/6530.0 Main%20Features22009–10?opendocument&tabname=Summary&prodno=6 530.0&issue=2009–10&num=&view=
12. Simone de Beauvoir, *Coming of Age* (New York: G.B. Putnam's Sons, 1972), p. 197.
13. Susan Feldman and Marilyn Poole, 'Positioning Older Women,' in *A Certain Age: Women Growing Older*, ed. by Susan Feldman and Marilyn Poole (Sydney: Allen & Unwin, 1999), p. 3.

14. Toni Calasanti and Kathleen Slevin, 'Introduction,' in *Age Matters*, ed. by Toni Calasanti and Kathleen Slevin (New York: Routledge, 2006), p. 3.
15. William Brown and Arvind Singhal, 'Ethical Considerations of Promoting Prosocial Messages Through the Popular Media,' *Journal of Popular Film and Television* 21:3 (1993), pp. 92–99.
16. Jane Cassidy, 'The Soap Opera That Changes Lives,' *British Medical Journal* (15 May 2008), p. 336.
17. Amanda Meade, 'South Africa's addiction to Soul City saves lives,' *The Australian* 6 (September 2010).
18. William Brown and Michael Cody, 'Effects of a Prosocial Television Soap Opera in Promoting Women's Status,' *Human Communication Research* 18:1 (1991), pp. 114–142.
19. Brown and Singhal, p. 95.
20. Household Expenditure Survey, Australia: Summary of Results, 2009–10 (cat. no. 6530.0).http://www.abs.gov.au/ausstats/abs@.nsf/Lookup/6530.0main+f eatures12009–10
21. Valerie Grove, 'Introduction,' in *Mrs Miniver* (London: Virago Press, 1989), p. x.
22. Ibid., p. xi.
23. Brown and Singhal, p. 97.
24. T.S. Eliot, 'East Coker,' in *The Complete Poems and Plays of T.S. Eliot* (London: Faber and Faber, 1969), p. 182.
25. Liz Byrski, *Bad Behaviour* (Sydney: Pan Macmillan, 2009).
26. Liz Byrski, *Last Chance Café* (Sydney: Pan Macmillan, 2011).
27. Liz Byrski, *In the Company of Strangers* (Sydney: Pan Macmillan, 2012).
28. Liz Byrsk, *Belly Dancing for Beginners* (Sydney: Pan Macmillan, 2008).
29. Liz Byrski, *Trip of a Lifetime* (Sydney: Pan Macmillan, 2008).
30. Liz Byrski, *Food, Sex and Money* (Sydney: Pan Macmillan, 2005).
31. Adrienne Rich, *Of Woman Born: Motherhood as Experience and Institution* (New York: W.W. Norton, 1995), p. 188.
32. Rosalind Coward, 'This Novel Changes Lives: Are Women's Novels Feminist Novels?' reprinted in Elaine Showalter (ed.) *The New Feminist Criticism* (New York: Pantheon, 1985), pp. 53–64.
33. Gayle Green, *Changing the Story: Feminist Fiction and the Tradition* (Bloomington: Indiana University Press, 1991), p. 2.
34. Leslie Heywood, *Dedication to Hunger: The Anorexic Aesthetic in Modern Culture* (Berkeley: University of California Press, 1996), p. xii.
35. Scott McCracken, *Pulp: Reading Popular Fiction* (Manchester: Manchester University Press, 1998), p. 1.
36. Ibid., p. 3.
37. Ibid., p. 5.
38. Ibid., p. 5.

2
Fiction or Polemic? Transcending the Ageing Body in Popular Women's Fiction

Imelda Whelehan

In this chapter I examine the representation of older female characters in contemporary popular fiction. I do this with reference to social and cultural discourses of ageing, feminist criticism and age studies, and the work of a selection of contemporary women writers of popular fiction from the UK and Australia. I reflect on how they depict ageing heroines and succeed (or otherwise) in relocating traditional relationship-based concerns of romance fiction, to focus on the needs, ambitions and aspirations of the central characters where often the 'romance' narrative is displaced or absent. I begin by analysing Elizabeth Buchan's *Revenge of the Middle-Aged Woman* (2002) and Fanny Blake's *Women of a Dangerous Age* (2012). These novels feature women in their late forties and fifties experiencing abrupt and unpredicted changes in their personal and professional lives; while their age is not explicitly cited as the cause of these changes, both novels exhibit a consciousness that images of retreat and decline are dominant in culture and that there is no acceptable way to behave as an older woman. The central part of my discussion will consider the fiction and criticism of Liz Byrski, who has spoken out about the near invisibility of older and old women[1] and whose novels explicitly position older women at the heart of the narrative. I will then explore responses to ageing in *Bridget Jones: Mad about the Boy* (2013) and examine whether Helen Fielding succeeds in having Bridget 'grow up'. In the latest addition to the cycle, Bridget Jones, to the dismay of many, has passed 50 and is no longer the hapless singleton she was in the 1990s. The possible conceptual disjunction between women growing older and women growing up, placed in the context of postfeminism's tendency to 'girl' both women and feminism, will shape the core critique offered in this chapter.

While most chick lit heroines contemplate ageing and being single past thirty with dread, late middle-aged and older characters in women's popular fiction are moving out of full-time childcare and sometimes full-time employment. They generally continue to fulfil the role of carer – to elderly relatives, to grown up children, or to men accustomed to having domestic affairs maintained by their partners. Often they are motivated by some unresolved past conflict or tension to travel somewhere, or divorce or bereavement may force significant life changes. This journey, physical or spiritual, is reminiscent of Leslie Kenton's notion of the 'crone's retreat': 'the first step in any initiation is isolation, some kind of withdrawal from our ordinary lives so that we can confront the changes taking place in our bodies and the transformations in our lives and so we can come to terms with what within us is dying and make way for something else to be born'.[2] Kenton's view is that the transitions of ageing are ritually honoured in ancient tribes and valuable to the women who can spend some time alone to reflect on the changes that have occurred to them now that their busiest years are drawing to a close. To focus on this stage of women's lives is to concentrate on an area still rarely depicted in popular or middlebrow fiction. If monogamous love and heterosexual desire to a large extent underpin what might broadly be defined as 'romance' in the popular fiction domain, what takes centre stage in the fiction that depicts an older woman's life? The portrayal of older characters in a genre that broadly favours narratives of courtship and unfettered romantic love raises feminist issues for the writer, regardless of their political affiliations. In diverse ways, in focussing on women in their 40s and beyond, each of the writers discussed in this chapter has to challenge the reductive stereotypes of the ageing woman, as these two-dimensional images prove inadequate for the realisation of a convincing central protagonist.

Mainstreaming middle age

Elizabeth Buchan's *Revenge of the Middle-Aged Woman* and Fanny Blake's *Women of a Dangerous Age* both focus on two women who share a man in common. In Buchan's novel Rose's long marriage to Nathan ends abruptly when he reveals an affair with her younger colleague and friend, Minty. In *Women of a Dangerous Age* Lou and Ali, in their late 50s and mid-40s respectively, meet on holiday in India, where they are both travelling alone – Lou to mark the transition out of a long marriage and Ali about to move in with her lover after years as his mistress. Their shared interest in fashion and design compensates for the fact that they are opposites in every other way: Lou, vibrant and untidy with a love of colours, vintage clothing and food; Ali, healthy, slim, chic and highly organised and a maker of bespoke jewellery. It gradually becomes clear that Lou's ex and Ali's (soon to be ex) lover are the same person. While the story of Rose and Minty in *Revenge of the Middle-Aged Woman* is one of enmity, and part of the pleasure of the novel is the element of revenge narrative promised by the title, Lou and Ali's accidental meeting grows into both a deep friendship and a professional relationship, which give them the strength to revisit and reimagine a past where their shared lover becomes irrelevant. Lou has to come to terms with the fact that her husband was a serial philanderer; Ali is reunited with an old lover whose support persuades her father to tell the truth about her mother's sudden disappearance and suicide, an event that blighted her teenage and adult life. While both these novels look to the future, the past and its reinterpretation also become an important theme. In Rose's case, meeting old flame Hal prompts consideration of the alternative directions her life might have taken, while reconciling her to the decisions she made.

Such reflections prompt important decisions – in Rose's case, she realises that she has devoted too much time to facilitating Nathan's social and professional progress at the expense of her own identity. Rose takes a career break while she evaluates her options; ultimately, this break gives her some flexibility and autonomy, allowing her the time to reconnect with friends and grown-up children, and it offers implicit recognition that women's lives can become clogged with domestic as well as career obligations. Self-evaluation, also, has a physical impact: the shock of the breakup causes Rose to lose weight, and a close friend encourages her to buy a chic new wardrobe. Mirror scenes recur in this book, and while the image reflected back is not the one she would prefer to see, there is an affirmation of its appropriateness. While bathing, Rose studies herself:

> I looked down at my partially submerged body. What did I expect to see? The gleaming bronze of a fountain whose lines flowed untouched and unmarked? My body had swelled in gestation. It had been stretched, ripped, sewn up. It had carried children, cradled them and, when the time had come, pushed them gently away. It had learnt to be endlessly busy, to snatch at repose to guard its silences in the hot, crowded demands of the family. How could all this activity not be written into the flesh?[3]

In one sense this description is a claim for the integrity of the ageing female body; but it requires the justifications of reproduction – of having performed a purpose which takes its toll – rather than acknowledging that age is inscribed into the flesh whether women are mothers or not, and it should not be a source of guilt. Seeking the self in the mirror serves another purpose – claiming space and visibility that really prizes only the young female. Rose finds this especially true once she is no longer part of a couple: 'it was as if a wand had been waved and I was invisible. From having a settled position, as a wife and all that that meant, I was suddenly the blurred figure in the background of a painting or photograph.'[4] It is a moment of triumph when, buoyed by her new career and an amicable reunion with Hal, she realises, 'I was not dead. I was not finished. Neither was I invisible, nor beaten.'[5] These two novels share a sense that the self becomes buried in the identities which marriage and motherhood thrust upon women; Rose's healing is as much a reconnection with the home as a place for her own 'crone's retreat', rather than a symbol of family unity or motherly self-sacrifice. The home subtly shifts from a site of female effacement, reimagined as a space for nurturance of the self.

Heterosexual family life is central in these novels, and there are no significant single or childless characters shown to be dealing with any other variety of invisibility through ageing. In *Women of a Dangerous Age* Lou and Ali's friendship is cemented because they both have family issues to resolve. Lou has to come to terms with her ex-husband's string of affairs and the news he fathered a child with someone else. Her moral determination to make him reveal this fourth child to her own children further fractures the family core. Family has its imprint and impact everywhere: even as Lou leaves her marital home, it is to go and live in the house of her recently dead sister. This focus on family life and its rituals, even when the nuclear family is breaking down, offers a clear link to chick lit's central themes, with careers in the media and fashion also featuring prominently. Rose, Minty and Lou have all been journalists; Lou moves into the quirkier side of the fashion industry when she opens her vintage clothes shop, which enables her to showcase Ali's handmade jewellery. These characters understand that women of a 'certain age' are burdened with the ideological obligation to age appropriately, involving careful self-policing and acknowledging some high-fashion statements scream 'mutton dressed as lamb'. For all Lou's eccentric fashion sense, the narrative underscores her awareness of appropriate apparel for her age:

> She went back to considering her wardrobe and decided on the fifties-style coral-coloured cocktail dress that she'd designed with a

sweetheart neckline not too low (cover the crêpey cleavage), elbow-length sleeves (flatter the flabby upper arms) and a pencil skirt (make the most of those pins) – an understated statement of a dress for a woman of a certain age.[6]

While style and taste unite Lou and Ali, Lou is beset by indignities and embarrassments that draw attention to her abject status as older woman. Her first contact with future lover Sanjeev is farcically described as he rescues her unglamorous control panties from an overflowing suitcase. It is impossible not to call to mind Bridget Jones's oversize panties (so legendary that they warrant further mention in the most recent instalment of her diary). In other ways Lou's misadventures recall the hapless chick lit heroine, adding a new spin to the 'dangerous age' of the title, ranging from a drunken one-night stand with her ex-husband to vomiting after a day out with Sanjeev promises intimacy. Not content with having Lou vomit on her doormat, Blake prolongs the agony as she 'pulled a grubby holed tissue from her mac pocket and blew her nose, despairing when the snot oozed through onto her hand. As she raised one foot to step over the puddle of vomit, she was all too aware of what a hideous sight she must look.'[7] In this scene Lou is watching herself and seeing a grotesque romantic failure, emphasising that even diligent self-scrutiny cannot always maintain the mask of femininity because the abject elements of the scene unseat the romance.

Negative female characters, such as the ex-wife of Ali's old flame, are straightforwardly depicted as excessive, inappropriate and ersatz:

[t]he visitor was smaller than Ali, slightly plumper, with a generous deeply tanned cleavage on show between the lapels of her open coat. Fading blondish hair like spun sugar was arranged around a face in which the features had already blurred with age, the flesh sliding south to settle on her jawline, and a pair of beady eyes clearly summing up what she saw in Ali.[8]

Old lover is compared with (younger) new, and representations of women are often produced this way, through the process of contrast rather than any clearer articulation of what being an 'older' woman means. The difference between the representation of men and women is stark. Don is described thus at their reunion: '[t]here was no mistaking Donovan Sterling. His wild black curls had been snipped into submission and had turned steely grey'; Hooker, Lou's ex-husband, '[u]nlike so many men his age... still looked good in jeans – not bagging round the arse and knees or disappearing under a beer gut'.[9] Physical descriptions underpin each woman's personality; for example, Lou's expansive, colourful exterior mirrors her warm and maternal generosity and her trusting nature; Ali's high degree of self-control and surveillance makes her determined and organised, but it is also used to highlight the psychological damage caused by her mother's disappearance. While Don is portrayed as a genuine and thoughtful lover, Hooker has spent years dissembling to his wife and other women. And yet both are simply represented as physically attractive and 'good for their age', their exterior offering no insights to their psyches.

Buchan's novel offers the pleasures of the revenge plot, but it also suggests that the primary relationship battles take place between the rival women involved. Towards the novel's end, Nathan is bewildered at his choice of Minty over his beloved Rose: 'I made the mistake of thinking sex was something it wasn't.' Rose condones and indulges his fecklessness by blaming herself: 'I thought I had you precisely right and I fitted myself around that strong notion sitting in my head. But I must have missed something, the bit of you that also longed for the green grass on the other side of the fence.'[10] Rose's triumph lies in actually improving her social and professional life as an effect of her separation from Nathan. There is surely a nascent feminist message to be gleaned here, albeit a troubling one for heterosexual women in monogamous relationships, as it suggests that family, more than anything, impedes women's potential. In *Women of a Dangerous Age* Lou's independence and drive conveys clear feminist-inspired choices, and on more than one occasion we are told that 'every feminist bone in her body' objected to certain attitudes of both her husband and son.[11] Her understanding of her marital breakup takes on rather conventional overtones; like Rose, Lou to some extent blames herself for her husband's indiscretions:

> They had been too busy keeping their heads above water, grabbing at whatever kept them afloat, that they had forgotten to put out a hand to help the other. She didn't blame Hooker for that. She had played her part in their game, obsessed as she had been with her work at *Chic to Chic*, then resentful at having to stay at home with the teenage children, however much she loved them. No wonder Hooker had looked for distraction elsewhere.[12]

The strength of this episode is in its psychological realism: it offers a position that a reader can judge adversely or empathise with. Either way, it implies that principles and ideals are derailed by our emotional investments and, for women in particular, the pulls of family versus professional commitments. By the end of both novels the idea that men and women inevitably play different roles in family life is entrenched; the radical critique posed, if not overtly commented on, is that only separation provides liberation and rejuvenation. Not only do these women learn to confront age in growing older; unlike their men, they are portrayed as able to finally grow up.

Popularising feminism: Liz Byrski

British-born Australian novelist Liz Byrski has written seven novels in the last decade and has garnered a readership hungry for representations of women over fifty. In this volume Byrski reflects on her own writing in the context of popular cultural representations of ageing women, and elsewhere she observes that the 'imaginative freedom to enjoy ageing, to recognise its possibilities and rise to its challenges, depends to a considerable extent upon how we see our ageing represented in the world around us.'[13] The older women Byrski found in much fiction were 'usually negative and stereotypical; bossy, interfering mothers-in-law, nosey neighbours, crotchety spinsters, pathetic empty nesters, or feeble and demented burdens, hampering the lives of the really important people; men, young women and children.'[14] Having written as a professional journalist, part of her novelistic ambition is pragmatic – 'I identified a gap and attempted to fill it'[15] – and as a writer coming to fiction relatively late in life her concerns are also closer to home. Her interest in the feminist consciousness-raising novel of the 1960s and 1970s, while failing to provide compelling representations of older women (see Byrski, this volume), provided a model to consider and extend, and her characters are presented as constantly developing and learning. There is emphasis on encouraging recognition of shared issues and problems with the reader, but there is an equal focus on the individuation of character as a counter to the cultural invisibility of the ageing woman. In this sense there is a utopian thread to Byrski's writing which is not so much about envisaging a better quality of life for older people (though it is that, too), but about imagining a societal change in Western responses to age so that decline and death – the long walk 'over the hill' – do not solely inform contemporary discourses of ageing.

I shall explore Byrski's attempts to rehabilitate and diversify fictional representations of older women, examining how narrative concerns shift to incorporate positive images of renewal and rebirth, focussing on change rather than stasis or nostalgic yearnings. The representation of the body in relation to perceptions of consciousness and mental states provides an intriguing point of comparison with Buchan and Blake, prompting further interrogation of Sontag's view that ageing is as much 'an ordeal of the imagination' as it is a lived corporeal experience.[16] Byrski's fiction problematises popular cultural obsessions with the youthful body and defies representations that trap older women in the prison house of biological inevitability. She concentrates on intimate and familial relationships, sexuality and friendships, and her work is imbued with feminist critique. Her narrative concerns extend beyond the purview of 'henlit' or 'mumlit' and the reader is encouraged to look at dominant social values askance, particularly as they relate to older women's experiences. Just as a number of feminist critics have addressed the 'girling' of popular culture through an exploration of the discourses of postfeminism, which as Diane Negra notes, 'thrives on anxiety about aging',[17] so Byrski addresses this exploration in her popular fiction by making ageing visible from the point of view of central characters in their fifties and beyond and by remodelling this part of a woman's life as one of choice, adventure and sometimes reconciliation and forgiveness.

The working title of Byrski's first novel was *Crone's Retreat*, in direct reference to Leslie Kenton's work on ritualising ageing as a positive journey, prompting one prospective publisher to ask, 'is this fiction or polemic because it can't be both.'[18] Conscious of the marketplace, Byrski changed her title to *Gang of Four* (2005), but her feminist voice remains, insisting on the right for fiction and polemic to sit together and convinced that popular fiction has always had the potential for a critical and challenging voice. The success of *Gang of Four* proved that Byrski's blend of gender politics and entertainment could engage her audience and her aim to paint a more nuanced, complete picture of the ageing woman is underpinned by quiet feminist determination. Whether the fiction can always contain the polemic, or whether it should, is a moot point.

The success of Byrski's work in Australasia, and more recently in Europe, suggests a buoyant and discerning market demand and a thirst for alternative views on ageing. Part of Byrski's strategy is to avoid fixing older women in contemporary, popular stereotypes, and to that end there are various 'facts' of ageing that she more or less avoids, including depictions of the physical effects of menopause. For the last 20 years or more, women have been bombarded by a slew of medical discourses about menopause and its effects, to the point that one might be forgiven for thinking that if menopause could be avoided, so could the ageing process. This discourse is so pervasive that few mainstream challenges are made to its assumptions or the social and ideological impact of positioning menopause as a disability heralding long-term decline. Hormone replacement and other therapies are, in this context, presented almost as a 'cure', the only way of retaining femininity. For Margaret Morganroth Gullette the 'menoboom' of the 1990s is inseparable from the backlash: '[m]enopause discourse flourishes at a moment when (some) women are seen to be powerful, rich, and attractive.'[19] With this cultural baggage in evidence, it is for good reason that menopause as a physical event or 'ailment' is not dwelt on in Byrski's work. She might more readily agree with Germaine Greer that the 'climacteric marks the end of apologizing. The chrysalis of conditioning has once and for all to break and the female woman finally to emerge.'[20] This dominant discourse of decline and diminishment associated with menopause is accompanied by upbeat but equally insidious narratives of 'successful ageing', which require both women and men to fight deterioration by absorbing and acting upon the many contradictory sources of advice – ranging from diet and exercise to brain training and positive thinking. As Byrski notes in this volume, it is a phony war that can only discourage and fill with dread those not yet arrived at the magic transition point where suddenly turning back time can be the only aspiration.

In Byrski's novels, mid to late life is reconceived as an opportunity rather than a threat. Most of the women portrayed are professionals and many have senior positions; often their professional status is contrasted to that at home. The focus on what they do and how they feel quite deliberately obscures questions of how they look and how people respond to their bodies. While characters lament increased inches around their waist, grey hairs and other typical signs of ageing, offering a realistic depiction of how many women internalise popular cultural physical norms around the desirable female body, detailed physical descriptions are rare. In *Belly Dancing for Beginners* (2007) Sonya, a novice belly dancer, worries that her flab will ruin the line of her costume and is assured that Marissa, the teacher, is much larger, though at no time is her size revealed or cast in negative terms. Biological effects of ageing, such as aches and pains and fatigue, do get a mention, and illness is a fact of life, but for many of the characters the journeys they are able to take are rejuvenating and allow them to reassess their own social and cultural positioning.

Byrski deals head on with an internalised, generalised disgust for the old by having her characters grieve and feel guilt over their own ageing or senile parents. Generational relationships are depicted to flesh out the complex caring and social roles which women over 50 play. While not all her characters are in marriages (or are heterosexual) those that have long-term intimate partners are often the most hungry for space and change. As Isabel in *Gang of Four* laments, the continuing ties to her grown-up family extend to all kinds of less physically strenuous but nonetheless demanding domestic labour – hosting family events, remembering birthdays, planning Christmas, renewing policies, etc. Reflecting on the imbalance of domestic chores in her marriage, Isabel blames herself for husband Doug's 'learned helplessness': 'Why did she always do for him what any adult should do for himself: take his clothes to the cleaners, make dental appointments and remind him to keep them, iron his shirts, book the car for service and deliver it? It wasn't even that she had more time. She too had always had a full-time job, only taking breaks to have the children.'[21] Doug, it is noted, maintained a 'benign dictatorship enabled by her', a phrase which recalls Sylvia Plath's depiction of marriage as a 'private totalitarian state'.[22] Reflections on the continued imbalance of domestic labour and the difficulties various characters experience in enacting their feminist values in all aspects of their lives recurs. In Byrski's writing and like Blake's novel discussed above, the reader is encouraged to reflect upon their individual circumstances and note how common this 'learned helplessness' might be. In *Belly Dancing for Beginners*, historian Oliver's work on Nazi wives prompts him to question why his friend Gayle stays married to a bullying, homophobic husband who disowns their gay son. Oliver remarks to another friend, 'women's conditioning sets them up for some of these awful moral dilemmas, you know, love and duty, being intimidated, bullied, unable to speak out', to which Sonya counters 'What is this? Feminism 101?'[23] By identifying the potential didactic tone of this exchange, Byrski betrays a moment of authorial reflectiveness that exposes the blurred line between fiction and polemic as well as the chasm between lived realities and our moral or theoretical ideals.

Byrski's work carries recognisable themes of women's popular culture, most notably that of the makeover. In chick lit this makeover is often portrayed as the point when the heroine's excess pounds miraculously fade away, a different outfit complements her body, or people around her finally appreciate her true worth. Byrski employs this trope to emphasise attitudinal and emotional changes in her characters (with outer transformations taking second place) and to explode what empty clichés prevail around the figure of the ageing woman. Here she exploits the relative silence about ageing to her distinct advantage. In her novels women confront themselves, are caught unawares, or are reflected through the eyes of their friends. The mirror is not only the heroine's candid assessment of self; it is also the lens through which cultural discourses of ageing set up expectations and corresponding disappointments. Vivian Sobchack speaks of her 'increasing inability to see myself – with any objectivity – at all'.[24] What is there for the mature woman to see except the shadow of the self she was where youth offers the singular model of female beauty?

In *Gang of Four* mirror scenes include one where Isabel, coached by new friend Sara on how to dress for travelling: 'surveyed herself in the fitting room mirror in a close-fitting cream T-shirt and khaki pants and was pleased at the effect'.[25] Later, Isabel once again gazes in the mirror to notice that she 'looked so different from the woman who had stared back at her from the mirror in her bathroom at home.'[26] Her friend Robin, desperately ill with cancer, looks up from her hospital bed to see a similarly transformed Isabel in front of her, but the details of the trans-formation are left for us to imagine. In *Belly Dancing for Beginners* when Gayle looks at her reflection in full belly-dancing costume, she is amazed at the transformation that marks a further step away from her stultifying marriage, so here the makeover expresses a renegotiation of the self. To see oneself accurately in the mirror is the beginnings of a rejection of ageism. The mirror is also a metaphor for realising one's life can be lived in other ways than those most commonly refracted through popular culture and the mass media, a symbol of the process of consciousness raising by sharing experiences and looking at social norms askance. As one of Byrski's characters says in *Gang of Four*, 'It's easy to have all those ideals and beliefs when we're not being challenged at a deeply personal level. But we only really find out how we feel when something thrusts its spanner into our own lives.'[27]

This process of becoming is at the spine of Byrski's writing and the journey motif figures strongly as part of that. Her characters' journeys, while treacherous, bring the comforts of greater understanding of both the self and the past. In each case it is the women that instigate change, often when they are released from other 'ties' by the departure of a child or the death of an elderly parent. In *Gang of Four* Isabel retraces the steps of her dead mother, a dancer who toured Europe in the 50s, to accidentally discover her mother's female lover; her friend Sally traces the baby she gave up as a young woman, but she has been severely physically and mentally disabled in a car crash; Grace takes a sabbat-ical from her academic job; Robin buys a house in a the country and abandons her legal practice in favour of a bookshop. By the end of the year that marks their various crone's retreats, Robin has died after being diagnosed with particularly aggressive cancer, and the dynamics of friendship and familial relationships have adjusted to incorporate the women's new selves.

While her novels are optimistic, life-enhancing portrayals of older women, they are also dialogues with social realities including death, illness and mourning. Isabel's quest infects her friends and while what they learn is important and life changing, part of what they learn involves mentally travelling backwards in time and addressing parts of themselves which have not aged but still remain locked in childhood or young adult traumas. In *Belly Dancing for Beginners* the most wise, giving person who is at home with her body is Marissa, but she is also the one nursing the most deeply buried trauma, the secret of a gang rape as a young woman. Chillingly, her glimpse of Gayle's husband and recognition of him as the ringleader of the attack alerts the reader to Brian's darker past. In this novel bodily awakening does prompt psychological changes in Gayle and Sonya and also in Oliver, who learns to tango in order to liberate himself from excessively coy behaviour around people whom he is attracted to. With changes in social behaviour and some loss of inhibition comes assertion and self-reliance, which, for many of the women portrayed in Byrski's work, is the greatest challenge of all.

If we agree with Judith Butler that the 'abject designates here precisely those "unlivable" and "uninhabitable" zones of social life which are nevertheless densely populated by those who do not enjoy the status of the subject'[28] we can see Byrski's work as an exploration of the abjection of ageing, recalling Byrski's reflections on herself and her contemporaries who 'pollute the tree-lined streets, the shopping centres, the many coffee shops, the footpaths and the parks with our oldness; a constant, unpleasant reminder to younger generations of what lies ahead.'[29] The still-active old are all too visible on the streets, she suggests, as opposed to the media landscapes where they quietly disappear into the background. Her project in writing fiction is to make those zones liveable again in the minds of older women who might be mourning the loss of their younger selves or remain unable to recognise their grown-up present selves when they catch sight of their reflection.

A born-again singleton

The third Bridget Jones novel, *Bridget Jones: Mad about the Boy* (2013) was published after a widely-circulated news 'spoiler' informed fans that Mark Darcy was to be killed off. While this spoiler came as a surprise to many, the structure of a novel in this genre that features a devoted husband has no narrative arc. As I have argued elsewhere, both chick lit and chick flicks rely on the prolonged absence of the love object so the heroine can assess his virtues with her friends as well as enjoy the most functional and sustaining relationships – those shared with friends.[30] Fielding has chosen to return Bridget, via tragedy, to her much lauded singleton role. While Bridget is a young widow, she is also an old singleton: at 51, with two primary school aged children, she also corresponds to an expanding demographic of older mothers who defer childbirth until their mid to late forties. At first sight the book seems to be a candidate for mumlit, best exemplified by Alison Pearson's *I Don't Know How She Does It* (2002), as if, in cyclical terms Fielding is imitating her imitators. But in this book Bridget represents something relatively untouched in mumlit – the fact of ageing in a world, and indeed in a fictional genre, that gazes at 50 but never normally crosses the threshold.

Bridget Jones's Diary (1996) is part of popular fictional history, and its status as a bestseller and the successful sequel and tie-in films developed a character with relevance beyond this time. In allowing Bridget to age, Fielding acknowledges that chick lit readers from the 1990s are facing this new phase in their lives. From the opening of the novel, it is clear not just that Bridget has aged, but also that the dating world has changed beyond recognition. Facebook, Twitter, e-dating and further advances in social media make Bridget's continued commitment to her diary seem even more outmoded. Bridget attempts to master these new forms of communication and her modest success leads her to become a very post-millennial ageing female stereotype – the cougar – dating a man over twenty years her junior. From the start Roxster loves Bridget because of, not in spite of, her tendency to be at the heart of comedically slapstick disasters. In recalling the Bridget of the first novel, these incidents make her seem as young as her lover. In fact, Bridget and her friends all seem to be in suspended animation, and when they gather to discuss their romantic encounters, they appear not to have aged a bit. What alerts us to the fact that time has indeed moved on is that they have all achieved degrees of professional success while failing to cleanse their messy love lives or indeed learning from their romantic mistakes. Jude, still haunted by horrid ex Vile Richard, 'practically runs the City', while quasi-feminist Shazzer, absent from this book, is married to a dot com millionaire and lives in Silicon Valley. Tom, dispenser of appalling relationship advice, is 'quite a senior psychologist'.[31]

Bridget's attempt at a career in screenwriting, adapting *Hedda Gabler*, draws reflexively on the adaptive nature of the Bridget Jones books which plundered themes and characters from *Pride and Prejudice* and *Persuasion* and reminds us of the significance of the successful film adaptations, themselves referred to in the new novel. The reference to Hedda, a character who asserts that her 'dancing days are over', gestures towards the huge, uncharted fictional landscape of the older woman and, in Bridget's ingenuously ironic words, to 'the perils of trying to live through men'.[32] Is this inability of Bridget and her friends to 'grow up' in their personal lives simply a narrative means of maintaining continuity with the successful formula of the first two books, or does it prove cause for reflection on whether romance narratives can express mature themes? Bridget regards herself as permanently out of sync with her married acquaintances, as if their lives operate on a completely different chronology, 'because I was at a different stage of life, even though I was the same age. It was as though there had been a seismic timeshift and my life was happening years behind theirs, in the wrong way.'[33] There is a tension between Bridget's role as a mother and as a lover, which cannot be reconciled in her relations with Roxster: he simply becomes an additional 'child' and playmate, their relationship ending when he feels the need to 'grow up' by finding someone nearer his own age.

Tensions between youth and age, past and present, are brought to bear on the character of schoolteacher Mr Wallaker, who refuses to pander to the needy, entitled behaviour of the parents, but rather manages the children with military precision. As the Mr Right of this volume, his encounters with Bridget are characterised by misunderstandings and bad timing, and his Darcy-like hauteur is explained by traumas experienced in the SAS in Afghanistan. A more age-appropriate match for Bridget and described as 'rather like Daniel Craig', this Bond reference marks him out as a 'man' rather than a 'boy'. The mixture of old school, discipline-oriented education versus new agey focus on the 'developing child' focusses on the anachronisms of his ageing masculinity, but also it shows the ease with which an attractive older man can be depicted in fiction.[34] Bridget, in contrast, is torn between the image of her youthful past and the future as embodied by her aged mother, also widowed. For Bridget 'middle aged' is the worst adjective in that it summons 'a certain past-it-ness non-viability', and her body acts as testimony to the realities of middle-aged spread: 'Am starting to look like a heron. My legs and arms have stayed the same, but my whole upper body is like a large bird with a big roll of fat round the middle that, when clothed, looks like it should be served up at Christmas with cranberry jelly and gravy.'[35] The two models of 'successful ageing' available to Bridget are in mutual contradiction; there is TV presenter Talitha, just turned 60, whose mantra is that it is 'better to die of Botox than die of loneliness because you're so wrinkly',[36] and her mother who lives in a retirement community which actively encourages fitness, socialising and adventure but is cringingly embarrassing in the generation gap it exposes. Ultimately, Bridget's salvation is in a new monogamous relationship with Mr Wallaker, consumated in a sexually charged penultimate scene that could do credit to Mills and Boon: 'Oh God. He was so masterful, he was such a MAN!'[37] Fielding airs some core concerns about ageing to represent Bridget two decades on; nevertheless the closure allows her the protection of coupledom to deflect the invisibility and lack of purpose felt by characters such as Rose in *Revenge of the Middle-Aged Woman*.

Conclusion

Byrski's work brings a critique of ageing to popular consciousness; she is unusual in that her fiction aligns with her criticism and wider political purpose. But these other novels which depict older women at the centre also allow us to assess the ways ageism is internalised and inscribed in conventions of representation of female characters. Byrski's work makes use of feminist critiques, but she is also aware, as Kathleen Woodward asserts, that 'ageism is entrenched within feminism itself'.[38] Blake and Buchan rely on psychological realism and Fielding on observational humour to allow the reader a different, critical perspective on age. My readings of all these writers have led me to realise the extent of the gap they are filling in women's popular fiction. Age studies is still taking on board the impact of gender; and feminism, ironically (like Madonna), has remained forever young, or forever the battleground of the young, where newer 'waves' of feminism deploy the language of generational conflict to expound why feminism has little relevance to them. In popular cultural studies a recent focus on the discourses of postfeminism and the 'girling' of women has further displaced considerations of age and ageing. After all, images of women displaying youth populate our cultural imaginary in ways that bring them to the forefront of our minds. On the other hand, images of ageing women collapse into a few reductive types, providing little direction to, in Betty Friedan's words, 'break through the cocoon of our illusory youth and risk a new stage in life, where there are no prescribed role models to follow, no guideposts, no rigid rules or visible rewards, to step out into the true existential unknown of these new years of life now open to us.'[39] In many ways feminism has spent so much time making itself relevant to the young that it is ill-equipped to face renewed challenges within an ageing western population. However, recent memoirs by prominent feminists such as Lynne Segal, who takes on de Beauvoir's legacy to focus on the 'psychology and politics of ageing', possibly herald a more nuanced feminist response to these issues.[40]

As Margaret Morganroth Gullette notes, despite the emergence of older women writers in both literary and popular culture in the early twentieth century, 'as feminism appeared to gain strength, so too did the subversive force of ageism'.[41] Feminists who started writing in the 1970s and 1980s are the baby boomers now swelling the ranks of the retired or soon to be retired, and yet it is as if they have been reluctant to look into the mirror and chart their own lived experiences. Woodward suspects that feminism, like popular culture, has remained ageist. If people cannot bear the sight of a naturally ageing female body on screen, or stomach the challenges of narrating ageing authentically in a fictional form shaped by romance and youth, the tasks Byrski has set for herself as a feminist *writing* the ageing body are clear. Importantly, Byrski's construction of this stage of a woman's life is as a turning point, the beginning of something, a quest, is echoed in writings such as those by Buchan and Blake. Dana Heller, writing about the female appropriation of the quest motif, argues that 'the feminisation of the quest begins in a word: "No." The female subject assumes the task of continuing to say no to domination, of continuing to speak in her own voice even when she fears that no one will comprehend her. Her fear is understandable, for her voice emerges always in relation to a historical absence that precedes her, an absence from which she still must proceed.'[42] The quests described in these novels, focussing as they do on the fictional portrayal of the life of the older woman, draw attention to an even greater historical absence, and the risk that no one will comprehend her words is felt much more keenly.

Notes

1. Liz Byrski, *Getting On: Some Thoughts on Women and Ageing* (Sydney: Momentum, 2012).
2. Leslie Kenton, *Passage to Power: Natural Menopause Revolution* (New York: Random House, 2011), p. 271.
3. Elizabeth Buchan, *Revenge of the Middle-Aged Woman* (London: Penguin, 2002), p. 71.
4. Ibid., p. 214.
5. Ibid., p. 342.
6. Fanny Blake, *Women of a Dangerous Age* (London: HarperCollins, 2012), pp. 150–151.
7. Ibid., p. 278.
8. Ibid., p. 359.

9. Ibid., p. 204; p. 97.
10. Buchan, pp. 323–324.
11. Blake, p. 99; p. 165.
12. Ibid., p. 392.
13. Liz Byrski, 'Getting Noticed: Images of Older Women in Australian Popular Culture,' *Australian Studies*, 2 (2010), p. 2.
14. Ibid., p. 3.
15. Ibid., p. 8.
16. Susan Sontag, 'The Double Standard of Aging,' in *The Other within Us: Feminist Explorations of Women and Aging*, ed. Marilyn Pearsall (Boulder, Colorado: Westview Press, 1997), p. 19.
17. Diane Negra, *What a Girl Wants?: Fantasizing the Reclamation of Self in Postfeminism* (London: Routledge, 2009), p. 12.
18. Byrski, 'Getting Noticed ... ,' p. 10.
19. Margaret Morganroth Gullette, *Declining to Decline: Cultural Combat and the Politics of the Midlife* (Charlottesville: University Press of Virginia, 1997), p. 99.
20. Germaine Greer, 'Serenity and Power,' in *The Other within Us: Feminist Explorations of Women and Aging*, ed. Marilyn Pearsall (Boulder, Colorado: Westview Press, 1997), p. 273.
21. Byrski, *Gang of Four* (Sydney: Pan Macmillan, 2005), p. 251.
22. Byrski, *Gang of Four*, p. 320; Sylvia Plath, *The Bell Jar* (London: Faber and Faber, 1981), p. 89.
23. Byrski, *Belly Dancing for Beginners* (Sydney: Pan Macmillan, 2007), p. 257.
24. Vivian Sobchack, 'Scary Women: Cinema, Surgery, and Special Effects,' in *Figuring Age: Women, Bodies, Generations*, ed. Kathleen Woodward (Bloomington: Indiana University Press, 1999), pp. 200–201.
25. Byrski, *Gang of Four*, p. 75.
26. Ibid., p. 115.
27. Ibid., p. 45.
28. Judith Butler, *Bodies that Matter: On the Discursive Limits of 'Sex'* (New York: Routledge, 1993), p. 3.
29. Byrski, *Getting On*, p. 53.
30. See Imelda Whelehan, 'Remaking Feminism: Or Why is Postfeminism So Boring?,' *Nordic Journal of English Studies*, 9:3 (2010), pp. 155–172.
31. Helen Fielding, *Bridget Jones: Mad about the Boy* (London: Jonathan Cape, 2013), p. 12; p. 13.
32. Ibid., p. 17.
33. Ibid., p. 65.
34. Ibid., p. 5.
35. Ibid., p. 67; p. 48.
36. Ibid., p. 32.
37. Ibid., p. 378.
38. Kathleen Woodward, 'Introduction,' in *Figuring Age: Women, Bodies, Generations*, ed. Kathleen Woodward (Bloomington: Indiana University Press, 1999), p. xi.
39. Betty Friedan, *The Fountain of Age* (London: Jonathan Cape, 1993), p. 33.
40. Lynne Segal, *Out of Time: The Pleasures and Perils of Ageing* (London: Verso, 2013), p. 4.

41. Margaret Morganroth Gullette, 'Creativity, Aging, Gender: A Study of the Intersections, 1910–1935,' in *Aging and Gender in Literature: Studies in Creativity,* ed. Anne M. Wyatt-Brown and Janice Rossen (Charlottesville: University Press of Virginia, 1993), p. 44.
42. Dana A. Heller, *The Feminization of Quest-Romance: Radical Departures* (Austin: University of Texas Press, 1990), pp. 13–14.

3
'Mrs Robinson Seeks Benjamin': Cougars, Popular Memoirs and the Quest for Fulfilment in Midlife and Beyond

Joel Gwynne

A one night stand with a 19-year-old. A seven-year affair with her 27-year-old estate agent. But is Wendy, 61, even a little bit ashamed of her passion for toyboys? Not a bit of it...[1] So begins Kathryn Knight's review in The *Daily Mail* of Wendy Salisbury's *The Toyboy Diaries: Sexploits of an Older Woman* (2007), a memoir that chronicles the trials and tribulations of intergenerational dating. Both summoning and yet disavowing the possibility of shame, Knight's words are revealing in gesturing towards the recognition of a very contemporary discord between the historical construction of older women's sexuality as taboo, and the reconfiguration of this taboo in the contemporary moment. Indeed, while critics such as Susan Sontag have long positioned the experience of ageing for the older woman within the decline narrative as 'a humiliating process of gradual sexual disqualification',[2] representations of sexually active older women have become increasingly visible over the past decade through the cultural ubiquity of the 'cougar': an older woman who seeks younger lovers. By celebrating a woman's capacity to 'flirt, flourish and fornicate into [her] fifties and beyond',[3] both Salisbury's debut memoir and its sequel, *The Toyboy Diaries 2: The Daily Male* (2009), ride the crest of the wave of this recent fascination with sexually agentic midlife women apparent across all aspects of contemporary cultural production.

Certainly, even though Lynne Segal as recently as 2007 identified the sexual agency of the older woman as a form of 'dissident desire',[4] it is clear that the desiring and desirable postmillennial midlife woman has now cast off at least some of her dissidence. Rather than a transgressive figure, she has instead become a central, perhaps even reactionary, archetype of popular culture – as Sharron Hinchliff demonstrates in her chapter in this book. One needs only to cast a cursory glance at any aspect of visual and print culture to see both the presence of the cougar and her deployment as a standard bearer of youthful postfeminism, for within this cultural discourse her sexual activity is invariably linked to her 'girling'. Postfeminist culture has, after all, reconstructed our entire understanding of the relationship between age and womanhood, as Sarah Projansky contends:

> If the postfeminist woman is always in process, always using the freedom and equality handed to her by feminism in pursuit of having it all (including discovering her sexuality) but never quite managing to reach full adulthood, to fully have it all, one could say that the postfeminist woman is quintessentially adolescent no matter what her age.[5]

Within this climate the cougar is able to legitimise her voracious sexuality as culturally acceptable because her literal age belies both her physical appearance and her embracing of the hedonistic pleasures of youth. Indeed, it is in this context that the representation of the cougar rose to discursive prominence in 1998 with the appearance of Kim Cattrall's hypersexual Samantha Jones in *Sex and the City* (1998–2004), a representation elevated within popular television from supporting character to protagonist via Courtney Cox's performance as Jules Cobb in *Cougar Town* (2009–Present). More recently, Claire Irvin's *Cougars: You're as Young as the Man You Feel* (2011) marks this subject position as emerging in contemporary popular fiction. Beyond popular entertainment, Google searches of terms such as 'cougar woman' yield not only the international dating websites *cougerlife.com*, *cougered.com* and *dateacougar.com*, but also clubs and societies such as *therealcougarwoman.net* for the 'smart, sexy, independent and proud' woman over 40 who is 'not afraid to try new things, and even if she is, does it anyway.'[6] The mission statement on the homepage of this particular website is revealing:

> The mission of *The Real Cougar Woman* is to re-connect women to their power. Too often women lose sight of their precious dreams because of the demands that life puts on them. Too often women are conditioned by old fashioned role models that put them last on the priority line. We want to refocus those priorities so they can soar to new heights.[7]

The cougar is thus constructed not merely as a subject position that signifies the reclamation of sexuality for the older woman, but also as one that invokes the complex 'politics' of postfeminism by emphasising individual empowerment while eliding the means by which empowerment is attained in the absence of collective feminist activism. Statements such as the one quoted above affirm the power of the older woman to take control of her life and 'soar to new heights', while offering no explanation of how, exactly, she is able to elevate her status in society and, more importantly, what her 'power' constitutes. The sheer pervasiveness of such statements across culture institutes what can be termed as a 'cougar discourse' which testifies to the nexus between postfeminism and neoliberalism, attributing a woman's success and status in society both to responsible self-management and to the execution of a positive, individualised life project. Even though such discourses not only perniciously dislocate empowerment from feminist politics, but also disregard the wider structural imbalances and inequalities experienced by older women, the cougar is nevertheless framed and marketed as an enduring symbol of postfeminist agency.

This chapter seeks to explore the conflict within cougar discourses between feminist politics and postfeminist disavowal. Focusing on Wendy Salisbury's memoir, *The Toyboy Diaries: Sexploits of an Older Woman*, and its sequel, *The Toyboy Diaries 2: The Daily Male*, I explore the depiction of an older woman who appears to fully capitulate to popular culture's prevailing message that female sexual desirability and subjectivity is inevitably bound up in discourses of youth. The chapter aims to underscore the problems that women confront when attempting to adhere to the narrow dictates of postfeminist desirability despite the somatic obstacles presented by ageing, and it seeks to answer the following questions: If women have historically been encouraged to 'eroticize the more distant, more powerful, father figure',[8] then what are the feminist implications of seeking a lover who is significantly younger? Does the 'coming out' of the older desiring subject signal a victory for feminism, or do 'May to December liaisons'[9] represent nothing more than, in the words of Ursula Owen, the 'odd prospect of happy fucks'?[10]

Resisting decline: the feminist implications of toyboy dating

Salisbury's debut memoir begins with a number of strong feminist declarations which serve to challenge many of society's expectations of the ageing woman, most notably by contesting the association of ageing with decline, restriction and dependence. Calling to mind Betty Friedan's hypothesis that women are especially resilient and adaptable during ageing due to the sustained discontinuity that has historically pervaded their lives,[11] Salisbury identifies her positive response to ageing as matrilineal: 'My mother at eighty-six is determined and acerbic still, frustrated even now if a day passes without achievement. The female work ethic rates highly in my family.'[12] By demonstrating female strength in adversity, Salisbury's memoir reveals its feminist politics at various junctures. It begins by placing particular emphasis on the importance of women's independence in later life, declaring the need for self-sufficiency 'determined by our actions, not those of others.'[13] The narrator positively interprets Gabriel García Márquez's dictum that 'The secret of a comfortable old age is to make a pact with solitude', asserting that, 'solitude, and even singledom, is fine – but loneliness is not.'[14] The manner in which she rejects a life of loneliness appears to mark her memoir as a feminist narrative, for rather than celebrate the importance of long-term male companionship in old age, the narrative instead begins by celebrating female solidarity among daughters and friends, the 'comforting bosom of my family and the Sisterhood':[15]

> My girlfriends are my rocks; there to cling to when the maelstrom gets too much... The dynamic between us is vibrant: a forceful flow of female energy so electric it would shock any bloke who dared to touch the fuse wire. Historically, we are likely to survive our men, and have in place contingency plans for the future. ... So a group of us are thinking of selling our respective homes, pooling our resources and buying one big house together.[16]

Salisbury's rejection of heterosexual, monogamous companionship in favour of singledom and sisterhood is predicated on a gendered double-standard of ageing, one that forces women to relentlessly pursue physical desirability while absolving men of this responsibility. While the narrator identifies herself and her female friends as 'attractive, sexy, vibrant older women', she laments the grim social reality that men of a similar age 'think they can pull you because they've got money and a pulse and that any single woman is desperate for a man at any cost.'[17] Rejecting marriage proposals from a number of wealthy older men, Salisbury espouses what could be perceived as a number of feminist lifestyle choices when she refuses to compromise her own independence in exchange for financial rewards: 'A whole house in Holland Park Avenue with 2.4 gardeners and a dog may be some girls' idea of heaven but it sounded to me like a slow comfortable death.'[18] By positioning companionship with an older man as 'a less challenging option', Salisbury announces her decision to date men who are considerably younger, declaring that she would rather 'eat one lavish meal' than have 'the security of bread.'[19] Even though the narrator is motivated by primarily the pursuit of sexual pleasure – 'any notches on the bedpost, even if they damage the woodwork, are better than no notches at all'[20] – she also asserts the feminist implications of her lifestyle. In her second memoir, published two years after the first, she declares: 'My sister compliments me hesitantly on my success, but she too is slightly disconcerted about what people might think. But there are many voices of approbation to counter these attacks, compliments and thanks from other women who claim I've "changed the way they look at life". A flattering flutter of fan mail arrives daily in my email inbox.'[21]

It is not difficult to understand why Salisbury may be an aspirational figure to some older women. Jeannette King persuasively argues that influential writers of fiction such as Doris Lessing insist on the continuing existence of older female desire, 'rejecting the expectation that with age a woman becomes degendered and content with a more cerebral or spiritual existence.'[22] If Lessing's novels depict older women protagonists struggling with their sexuality in ways rarely seen before,[23] then Salisbury's memoir is arguably even more radical and potentially more impactful, given both its status as a work of nonfiction and its highly explicit representation of the desiring ageing body. Moreover, in foreshadowing her representation of sexual subjectivity, Salisbury's depiction of the ageing body as an object of desire is also significant, urging the reader to dispel any imaginative investment in the pervasive stereotype of 'a little lady with a tight grey perm queuing up for her pension' by invoking a comparison between herself and images of energetic stardom: 'Helen Mirren, Susan Sarandon, Catherine Deneuve, Goldie Hawn, Diane Keaton, Judi Dench, Joanna Lumley – sexy sirens one and all.'[24] If critics such as E. Ann Kaplan have noted the invisibility of the ageing female body in terms of desirability and cultural representation,[25] then Salisbury's memoir aims to correct this pattern by announcing the manifold allures of the older woman: 'carnal experience, worldly wisdom, financial security, maternal nurturing and abandoned sexuality.'[26]

As I will discuss in more detail later, Salisbury's pronouncements on the desirability of the older woman are often overly deterministic, essentialist, and supportive of certain cultural stereotypes surrounding transgressive female sexuality. However, it remains difficult to deny the positive intent of her memoir, for the narrator's exuberant celebration of sexual desire and sexual performance provokes both the reader and social convention: 'I bucked urgently against his face and exploded all too quickly as his hungry mouth consumed the flow of pent-up juices pouring forth from me.'[27] Descriptions of sex dominate the narrative, and this type of content, written by a sixty-year old woman, is undeniably difficult to find in popular culture. The equation of beauty with youth – and beauty as a prerequisite for sex – is a gendered equation, and one which fosters a culture of hostility towards older women embarking on intimate relationships. As Jacqueline Zita notes, the ideology of ageism represents 'the old female as asexual if not antisexual',[28] and Salisbury's memoir makes positive use of feminism's discursive inroads into the fraught territory of female sexuality in order to resist this particular form of ageism. If, as feminists have long established, the 'vocabulary of sex is much more concerned with describing what happens to a man's body during sexual arousal than a woman's',[29] then Salisbury's mapping of older women's desire is doubly significant; not only does her memoir contribute to a corpus of feminist literature expressing a frank articulation of female desire, it also works towards remedying the elision of older women's sexual subjectivity within culture.

Chasing youth

Lynne Segal has suggested a number of reasons why older women may be able to occupy a dominant position in relationships with younger men, positing that masculinity is achieved through the 'flight from the mother, from childhood dependency'.[30] To this aim, Salisbury exploits her position as an older woman by presenting an image of maternal constancy and support, enabling the manipulation, use and disposal of younger men. At one particularly noteworthy moment in her debut memoir, a younger lover rejects her application of the term 'toyboy': 'It makes us sound like you just want to use us and throw us away'. Salisbury's riposte marks her as a stridently feminist avenger, pointing out that by doing so she is merely 'redressing the balance'.[31] While it is difficult to deny the feminist imperatives of her articulation of sexual desire and casual sex, what remains more problematic, however, is the manner in which sex is positioned by the author as the older woman's *primary* route to empowerment. It is in this way that the feminist politics of the memoir are co-opted by postfeminism. Kathrina Glitre has argued that 'the postfeminist sensibility encourages self-indulgent pleasure to be mistaken for empowerment',[32] and Salisbury too often confuses sexual pleasure with material liberation. Enthusing that modern 'single sirens are free to celebrate their sexual freedom in whichever way they choose', the narrator sees the sexual permissiveness of contemporary society as affording new possibilities for the postfeminist older woman who, in the past, 'didn't get many firsts after fifty except perhaps fittings for false teeth or a hot flush in the Fuller Figure department.'[33] Understanding sexual freedom as the most significant outcome of the women's movement, Salisbury frames her sexual adventures within the ironic vernacular of popular feminism: 'I'd pulled a handsome, young buck and it was my moral duty to validate that for the sake of the sisterhood.'[34]

In Salisbury's memoir, then, sex with younger men is understood as both a positive outcome of the feminist movement and as a validation of the narrator's self-identification as a feminist. While this is by and of itself a highly reductive conceptualisation of political feminism, it is also problematic for other reasons. By expressing her feminism within the context of sex and the pursuit of younger men, Salisbury is also forced to pursue a youthful appearance, and her lifestyle loses its political charge in its corresponding celebration of youth culture and consumption as the vehicles of empowerment. Accompanying postfeminism's foregrounding of youth is the admonishment to older women urging them to extend theirs, or at least the appearance of youth, for as long as possible. Likewise, Salisbury's memoir presents a dramatisation of neoliberalism's figuring of women as rational, calculating individuals whose autonomy is measured by their capacity for 'self-care', manifested as a strict adherence to contemporary fashion trends and punishing grooming rituals. The narrator notes that while 'Time is a thief', she has 'fought it tooth and manicured nail with a dedicated beauty routine and the blessing of good genes from [her] Russian-Jewish ancestors.'[35] Her commitment to bodily self-management is worth quoting at length:

> I imposed upon myself a week-long regime of self-denial and physical abuse. Semi-starvation to get my stomach flat consisted of a fruit and veg only detox diet which left me raving and craving (chocolate, of course, what else?). To look fit and fabulous: full body exfoliation, deep-tissue massage, hours of diligent fake tanning during which I had to walk around naked like I'd lost my horse and both water melons, a sphincter-clenching Hollywood waxing, manicure, pedicure, highlights, pelvic floor lifts, push-ups, stretches, *kvetches*, underarm shaving, nipple and eyebrow plucking, morning and night-time applications of a new gel called Face Lift (at £33? I don't think so...).[36]

Salisbury's regime is not unusual given contemporary culture's emphasis on femininity as a pathological condition that necessitates relentless body work, yet her valorisation of youth, young bodies and youth culture denies the possibility of any positive conceptualisation of ageing. From changing 'out of my grown-up gear into my lilac Juicy Couture track-suit'[37] to dating younger men who 'mirror the me I'd like to be', the narrator reveals her addiction to youth: 'youth by association. Youth by injection. Better than botox any day'.[38] Younger lovers allow Salisbury to deny ageing and to instead experience youth by proxy, as she illustrates in one of her many post-rendezvous reflections: 'All my youthful vigour I had so missed sprang out of him and into me and though he treated me like a lady, he made me feel like a teenager.'[39] She is thus complicit in affirming the visibility of youth and the invisibility of older women, and she even concedes that there is 'something inside me left over from my teens that says if you're not in Leicester Square on a Saturday night, you don't really exist.'[40] Her dependency on youth and the experiences associated with it is not just social but also medical, for while feminist belief in the possibilities of positive ageing is contingent on resistance to youth culture, Salisbury's understanding of positive ageing rests on the transformative effects of chemical intervention: 'Following a hysterec-tomy at the age of 45, I was put on HRT to which I have an unswerving devotion. My gynecologist says I can stay on it until my dying day and if I'm honest, I fear giving it up lest I awake one morning with a tight grey perm and loose grey skin.'[41]

Salisbury's resistance to ageing is understandable, for in a climate where age is stigmatised the desire to consider oneself young may enhance a sense of personal wellbeing. Yet, as Betty Friedan has asserted, the pursuit of youth is nevertheless a particularly antifeminist and disempowering strategy of resistance, serving only to enhance social gerontophobia by casting ageing as nothing more than degeneration.[42] Likewise, Barbara Macdonald and Cynthia Rich contend that 'youth is bonded with patri-archy in the enslavement of the older woman',[43] and in so doing gesture towards the inability of the older woman to assert her subjectivity in her advancing years, relegated to the space of youth's abject 'other'. In the next section of this chapter, then, I will explore how Salisbury's celebration of youth and youth culture can largely be attributed to her memoir's construction of a highly pessimistic perception of ageing that situates her narrative firmly within discourses of decline.

Beyond youth

The untenable pursuit of lifelong sexual desirability inevitably obstructs the actualisation of more material forms of empowerment and self-development, allowing critics such as Germaine Greer to come to the conclusion that 'To be unwanted is to be free.'[44] Greer encourages women to reconceptualise ageing by rejecting heterosexual romance and by celebrating the opportunities presented by old age, not least the formation of stronger bonds with fellow women. For Greer, old age represents the ultimate opportunity for women to reclaim the self. Yet, in Salisbury's memoir, the pursuit of youth is largely explained by the narrator's refusal to perceive ageing as anything other than deterioration, despite the encouragement of friends who share with Greer a more affirmative understanding of ageing as a cessation of the limitations imposed by motherhood. At an important textual crux in Salisbury's debut memoir, her daughter, Lily, leaves to attend university, forcing her mother to confront the crisis of the 'empty nest'. While the narrator's friends urge her to enjoy the prospect of 'space and freedom, no faddy meals to cook, full power over the remote control, no teenage hormones to deal with, [and] no blaring music', Salisbury experiences the event not as the 'first day of the rest of [her] life', but rather as the 'last day of the best of [her] life.'[45]

The narrator's pessimism regarding her future in many ways reflects the perspective of Simone de Beauvoir in *The Second Sex* (1949), whose analysis of the period from maturity to old age moves from the notion of femininity to the notion of maturity. Recognising that the older woman is liberated from the patriarchal bonds of motherhood and childbearing, de Beauvoir nevertheless perceives this as a 'useless freedom'.[46] For Salisbury, the liberation presented by old age is also useless if it cannot be enjoyed in the company of a man, and her memoir represents the narrator as entirely incapable of autonomy and self-sufficiency, perceiving herself as having no future beyond a romantic and/or sexual relationship. Shortly after she separates with one of her younger lovers, the narrator experiences a psychological meltdown and cries 'every day for the first year', feeling 'fragile and frightened to be alone again at fifty-six.'[47] Indeed, when not celebrating her sexual adventures, Salisbury's memoir is concerned with primarily 'the depths and shallows of being single again at a very uncertain age.'[48] Lonely and unattached, Salisbury enters into states of depression, and the physical environment transforms in accordance with her state of mind: 'The old gold trees leaned into autumn like ageing spinsters drying, dying... The windscreen wipers swished back and forth like a monotonous metronome: *you'll be all alone... you'll be all alone...* they seemed to say.'[49] In defence of Salisbury, it is difficult to disagree with her conviction that 'there's not a mother alive, whether married or single, who is ever really ready for the empty nest',[50] and the description of her emotional state when her daughter leaves for university is affecting: 'On the drive west, the girls chattered excitedly about their futures, whilst I sat huddled in the back watching the autumn landscape whizzing past the window.'[51] The pursuit of sexual pleasure as a form of compensation for the absence of familial companionship appears to drive the memoir, and what remains especially troubling is how the narrator's fear of loneliness in old age motivates her to reject other forms of independence, intimacy and bonding. When reflecting on the recent loss of a lover, she concedes:

> It may sound trivial but out at the cinema on a Saturday night, if I saw a group of women together, I'd hold his hand a little tighter and thank God I wasn't one of them. Because despite being the autonomous person I have since become, I still believe that having a man on your arm gives you validation and status...and it was ever thus.[52]

Salisbury's confession is interesting not merely in revealing her belief that a single woman is unable to attain status in society – an observation that is certainly doubly true of the *ageing* single woman – but also for its contradictory claims of autonomy. Statements such as the above compel the audience to read the memoir against itself, for while the narrator's feminist politics rest on the independent assertion of casual sex as a subversive lifestyle choice, she far too often appears chaotic, dependent and unstable. She admits that her first toyboy experience occurred shortly after a painful divorce from her second husband, and while seeking comfort in a relationship to recover from the loss of another is understandable, the memoir documents this behaviour as a problematic pattern. Even after declaring her status as an 'autonomous person' in command of her life choices, Salisbury admits: 'Sometimes I ask myself what the hell I'm doing with my life.'[53] Her lack of direction, control and purpose is especially clear at two points in her debut memoir, first when she begins a series of blind dates after placing an advertisement in a paper – 'What the hell did I think I was doing waiting for strange, young men on street corners?';[54] second when pursuing a sexual conquest with almost no genuine investment in the encounter – '"I could lend you the decanter and glasses," I offer immediately. "As long as I get them back." That's another twice I'll have to see you, I thought. God knows why because I really wasn't that into him.'[55] These examples run contrary to Salisbury's initial presentation of her lifestyle and sexual object choices as the outcome of a cognizant decision to pursue hedonism and to resist social convention ('I embraced my single status with a backstage pass that read: Excess All Areas'.[56]), thus undermining the political potential of her memoir.

In other ways, too, the memoir is difficult to position as political. Salisbury's reclaiming of the sexual subjectivity of older women is certainly positive, yet her way of articulating sexual desire is often reactionary rather than revolutionary, and it should be understood in the context of Carole Vance's assertion that the sexuality of marginalised groups is often represented 'inaccurately through caricature or other distortion'.[57] Even though Salisbury's memoir disrupts and exposes the instability of the discursive boundary that separates the young and insatiable from the old and celibate, it also supports Vance's contention by presenting the narrator as a hypersexual predator, negating the subversive potential of older women's desire through self-ridicule and hyperbole. Salisbury asserts that she is 'neither a lush nor a sexual predator',[58] yet her memoir is punctuated with images, analogies and metaphors of predation. Her description of seduction involves prowling 'like a panther approaching a grazing gazelle',[59] while at other times she describes how a 'lascivious smile curled at the corners of [her] mouth.'[60] Moreover as the litany of sexual conquests roll on, it becomes clear that Salisbury's lovers are not autonomous and egalitarian agents who are actively seeking an attractive older woman, but rather young men down on their luck who have simply 'slid into [her] frying pan like a fresh egg into hot butter.'[61] While it is always problematic to describe consenting sexual relationships as exploitative in nature, it is impossible to ignore the social and economic disparities between Salisbury and her lovers. In Kathryn Knight's review in *The Daily Mail*, she describes Salisbury as 'raised by a high-achieving family who made their fortune from textiles',[62] and the memoir documents her wealth at various points.

Indeed, by detailing the contents of her fridge 'full of gourmandises from the hugely expensive local deli'[63] and by purchasing her younger lovers' clothes from Gucci in Bond Street, Salisbury showcases her affluence with flamboyancy and opulence. This display is important, for in the social hierarchy of gerontocracy men exert greater power and capital with the coming of age, hence older men's ability to attract younger lovers. Salisbury's pedigree and economic independence functions, then, as a form of substitute masculinity, and it forces the reader to ask important questions concerning not only the feminist politics, but also the ethics of her arguably exploitative lifestyle. Earlier in this chapter, I noted the feminist imperatives of Salisbury's refusal to compromise her own expectations and independence in exchange for financial rewards. Yet, it is clear that her younger lovers occupy the subordinate position she rejects, thus undermining any positive understanding of equality. The narrator's status as a sexual predator is therefore enhanced by her social status, for even though she is of the requisite stock to attend cocktail parties at the Bolivian Embassy, her lovers curiously include struggling men such as James, 'potless, single and living in a shared rental in Tooting'.[64] Another lover, Marc, who 'had family problems and unexpectedly found himself homeless' moves into Salisbury's house 'until he got himself sorted out', a living arrangement described by the narrator as 'like putting a juicy, fat steak just out of reach of a starving carnivore.'[65] While it is clear that Salisbury employs such analogies for comic effect, this strategy proves counterproductive in terms of recalibrating the invisibility of older women's sexuality. As Susan Bordo has noted, the exaggeration of sexuality or sexual desire for comic impact often functions to neutralise the subject's political potential.[66] Affirming the caricature of the wealthy, predatory older woman, Salisbury thus counters the cultural invisibility of older women's sexuality with an equally problematic and hysterical amplification of desire. Her memoir does not express the sexual desires of an older woman with sincerity and authenticity, but rather relegates older women's sexuality to the comedic space of social transgression, and by doing so potentially alienates the female reader. Moreover, it is also important to stress that commensurate with the postfeminist privileging of white, middle-class women, the memoir offers no model of agency for the older female reader who does not share with the narrator the financial means to pursue both the appearance of youth and the bodies of young men. What, then, do both Salisbury's debut memoir and its sequel offer the older female reader, and how can they be positively interpreted?

Conclusion: fulfilment beyond sex

Published two years after her first memoir, Salisbury's sequel, *The Toyboy Diaries 2*, represents something of a departure in terms of the author's own attitudes to ageing. It begins in familiar fashion, with the author espousing the merits of younger lovers. Yet, rather than focussing on corporeal pleasures, there is a pronounced shift towards emphasising the nonphysical rewards of intergenerational dating. The narrator relays the negative experiences of friends in relationships with domineering older men and suggests that younger men are 'more interested in women as equals'.[67] In fact, this decentralisation of the body as the primary route to fulfilment applies not just to the narrator's sex life, but also to her own body. According to Germaine Greer, it is especially essential for women as they age to think of themselves as subjects rather than bodies, and central to this subjectivity is the vanquishing of their lifelong project of constructing sexual selves.[68] To this aim, Salisbury's second memoir represents a return to the self by casting off the exigencies of the body: 'A more sedate and settled life could be the way forward. It might be a relief to get up in the morning and slip into some comfi-fit slacks and a floral blouse instead of squeezing my derrière into a pair of skinny jeans and my boobs into the latest Wonderbra.'[69] This decentralisation of the body facilitates a form of soul searching, and the narrator is forced to reassess her identity as a mother, daughter, aspiring writer and 'experienced older woman': 'Like most women, I assume many roles... I enjoy these multi-personae but I occasionally wonder: which one of them is the real me?'[70] This reflection is highly significant, for it suggests that, between the space of writing two memoirs, Salisbury has matured from 'girl' to 'woman', a maturation process that necessitates the abrogation of her formerly hypersexual self.

Salisbury's second memoir begins, then, as more of a meditation on rather than a celebration of the hedonistic pleasures of toyboy dating. The narrator even confesses that she 'seems to be growing up (that's UP, not OLD!)',[71] and this maturity is reflected in her greater independence. After a trip to Ecuador following the breakdown of a relationship, Salisbury reflects on the need for men in her life and asks several important questions: 'I feel more comfortable in my skin, with just being me. So do I really need a man around? Do I need to compromise, settle down with someone I'm not sure about, just for the sake of "society", just for the sake of "it"? Is that fair on me – and is it fair on him?'[72] More significantly, the source of the narrator's newfound sense of self is precisely a rejection of the casual sex that dominates most of her first memoir: 'All in all, my attempt to have a zipless fuck à la Erica Jong fails miserably and leaves me feeling hollow and empty.'[73] By arriving at this conclusion, Salisbury's second memoir works towards establishing fulfilling bonds beyond the sexual contract, affirming Betty Friedan's hope for new forms of intimacy in old age. For Friedan, since the 'continued exercise of our unique human capacity for caring' is 'key to vital aging versus decline', women 'must be able to evolve beyond the sexual and family ties of youth.'[74] Likewise, Salisbury comes to the realisation that family, friends and children offer infinitely more fulfilment than casual sex: 'I collapse onto the grass exhausted, thinking how blessed I am to have these darling children in my life. This is what reality is made of – not hankering after some age-inappropriate brain fuck that brings me more grief than relief.'[75]

The Toyboy Diaries 2 can, therefore, be reasonably positioned as what Margaret Morganroth Gullette has termed a 'midlife progress narrative'.[76]

Both Salisbury's debut memoir and its sequel stand as problematic celebrations of the current status of the older woman within culture, oscillating between feminist affirmation and postfeminist disavowal. Characteristic of popular cultural texts that embody the contradictory politics of postfeminism, Salisbury's memoirs are difficult to situate on any 'feminist' or 'antifeminist' continuum. It is certainly feasible to argue that Salisbury's particular brand of feminism not only supports the apolitical and individualised trajectory of postfeminist discourse, but is perhaps more insidiously predicated on fetishising other forms of inequality. And yet, it is also reductive and unrewarding to even attempt to fix the memoirs to a political position in any conclusive sense, for their value is manifested in the inability to do so by providing a testimony of the complexities of ageing as a sexual subject in contemporary culture. Rather than extolling Salisbury as an aspirational model or condemning the faultlines of her lifestyle politics, I would like to instead close this chapter with a quotation from her second memoir, which I feel underscores the feminist potential of this genre of writing and conveys the vital importance of sexual narratives produced by older women in the contemporary moment: 'Older women's lives are, thankfully, changing with the speed at which the "Send Message" button can be pressed on an Internet-dating website. We are less invisible now, more respected. Society and the media are finally acknowledging that the sophisticated siren has her own story to tell – and a fascinating one it is too.'[77]

Notes

1. Kathryn Knight, 'Here's to Me, Mrs Robinson! I'm 61 but Younger Men can't Get Enough of Me,' *Mail Online*, available at http://www.dailymail.co.uk/femail/article-464805/Heres-Mrs-Robinson-Im-61-younger-men-me.html (Accessed 15 May 2013).
2. Susan Sontag, 'The Double Standard of Ageing,' in *The Other within Us: Feminist Explorations of Women and Ageing*, ed. Marilyn Pearsall (Boulder, Colorado: Westview Press, 1997), p. 20.
3. Wendy Salisbury, *The Toyboy Diaries: Sexploits of an Older Woman* (London: Old Street Publishing, 2007), p. 3.
4. Lynne Segal, 'Forever Young: Medusa's Curse and the Discourses of Ageing,' *Women: A Cultural Review*, 18 (2007), p. 48.
5. Sarah Projansky, 'Mass Magazine Cover Girls: Some Reflections on Postfeminist Mothers and Postfeminist Daughters,' in *Interrogating Postfeminism: Gender and the Politics of Popular Culture*, ed. Diane Negra and Yvonne Tasker (Durham: Duke University Press, 2007), p. 45.
6. www.therealcougarwoman.net (Accessed 17 May 2013).
7. Ibid.
8. Segal, p. 47.

9. Knight's review, see Note 1.
10. Ursula Owen, 'When the Machinery Stops Working,' in *A Certain Age: Reflection on the Menopause*, ed. Joanna Goldsworthy (New York: Columbia University Press, 1995), p. 88.
11. Betty Friedan, *The Fountain of Age* (London: Vintage, 1994), p. 112.
12. Salisbury, *The Toyboy Diaries 2: The Daily Male* (London: Old Street Publishing, 2009), p. 2.
13. Ibid., p. 53.
14. Ibid., p. 93.
15. Ibid.
16. Ibid.
17. Ibid., p. 240.
18. Ibid., p. 64.
19. Salisbury, *The Toyboy Diaries 2*, p. 109.
20. Salisbury, *The Toyboy Diaries*, p. 59.
21. Salisbury, *The Toyboy Diaries 2*, p. 159.
22. Jeannette King, *Discourses of Ageing in Fiction and Feminism: The Invisible Woman* (Basingstoke: Palgrave Macmillan, 2013), p. 155.
23. See Ruth Saxton, 'Sex over Sixty? From *Love, Again* to *The Sweetest Dream*,' *Lessing Studies*, 24 (2004), p. 44.
24. Salisbury, *The Toyboy Diaries*, p. 1.
25. See E. Ann Kaplan, 'Trauma and Ageing: Marlene Dietrich, Melanie Klein, and Marguerite Duras', in *Figuring Age: Women, Bodies, Generations*, ed. Kathleen Woodward (Bloomington: Indiana University Press, 1999), pp. 171–194.
26. Salisbury, *The Toyboy Diaries*, p. 3.
27. Ibid., p. 10.
28. Jacqueline Zita, 'Heresy in the Female Body: The Rhetorics of the Menopause,' in *Menopause: A Midlife Passage*, ed. Joan C. Callahan (Bloomington: Indiana University Press, 1993), p. 73.
29. Diane Richardson, 'Constructing Lesbian Identities,' in *Feminism and Sexuality: A Reader*, ed. Stevi Jackson and Sue Scott (Edinburgh: Edinburgh University Press, 1996), p. 279.
30. Segal, p. 47.
31. Salisbury, *The Toyboy Diaries*, p. 240.
32. Kathrina Glitre, 'Nancy Meyers and Popular Feminism,' in *Women on Screen: Feminism and Femininity in Visual Culture*, ed. Melanie Waters (Basingstoke: Palgrave Macmillan, 2011), p. 28.
33. Salisbury, *The Toyboy Diaries*, p. 3.
34. Ibid., p. 20.
35. Ibid., p. 2.
36. Ibid., p. 240.
37. Salisbury, *The Toyboy Diaries 2*, p. 72.
38. Salisbury, *The Toyboy Diaries*, p. 3.
39. Ibid., p. 268.
40. Ibid., p. 199.
41. Salisbury, *The Toyboy Diaries 2*, p. 161.
42. Friedan, p. 62.
43. Barbara Macdonald and Cynthia Rich, *Look Me in the Eye* (London: Women's Press, 1985), p. 39.

44. Germaine Greer, *The Change: Women, Ageing and the Menopause* (London: Hamish Hamilton, 1991), p. 67.
45. Salisbury, *The Toyboy Diaries*, p. 26.
46. Simone de Beauvoir, *The Second Sex*, translated by H.M. Parshley (New York: Knopf, Vintage Books, 1974), p. 301.
47. Salisbury, *The Toyboy Diaries*, p. 39.
48. Ibid., p. 49.
49. Ibid., p. 25.
50. Ibid., p. 24.
51. Ibid.
52. Ibid., p. 45.
53. Ibid., p. 226.
54. Ibid., p. 128.
55. Ibid., p. 216.
56. Ibid., p. 2.
57. Carole S. Vance, 'Pleasure and Danger: Toward a Politics of Sexuality,' in *Pleasure and Danger: Exploring Female Sexuality*, ed. Carole S. Vance (London: Routledge, 1984), p. 13.
58. Salisbury, *The Toyboy Diaries*, p. 99.
59. Ibid., p. 84.
60. Ibid., p. 74.
61. Ibid., p. 236.
62. Knight's review, see Note 1.
63. Salisbury, *The Toyboy Diaries*, p. 60.
64. Ibid., p. 86.
65. Ibid., p. 22.
66. Susan Bordo, *The Male Body: A New Look at Men in Public and in Private* (New York: Farrar, Straus and Giroux, 1999), p. 87.
67. Salisbury, *The Toyboy Diaries 2*, p. 39.
68. Greer, *The Change*, p. 60.
69. Salisbury, *The Toyboy Diaries 2*, p. 9.
70. Ibid.
71. Ibid., p. vii.
72. Ibid., p. 242.
73. Ibid., p. 178.
74. Friedan, *The Fountain of Age*, p. 55.
75. Salisbury, *The Toyboy Diaries 2*, p. 117.
76. Margaret Morganroth Gullette, *Declining to Decline: Cultural Combat and the Politics of the Midlife* (Virginia: University of Virginia Press, 1997), p. 12.
77. Salisbury, *The Toyboy Diaries 2*, p. viii.

4
Sexing Up the Midlife Woman: Cultural Representations of Ageing, Femininity and the Sexy Body

Sharron Hinchliff

Women's sexuality at middle and late adulthood

8 March 2013 saw the launch of a compendium of essays which highlighted the challenges and opportunities of ageing for women in the UK and across the globe.[1] The 38 essays, written by a range of authors (including politicians, policy-makers, academics and campaigners) discussed topics around health and wellbeing, finances and work, care and caring, social isolation, and intimacy and relationships; many acknowledged the significant, yet often overlooked, contributions that older women make to their families and wider society. It was released to mark International Women's Day, and the title *Has the Sisterhood Forgotten Older Women?* reflected recently raised concerns that feminism has neglected older women because of a focus on advancing the rights of younger women. While the consensus of the compendium was that the 'sisterhood' had certainly not forgotten older women, the recognition that it needed to catch up with the issues that are pertinent to this older generation of women today was clear.

One area that should be part of the feminist agenda, as I argued in this compendium,[2] is the sexuality of women at middle adulthood and beyond. This absence is perhaps not surprising in that it reflects the trajectory of societal interest in sex over the late twentieth and early twenty-first centuries. In most western societies, the attention paid to sexual activity, sexual expression, and a 'sexy' physical appearance has been aimed mostly at young people, and in particular young women. Advertisements that use sexual imagery to sell their products almost always include people who are in their late teenage years or early twenties. Television programmes and big screen films that include sexual activity and sexual expression in their storylines connect them mainly with young adults. Messages about safe sex are predominantly directed at young people, and government policy on sexual health and well-being in the UK, for example, has tended to exclude people over 30. The message that sexuality is the province of the young remains a powerful one, fuelling negative stereotypes about older people and sex.

Clearly, the significance attached to sexuality is cultural: it reflects and reinforces the dominant ideas and values about sexual activity, sexual attractiveness, and sexual expression in a culture at a given time. It is also, thus, historical. Assumptions about sexuality have been observed to change over different time periods and Gail Hawkes has drawn attention to the western societal shift that took place over the twentieth century where sexual activity, particularly penile-vaginal intercourse, came to be seen as a necessary part of adult health and wellbeing.[3] The assumption that 'good' sex was good for you continued with fervour and it was not long before its advantages for ageing health were being declared. In 1982 the authors of the *Starr-Weiner Report on Sex and Sexuality in the Mature Years* argued that:

> Energy needs a place to go. When sexual energy is denied the outlet of behaviour that can provide sexual release, it goes into other areas. This process, called displacement, may result in illness – diarrhoea, ulcers, heartburn, arthritis, neuralgia, and many other complaints familiar to older people.[4]

The message was clear: if older people were not sexually active, then they risked becoming ill. While the argument that the poor health of older adults can be explained by their inactive sex lives does not hold much authority today, academics have noted that the association between sex and health still underpins contemporary discourse. Stephen Katz and Barbara Marshall traced the way that sexology, with its positive health promotion messages about sex, crossed paths with gerontology to make the claim that sexual activity was not only a necessary but also a healthy part of successful ageing.[5] This shift was significant in the field of ageing sexuality as it marked a move away from previous expert advice that individuals should accept changes in sexual capacity related to getting older – that is, decline and dysfunction – and consequently sexually retire.[6] New narratives were thus created, extolling the benefits of inter-course for ageing health, and sexual activity became part of the ageing-well agenda. Early indications of this agenda were observed at the turn of the millennium when the UK Government's 'old age tsar' actively promoted – and therefore legitimised – sex as key to a long and healthy life. Again, this message holds currency today as sexual intercourse is promoted for not only its potential to improve life expectancy, but also its ability to help people look physically younger.[7] Merryn Gott has taken note of these changes and argued that the backlash to the asexual old age stereotype created a new stereotype: that of the 'sexy oldie', where sexual intercourse – built on the assumption that sex is always pleasurable and an expression of love – came to be seen as the ideal for *all* older people.[8] This new view was bolstered by the medicalisation of sex which, through the pathologisation of sexual abstinence, created an environment that normalised sexual intercourse at all stages of the adult life-course. Indeed, the relationship between ageing, sexuality, and medicalisation has progressed rapidly over the twenty-first century, and older adults now find themselves a primary target for biotechnologies that have been developed to enhance sexual function.[9] Changes in sexual ability as a result of ageing are still viewed in terms of decline, but the 'pharmaceutical imagination' can fix it,[10] enabling individuals to rebuild their 'dysfunctional' sex lives.

Changes were also beginning to be seen in mainstream media. Tiina Vares has drawn attention to the way that, from the 1990s, advertisements, television, and film started to depict older bodies as sexual but in a romantic rather than erotic way.[11] This trend has continued, and now ageing sexuality is often represented in television and film in ways that break free from the desexualisation of mid and later life – a shift most noticeable where 'older' women are concerned. As I will explore in the following section, the sexualisation of culture – where increasing attention is focussed on sexual behaviours and sexual appearance by the media, the fashion and music industries, and the manufacturers that operate within this framework to sell their products – has played a part in the new visibility of female sexuality in middle and, to a lesser extent, late adulthood. The focus of the remainder of this chapter is on midlife women, and I argue that the increasing attention paid to women in their forties and fifties in terms of sexual agency, sexual attractiveness, and sexual expression, in films, music, videos and television programmes, is indicative of the sexualisation of midlife. It is an extension of the sexualisation of younger women that has been observed over recent years in western societies: one that has simply moved further along the life-course. Yet, the sexualisation of midlife women appears to have slipped past the feminist gaze as those with an interest in sexuality have been concerned with the sexual objectification and subjectification of girls and young women. The aim of this chapter is, therefore, to set out a theoretical framework for understanding contemporary constructions of ageing female sexualities.

Reconfigured representations of female sexuality

A key focus of the recent scholarship and activism carried out by feminists with an interest in sexuality has been the causes and consequences of the sexualisation of western culture. This topic has received a lot of attention from a diverse range of sources (academics, parenting groups, and government bodies) who have been concerned primarily with the impact that sexualisation may be having on children's and young people's developing sense of themselves as sexual beings. Unease has been voiced about the downsizing of 'sexy' women's clothing (e.g., padded bras) for little girls, to the sexual dance routines (e.g., pole dancing) that are remodelled into fitness regimes for women,[12] as well as the many images and narratives displayed through contemporary advertising on our streets, and in our homes via magazines and television. There is no doubt that sexualised messages are part of everyday life, but sexualisation permeates at a deep level: it is lived as well as experienced, particularly by women and young girls who are the primary recipients of these messages. Indeed, the current cultural climate prioritises sexual pleasure in many ways and women have increasingly been targeted as sexual consumers.[13] We can see evidence of this in the rise of Internet shops that sell sexual products and are aimed solely at female customers,[14] the UK television programmes that tell their (primarily female) audiences how to have the 'best sex ever' (e.g., *Girls Guide to 21st Century Sex*, in the UK (2006)), and Internet blogs where women write candidly about their sexual experiences that take place outside the boundaries of the traditional heterosexual committed relationship. For example, the hugely popular blog *Girl with a One-Track Mind* by Abby Lee detailed the author's sex life as a single woman when she was living in London at the start of the millennium. (She later stated that an aim of the blog was to rebalance the sexual double standard that had long been applied to heterosexual women.) So, the discourses that foreground women's sexual agency and the high visibility of women's sexual pleasure have become regular parts of the cultural landscape, gracing the pages of women's magazines, the adverts we see in them and the shows that air on television. According to Angela McRobbie, female sexuality has been 'reconfigured within the realms of the "new femininities"' so that now the social production and construction of gender requires women and girls to *perform* specific sexualities.[15] For young women in particular, desirability is required to be visible through the ways they dress and act, so part of this performance entails showing that they are always 'up for it'.[16]

But one reconfigured representation of female sexuality we are seeing more of on our television screens and magazine pages (and in my view, on our city streets) relates to the midlife woman. Traditionally, female sexuality has been firmly connected with young adult bodies, rendering older female sexuality invisible and taboo. With the exception of Mrs Robinson in the 1967 film, *The Graduate* (who was a 36-year-old actor portraying a much older woman), women in middle adulthood have been denied sexuality based on the very definition of what constitutes 'sexiness'. According to Rosalind Gill older women have not been granted sexual subjecthood in television, film and advertising, and have been excluded from the sexualisation of culture per se.[17] She has argued that 'Sexual desire is frequently depicted as inappropriate – indeed as repulsive and disgusting – when the woman experiencing it is over 40.'[18] Thus, to be a woman at midlife is to stand outside the position of desiring sexual subject.

A recent shift in media culture, however, is the construction of the sexy midlife woman. Currently, a number of television shows and films (e.g., *Cougar Town* (2009–present), *Sex and the City* (1998–2004), and *It's Complicated* (2009) – although they are the exception rather than the rule – construct 'older' women as sexually agentic, and by doing so they disconnect from the traditional stereotypes of female ageing that featured in earlier versions of women-orientated entertainment. While these productions are not without criticism (only middle-class, heterosexual, white, and able-bodied women tend to be constructed in this way), the 'sexing' of these age groups clearly connects to shifts in the acceptability of 'older' female sexuality. Some of the main characters exhibit and are not ashamed of their sexual power and agency. They are sexually confident, sexually desiring, and not constrained to have sex only within committed relationships. (And in this way they also break free from the restrictions of traditional gender relations and the heterosexual expectations that accompany them.) To be sexually agentic *and* single is a marked shift as women at midlife have traditionally been cast in asexual and gender-stereotypical roles unless in comedy films where the most positive portrayals of female sexuality at midlife have been found.[19] Based on this evidence, there is no denying that this is a 'new' construction of female sexuality, and the discourses circulating in contemporary society reflect this shift. The midlife woman who takes a younger male partner is referred to in popular culture as a cougar: a label which is part of, and at the same time reinforces, the sexualisation of 'older' women. With connotations of sexual prowess, the cougar woman is said to display her power by preying on and capturing a younger lover. During one of the early episodes of *Cougar Town* (3:1), the main character Jules (Courtney Cox), prepares for a date with a younger man: she is 40; he is in his early 20s. It's their tenth date, and Jules has a 'tenth date rule' that means they will have sexual intercourse. The three main female characters (Jules; Ellie, her best friend, also 40; and Laurie, who is in her 20s) are in Jules' kitchen talking:

Jules: [biting into a bagel] and this will be my last bite of food so that my stomach looks *super flat* tonight...

Ellie: So what time is your gentleman caller arriving tonight?

Jules: I told him to show up at eight o'clock.

Ellie: Is that enough time to prepare?

Laurie: It's ten in the morning! Is she *serious*?

Jules: We're 40 Laurie. For us getting ready for sex is like prepping for a space mission.

Laurie: Well I already scheduled your mani-pedi. My Russian eyebrow lady was murdered – long story – so I was thinking you could just have the same girl that does your bikini wax do your brows.

Jules: You can't use the same person for both things! One's a gardener, the other's an artist. [Turning to Ellie] Oh if I'm gonna get waxed I've gotta tidy the den before the maid comes.

Laurie: What the *hell* does that mean?

Ellie: Oh, it means that Jules is so crazy that she has to give herself a trim before she gets waxed so her waxer doesn't think she's a cavewoman.

Jules: I've also gotta blow out my hair, buy candles, wash my sheets, I gotta do a thousand sit-ups and buy a bra that doesn't squeeze my back so tight that I get, you know, back boob.

This interchange vividly captures the anxieties of Jules who is about to have sex for the first time with her lover, but it does little to support the connotations of female sexual power that accompany the cougar label. And while offering a humorous account of preparing for a date, a lot more can be read from this storyline: for example, that a lack of spontaneity comes with age. Indeed, preparing for sex is compared to preparing for a mission to outer space as Jules needs to plan ahead and spend a lot of time getting her body, and her bedroom, ready for the sexual encounter. We could read this focus on self-preparation in relation to Jules being an 'older' woman: she is aware that her body may be different from the bodies of the women of her male partner's age group – the women we can assume that he usually dates – and thus believes that it requires extra 'work' before it can be revealed to her young lover. In this way, the 'older' female body is an unruly body, one that needs to be carefully managed if it is to be desirable. An alternative reading, yet one that cannot be clearly disentangled from that just described, is that it reflects a continuation of the self-policing of women's bodies: something that is no different whether women are 22 or 42 years of age. Previously released films such as *Bridget Jones Diary* (2001) support this interpretation, where Bridget (in her early 30s) exhibited the same anxieties as Jules and engaged in similar bodily preparations prior to a date. However, the *Cougar Town* story has an interesting juxtaposition: it positions Laurie's lack of understanding of what her friends Jules and Elli are talking about alongside *their* shared understanding, which works to demarcate the distinction between young and 'old'. Clearly, the comedy serves to critique the absurdity of such grooming practices. Whichever way we read it, there is no doubt that the *Cougar Town* storyline reflects the social realities that many women face while at the same time produces a narrative which serves to reinforce heteronormative femininity. It also provides a clear example of what Alison Winch has termed the 'girlfriend gaze', where female friends are an active and overt part of the policing of bodily perfection.[20]

We have seen that the boundaries around the age at which women are identified for their 'sexiness' are blurring, pushing forward to render midlife a period of sexual objectification and subjectification. Midlife women are being sexualised in media culture but, along with their younger counterparts, only if they meet very strict criteria. In the following section I will explore how this reconfigured representation of female sexuality can be viewed as offering freedoms (from the stereotype of asexuality) and opportunities (for new types of relationships) but also how, upon closer inspection, it comes with added responsibilities and dangers.

Treading the postfeminist path

'How should we read these figures, all of whom are constructed as powerful and agentic women?' asks Rosalind Gill in response to the way that advertisers currently construct young women's sexuality.[21] It is a question that is pertinent to this chapter because it allows us to trace how we have arrived at the sexy midlifer and to identify the dangers of this new construction of female sexuality. The recent societal shift in sexuality, the move from objectification to subjectification, characterised by a refocus on an actively desiring body,[22] is a key consideration here. The body has been central to ideals of female attractiveness for a long time, but in contemporary society it is imbued with much more: having a 'sexy' body has come to be understood as a 'key source' of women's identity.[23] A sexy female body is one that meets socially constructed ideals of sexual attractiveness and women who do not correspond to this narrow standard of beauty and sexual allure do not feature on television as sexually agentic midlifers. Imagine Jules and her friend Ellie from *Cougar Town* at 56 pounds heavier. While the fictional characters that portray sexy midlife women tend to be powerful both economically, through their successful careers, and socially, through their established friendships and networks, it is the extent to which they correspond with dominant standards of sexual appeal that frames their identity.

The television shows that present midlife women as sexually agentic did not come about by chance. As well as significant events that fed into their development (for example, more women gaining positions of power, the increased opportunities presented to young women, and the 'discovery' of girls as consumers[24]), women had called for sexual agency and for more accurate representations of their lives. In the same way that advertisers began to acknowledge the anger many women expressed at being objectified and presented with ideal images of femininity that were unattainable, and as a consequence re-examined how they engaged with female consumers and how they represented women,[25] television producers had to likewise reconsider how they connected with midlife female viewers. To increase audience figures for their channels, they could no longer portray 'older' women in age-stereotypical roles that did little to reflect their lives, and it can be argued that the producers achieved that goal, that shows like *Cougar Town* do reflect women's lives in the issues they raise. (However, the media-constructed sexy midlife woman is endowed with agency and exists in an environment of equality and egalitarian gender relations which clearly does not represent the lives of many women for whom inequality based on gender, race or age are very real issues.) But the media response to feminist critiques came at a price. As Susan Douglas has argued, women were sold a specific sexuality; that it is through sexual display that they have the power to get what they want 'and because the true path to power comes from being an object of desire, girls and women should actively choose – even celebrate and embrace – being sex objects.'[26] According to this argument, choosing to look a certain way gives women control over how they look to others, especially heterosexual men, and thus the normative beauty standards become empowering. Central to the shift from sexual objectification to subjectification, therefore, is the discourse of choice and pleasing oneself where women must recognise their own objectification as one they have chosen and which gives them pleasure.[27] In this way, sexual agency has become a 'regulatory project...part of the apparatus that disciplines and regulates feminine conduct, that gets "inside" and reconstructs our notions of what it is to be a sexual subject.'[28] Douglas warns us that this version of empowerment is based on the idea that women's liberation has been accomplished, that women now 'have it all', are more in control sexually, are stronger, are fearless, are more successful, and are held in awe more than they really are.[29] Empowerment is thus an illusion.

It is clear that changes in the cultural landscape have provided conditions within which the representation of the 'sexy' midlifer blossomed. The sexy midlife woman expresses her sexual agency; she does not hide her sexual desire; and she is no longer denied an 'autonomous sexual voice'.[30] However, while the taboo around sexuality in middle adulthood is slowly breaking down, there remains clear disdain of 'older' bodies. Naked midlife bodies are not shown in television or film in the same way as naked young bodies when it to comes to sex: they remain partially clothed or covered by sheets, as opposed to the more revealing nude shots of younger women. It is interesting to note that 'older' women, when presented thus, are disembodied akin to the way that younger women's bodies tend to be presented in advertisements for beauty products where just the legs, abdomen or breasts are shown. A difference is that younger women are objectified in these advertisements, whereas 'older' women are not. In this highly visual culture, there is a reluctance to view the flesh of the older female body, so being partially covered works to hide, rather than objectify, the older woman.

Contradictions thus characterise contemporary Western understandings of ageing female sexuality when midlife women can be sexual but their display is heavily policed. Indeed, the sexualisation of midlife women sits alongside the pathologisation of the ageing female body. Popular television programmes such as *Ten Years Younger* (2004–present) in the UK and *The Swan* (2004) in the US occupy primetime slots and their challenge is to alter the unacceptable, grotesque, aged female body into a culturally acceptable younger version. Viewers are left in no doubt that the 'older' female body is abject, but it can be nipped and tucked to minimise the impact of ageing upon how women look. Susie Orbach has drawn attention to the current rhetoric where women must be watchful of their bodies so much so that looking after them has become a moral value.[31] Women are accountable for their bodies and judged by them: in this way, the body project has become a personal responsibility. And through the rhetoric of choice, it is a way of producing an 'acceptable' body, one that can be remade if women follow the diet and exercise tips and cosmetic surgery procedures that feature in daily newspapers and women's magazines as a means to look *and* feel better.[32] The paradox of the sexualisation of culture is that it feeds off an anti-ageing narrative, evidenced by youthful standards of beauty and 'sexiness' being applied to women at midlife. Women are disproportionately disadvantaged regarding ideals about what constitutes a sexy body, and a consequence of the internalisation of socially constructed ideas of 'sexiness' is that they may adhere to the current sexual ideal as a way of actively distancing themselves from being viewed as 'old'. As Susie Orbach has noted, the 'language of empowerment and choice linked in with visual culture suggests to the individual woman that it is in her power to transform herself, to become the image held before her.'[33] Many women negotiate embodied ageing by changing the appearance of their bodies and in the UK there has been a year-on-year increase in 'anti-ageing' cosmetic procedures. When the *British Association of Aesthetic Plastic Surgeons* released their annual figures for the number of cosmetic surgery procedures carried out during 2012, demand for 'anti-ageing' procedures had seen a 'double-digit rise'. These included face lifts (up 14 per cent), brow lifts (up 17 per cent), eyelid surgery (up 13 per cent), and fat transfer (up 13 per cent).[34]

It is interesting to note a shift in the cosmetic surgery discourse where the term 'anti-ageing' has been replaced with 'rejuvenation'. Rejuvenation procedures are sold for their ability to restore youthfulness rather than halt ageing, and recent research indicates that this discursive turn may have taken place in order to avoid the tension that arises when people opt for surgery to look better but not to counter ageing. In Bridget Garnham's study, the participants underwent cosmetic surgery to remodel their bodies and look better but not younger. Here, cosmetic surgery was viewed as a way to design 'older' bodies rather than deny ageing: the latter was viewed as the impetus behind anti-ageing procedures and thus worked to perpetuate ageism.[35] This study provides a fascinating insight into the reasons why older adults opt for cosmetic procedures, and a new perspective on what it means to surgically alter an aged appearance. Yet it is important to remember that looking 'better' entails looking younger as the former is defined through dominant standards of beauty which are still based on youthfulness – otherwise these cosmetic procedures simply would not exist. As Kathryn Bayer has argued, in a culture that views ageing with disdain, to look younger as an older woman is to look good, and it is now socially acceptable to do so.[36] Rosalind Gill has drawn attention to the ways that young women's subjectivity is being remoulded to fit postfeminist ideas where they should be beautiful and sexy,[37] which applies to midlife women as well. But there is an added dimension for the midlifer: investing in beauty and a 'sexy' appearance has become a marker of successful ageing. Not only are women praised for looking younger at midlife (e.g., celebrities are rewarded in newspapers and celebrity gossip magazines with headlines such as 'Turns back the clock'[38]), looking younger has been shown to improve social and professional standing.[39] In a climate where it can be difficult for women to retain a sense of themselves as powerful as they age, taking steps to look 'better' (younger) may be a meaningful choice from a pool of very limited options.

The media constructions that typify the sexualisation of midlife women resist the cultural script of ageing as decline, which is clearly a positive step forward in societies where 'older' women are devalued. The female artists in their 40s and 50s who actively express their sexuality on stage and in music videos challenge expectations about what it means to be a midlife woman (I am thinking about Madonna's 'Hung Up' video where she wore a retro pink leotard and footless tights as she danced in a ballet studio: she was 47. Although, she did receive criticism for her outfit which, when compared to the contemporary clothes of the other women, served to highlight her youthful body in relation to her age). But quite often these representations conform to a younger version of female sexuality, and thus they support, inadvertently perhaps, what the women appear to be fighting against. While they show a resistance to the negative connotations of ageing sexuality, they are operating within the boundaries of heteronormativity, and therefore we can understand this level of resistance as women 'doing' gender in the context within which they work. Female celebrities are likely to have a vested interest in maintaining a youthful appearance as they are 'required' to visibly age as little as possible in order to be cast in prominent roles or to appeal to the public who buy their music. Looking youthful and 'sexy' enables them to retain currency in the television, film, and music industries that set parameters where 'sexiness' equals success. Indeed, we must question the extent to which these new sexy midlifers own their sexuality because this reconfigured representation of female sexuality sits within a heterosexual framework. The discourses of choice and empowerment, when viewed in this way, work to complicate rather than produce a clear counter-discourse.

There is no doubt that the media, in defining the standards which women should meet, plays a powerful role in shaping identities and ambitions.[40] But not all midlife women will express their sexuality in line with this socially constructed ideal of midlife 'sexiness'. Alternative readings of midlife sexuality are being made by women who define their own version of 'sexiness', or reject it altogether. Women that we could consider here include Lulu Guinness, Oprah Winfrey, Cheryl Crow, and many others, including those we see in our towns and city centres. To draw from Susan Faludi's observation of the 'cookie-cutter' version of femininity,[41] some midlife women appear to actively resist the 'sexy midlifer' mould that is being created for them by the powerful media agents.

Conclusion: feminism and the sexy midlifer

In this chapter I have argued that midlife, once understood as a time of freedom from societal pressures (to have a specific 'sexy' appearance) and a relaxation of body anxieties, is being redefined as a period of life where these concerns remain in sharp focus. The attention that is currently being paid to midlife women's bodies within media culture is a continuation of the surveillance faced by younger women. Through a constant feeding into women's subjectivities that their value comes predominantly from how they look, it seems that women will never be set free from the constraints that are closely tied to idealised representations of femininity. To repeat Susie Orbach, success means viewing the body project as a never-ending pursuit.[42]

It is without question that advertisers who significantly shape the content of contemporary media[43] recognise the financially privileged position of many midlife women and through the television networks encourage them to spend money to achieve a better/youthful appearance. As Susan Douglas has pointed out in relation to reality television shows such as *The Bachelor* (which can be applied to popular sitcoms like *Cougar Town*), 'such shows provide an excellent selling environment for the multibillion-dollar diet and beauty industry that needs us always, always, to envy the future selves we will become if we just use Oil of Olay or Dexatrim.'[44] But the societal shift in attitudes towards ageing and sexuality appears to be in a state of flux as women encounter competing discourses: that midlife is a time when concerns about physical appearance ease (because they are no longer part of the young demographic) but women must continue to pay close scrutiny to their bodies if they are to age successfully. The sexualisation of midlife is given to women as something to attain, something that women should desire because it gives them power, and thus the connection between youthfulness and power, rather than success (at work), achievements (in family life), or wisdom (from life experience), is reinforced. A theoretical framework for understanding ageing female sexualities should therefore incorporate social and cultural ideas about ageing, beauty and 'sexiness'; it must account for diversity as women negotiate their own ageing and construct alternative versions of the sexy midlifer including a rejection of 'sexiness' per se. When it comes to women, ageing and sexuality, a plurality of stories is required. A theoretical framework should also incorporate women's own perspectives on midlife to enhance current theoretical insights. When the boundaries shift and the age to which (heterosexual) standards of beauty and 'sexiness' have moved along the life-course, only research with women will enable us to understand how they interpret the new representation of midlife female sexuality, how they negotiate midlife when competing discourses sit alongside each other, and how they feel about having limited chances of escape from its consequences.

Notes

1. Sally-Marie Bamford and Jessica Watson, eds, *Has the Sisterhood Forgotten Older Women?* (London: International Longevity Centre UK, 2013), p. 7.
2. Sharron Hinchliff, 'Sexuality and Intimacy in Middle and Late Adulthood,' in *Has the Sisterhood Forgotten Older Women?* ed. Sally-Marie Bamford and Jessica Watson (London: International Longevity Centre UK, 2013), p. 104.
3. Gail Hawkes, *A Sociology of Sex and Sexuality* (England: Open University Press, 2002).
4. Bernard D. Starr and Marcella Bakur Weiner, *The Starr-Weiner Report on Sex and Sexuality in the Mature Years* (New York: McGraw Hill, 1982), p. 10.
5. Stephen Katz and Barbara Marshall, 'New Sex for Old: Lifestyles, Consumerism and the Ethics of Aging Well,' *Journal of Aging Studies*, 17:1 (2003), pp. 3–16, p. 7.
6. Ibid.
7. David Weeks, 'The Benefits of Sexual Activity for Later Life,' *British Psychological Society*, available at http://www.bps.org.uk/news/benefits-sexual-activity-later-life (Accessed 10 September 2013).
8. Merryn Gott, *Sexuality, Sexual Health and Ageing* (England: Open University Press, 2005), p. 23.
9. Barbara L. Marshall, 'Science, Medicine and Virility Surveillance: "Sexy Seniors" in the Pharmaceutical Imagination,' *Sociology of Health and Illness*, 32:2 (2010), pp. 211.
10. Ibid.
11. Tiina Vares, 'Reading the "Sexy Oldie": Gender, Age(ing) and Embodiment,' *Sexualities*, 12:4 (2009), p. 504.

12. Feona Attwood, 'Fashion and Passion: Marketing Sex to Women,' *Sexualities*, 8:4 (2005), p. 399.
13. Stevi Jackson and Sue Scott, 'Sexual Antinomies in Late Modernity,' *Sexualities*, 7:2 (2004), pp. 233–248.
14. Attwood, p. 392.
15. Angela McRobbie, 'Preface,' in *New Femininities: Postfeminism, Neoliberalism and Subjectivity*, ed. Rosalind Gill and Christina Scharff (Basingstoke: Palgrave Macmillan, 2011), p. xiii.
16. Attwood, p. 403. Rosalind Gill, 'Empowerment/Sexism: Figuring Female Sexual Agency in Contemporary Advertising,' *Feminism and Psychology*, 18:1 (2008), p. 35.
17. Ibid., p. 44.
18. Rosalind Gill, 'Beyond the "Sexualization of Culture" Thesis: An Intersectional Analysis of "Sixpacks", "Midriffs" and "Hot Lesbians" in Advertising,' *Sexualities*, 12:2 (2009), p. 154.
19. Rose Weitz, 'Changing the Scripts: Midlife Women's Sexuality in Contemporary U.S. Film,' *Sexuality and Culture*, 14:1 (2010), p. 17.
20. Alison Winch, 'The Girlfriend Gaze,' *Soundings*, 52 (2012), p. 1.
21. Gill, 2008, p. 37.
22. Ibid., p. 41.
23. Ibid., p. 42.
24. See Susan Douglas for an excellent analysis of this issue: Susan J. Douglas, *Enlightened Sexism: The Seductive Message that Feminism's Work is Done* (New York: Times Books, 2010).
25. Gill, 2008, p. 39.
26. Douglas, p. 156.
27. Gill, 2008, p. 42.
28. Ibid., p. 53.
29. Douglas, p. 5.
30. Gill, 2008, p. 43.
31. Susie Orbach, *Bodies* (London: Profile Books, 2009), p. 4.
32. Ibid., p. 82.
33. Orbach, p. 93.
34. British Association of Aesthetic Plastic Surgeons, 'Britons Raise a Few Eyebrows', available at http://www.baaps.org.uk/about-us/press-releases/1558-britons-raise-a-few-eyebrows. (Accessed 19 September 2013).
35. Bridget Garnham, 'Designing "Older" Rather Than Denying Ageing: Problematizing Anti-Ageing Discourse in Relation to Cosmetic Surgery Undertaken by Older People,' *Journal of Aging Studies*, 27:1 (2013), p. 43.
36. Kathryn Bayer, 'Cosmetic Surgery and Cosmetics: Redefining the Appearance of Age,' *Generations*, 29:3 (2005), p. 14.
37. Gill, 2008, p. 35.
38. *Daily Mail*, 'Bronzed and Beautiful: Rachel Hunter, 44, Turns Back the Clock in Metallic Bandeau Dress at *Marie Claire*'s 25th Birthday' (17 September 2013), available at http://www.dailymail.co.uk/tvshowbiz/article-2424079/Rachel-Hunter-44-turns-clock-metallic-bandeau-dress-Marie-Claires-25th-birthday.html#ixzz2fcQdnBHt (Accessed 22 September 13).
39. Bayer, p. 14.
40. Douglas, p. 18.

41. Susan Faludi, *Backlash: The Undeclared War against American Women* (New York: Anchor, 1991), p. 212.
42. Orbach, p. 111.
43. Rosalind Gill, *Gender and the Media* (Cambridge: Polity Press, 2007).
44. Douglas, p. 201.

5
Paternalising the Rejuvenation of Later Life Masculinity in Twenty-First Century Film

Hannah Hamad

This chapter deals with a representational recurrence in twenty-first century film towards the depiction of later life masculinity in pronounced paternal terms. This is a phenomenon that can be productively interrogated as symptomatic of a number of wider cognate discursive trends. These include the sharp rise in the cultural visibility of old age, broader trends in postfeminist culture with respect to the configuration of masculinities in terms of fatherhood, the powerful appeal of this discourse of masculinity in effecting the recuperation of troubled or maligned masculinities, and the attendant stakes raised for feminism by all of these issues, especially with respect to the troublingly gendered cultural double standards of ageing revealed by their easy negotiability.

The turn towards later life in contemporary US film

The early twenty-first century has seen an upsurge in films that deal directly with the experience of ageing into later life, a phenomenon that has piqued the interest of numerous scholars, critics and journalists. In part, this interest is responsive to the cultural and economic traction of the so-called 'grey dollar' (referring to the spending power and leisure time of ageing baby boomers) that has seen popular cinema increasingly marketed towards older demographics. This trend, too, speaks to the fact that numbers of cinemagoers over 50 have skyrocketed in recent decades.[1] Historically, age as an identity paradigm has been noteworthy for its relative cultural invisibility, so the unprecedentedly high levels of attention that are being paid in popular culture to the experience of ageing are remarkable. With respect to mainstream and middlebrow film in particular, Jacques Mandelbaum observes 'The number of films dealing with age is rising as older people take [*sic*] up more of the cinema-going audience.'[2] Mandelbaum points not only to the maudlin and much discussed tendency of filmic depictions of old age to frame the experience in terms of decline, decay, death and loss, as is pointedly the case in films like *Iris* (Richard Eyre, 2001), *Venus* (Roger Michell, 2006), *Away from Her* (Sarah Polley, 2006) and *Amour* (Michael Haneke, 2012), but also to the equally strong tendency towards whimsy, fantasy and utopianism. *Cocoon* (Ron Howard, 1985) is a now historical example, but more recent instances of this include *The Curious Case of Benjamin Button* (David Fincher, 2008), *The Best Exotic Marigold Hotel* (John Madden, 2012), *Robot and Frank* (Jake Schreier, 2012) and *Quartet* (Dustin Hoffman, 2012), none of which actually evades the ubiquitous discourse of decline that undergirds these filmic narratives of later life.

With respect to the increasing cultural visibility of the later life performer, the Academy Awards categories of 'Best Actor in a Supporting Role' and 'Best Actress in a Supporting Role' have long served as staging grounds for the Academy's intermittent tendency to pay homage to later life comeback performances of former stars or aged character actors. Noteworthy examples include Jessica Tandy, for her role in *Fried Green Tomatoes* (John Avnet, 1991) as a senescent nursing home resident narrating the events of her life to a younger woman channelling the viewpoint of the audience; Gloria Stuart, who frames the narrative of *Titanic* (James Cameron, 1997) and plays the elderly Rose (played elsewhere in the film by Kate Winslet); and Jack Palance for *City Slickers* (Jon Underwood, 1991), in which he caricatured his classical Hollywood western persona as aged cattle driver Curly Washburn. Commensurate with the high levels of popular cultural interest in both later life and the experience of ageing that this volume responds to, this tendency is also manifest in the higher profile 'Leading Role' acting categories. 85-year-old Emanuelle Riva, for example, was the oldest person ever nominated for her role in *Amour*. Correspondingly, a talking point of the 2012 Academy Awards was the critical buzz surrounding the nominations for 'Best Actor in a Supporting Role' of Max von Sydow and Christopher Plummer – von Sydow for his role in post-9/11 drama *Extremely Loud & Incredibly Close* (Stephen Daldry, 2011), adapted from Jonathan Safran Foer's novel of the same name – and Plummer (who won), for offbeat indie comedy drama *Beginners* (Mike Mills, 2010). In the former, von Sydow plays a lifelong absent father who redeems his maligned masculinity by befriending his grandson Oskar (Thomas Horn) following the death of his beloved father in the World Trade Center. In the latter, Plummer's septuagenarian widower, Hal, renews his heretofore emotionally detached and distant relationship with his son Oliver

(Ewan McGregor) after coming out as gay following the death of his wife. His later life reconceptualisation of himself affords Hal the opportunity to become a better father as he develops a more open, honest and emotionally reciprocal relationship with Oliver in the last (and, we are invited to understand, best) stages of his life. Hal's wilful reinvention of his relationship with Oliver is seen in flashback as he melancholically ruminates on his memories of his father. Through these flashbacks the surface affability and buttoned up denial that characterises the younger Hal is contrasted with the emotional candour of Hal at seventy-five, as he strives to build a genuine friendship with Oliver through late-night telephone chats, shopping trips, tactile affection and heartfelt bedside exchanges. The commonality across these films of the later-life paternal renewal and recuperation of a major male character is also a unifying trope identifiable in an otherwise diverse cluster of recent films dealing with later-life masculinity, including western melodrama *An Unfinished Life* (Lasse Hallstrom, 2005), British drama *Is Anybody There?* (John Crowley, 2008), Disney Pixar animation *Up* (Pete Docter, 2009) and futuristic family drama *Robot & Frank*.

Theorising intersections of age and gender in film

Alongside the robust and continually growing corpus of scholarship on ageing femininities in contemporary culture, to which scholars like Deborah Jermyn, Josephine Dolan, Estella Tincknell, Ros Jennings and Abigail Gardner have recently made noteworthy inroads in the fields of stardom, celebrity, popular music studies and television studies,[3] ageing masculinities are now also increasingly subject to scholarly scrutiny. In studying popular cinema this work was spearheaded by Chris Holmlund's take on the ageing masculinity of Clint Eastwood. Eastwood's stardom, she suggests, articulates dominant discourses of ageing as decline and decay, in terms of the physical and discursive markers of age that inflect his star text, but she negotiates them successfully by positioning his advancing years in more optimistic terms as 'ripening' rather than 'rotting'.[4] The influence of this work can be seen in more recent scholarship that addresses the contemporary spike in movie treatments of male ageing, such as Donna Peberdy's on the figure of the ageing baby boomer. Peberdy links the new cultural visibility of ageing men at the turn of the millennium to the retirement en masse of men of the baby boom generation (which, along with increasing life expectancies, is also a contextually specific and generational factor pertinent to the current glut in depictions of grandfatherhood) and its historical concurrence with the emergence of Viagra in the marketplace. These things, she argues, are bound up with an emergent preoccupation in American film that intersects between ageing and masculinity. She illustrates this intersection by highlighting the cultural need manifest in films such as *About Schmidt* (Alexander Payne, 2002) and *Something's Gotta Give* (Nancy Meyers, 2003) to position ageing masculinity on either side of a binary – following Holmlund's 'rotting'/'ripening' dichotomy – of having aged either badly (in terms of decline and decay) or well (in terms of renewal and rejuvenation).[5] Harvey O'Brien turns our attention to more recent phenomena within the current proliferation of ageing masculinity narratives with his discussion of 'old guys' in twenty-first century action films such as *RED* (Robert Schwentke, 2010) and *The Expendables* (Sylvester Stallone, 2010). Following the representational paradigms for the depiction of ageing masculinities outlined above, he positions them in terms of renewal, linking the restored viability of ageing 1980s action stars both to the evolution of the genre and to the restored negotiability of the ideological values they embody.[6] Dealing with a comparable corpus of films in my own work on film stardom and the paternalisation of ageing masculinity, I argue elsewhere that the recent career renaissances of male stars such as Sylvester Stallone, Bruce Willis, and Clint Eastwood have been enabled by the recuperative paternalisation of their formerly culturally out of step screen masculinities.[7]

The recuperability of deficient, problematic or culturally obsolescent masculinities through fatherhood is, I have argued, symptomatic of a much broader tendency of a postfeminist culture that – presenting feminism as moot – declines to configure struggles for gender equity in the labour share of parenting as a feminist issue. This tendency, correspondingly, conceptualises ideal masculinity in paternal terms and negotiates feminist challenges to patriarchal hegemony by restabilising the status quo. This restabilisation takes place through common sense appeals to the disingenuous feminism of a configuration of masculinity that appears responsive to second-wave feminist critiques of separate-spheres parenting, and their calls for fathers to become more engaged and affectively invested in the practice of parenthood.[8] However, in popular cinema the appropriation, marginalisation or outright elision of motherhood from narratives that centralise fathers gives lie to the feminist credentials of postfeminism's normalisation of fatherhood as a masculine identity paradigm with near universal negotiability.[9] This phenomenon of representation highlights the continuing need for scholars to defamiliarise the new norms of postfeminist culture and to subject them to feminist critical scrutiny.

Such is the powerful and unifying appeal of this discourse of masculinity that time and again in popular cinema it is successfully articulated across intersecting axes of masculine identity, including age. Fatherhood therefore increasingly compulsorily negotiates cinematic transformations of masculinity at intersections with ageing across all stages of the adult male lifecycle. And they invariably do so in ways that re-centre fathers, at the expense of the cultural legibility of mothers and at odds with the feminist drivers of such ostensibly ameliorative transformations of masculinity. These range from narratives that chart protagonists' transitions from abject immaturity to mature manhood, such as *Knocked Up* (Judd Apatow, 2007); to those that resolve middle-aged identity crises, such as *The Descendants* (Alexander Payne, 2011) and *Delivery Man* (Ken Scott, 2013); and to those that work to negotiate the paternalisation of later life. In the cluster of films under discussion in this chapter, this part of the adult male lifecycle is presented as a staging ground for the renewal and revitalisation of abjectly senescent masculinities. This revitalisation takes place through a late in life chance at surrogate or symbolic fatherhood, a crucial component of the masculine life script to which they have thus far failed either to adhere (they are childless) or to adequately fulfil (they were or are bad fathers). This at once offsets the destabilisation to masculine hegemony posed by the corporeal abjection and social obsolescence that accompanies advanced old age, at the same time as figuring their respective recuperations in the standardly drawn paternal terms that postfeminist culture tends to take for granted as legibly and credibly feminist. There is thus an observable strand of contemporary popular cinema in which the heightened visibility and cultural traction of depictions of later life is paired with the discursive currency of fatherhood. This produces narratives in which abjectly ageing masculinities are recuperated and socially re-enfranchised through a process of rejuvenating paternalisation.

Interrogating the paternalisation of later life masculinity in twenty-first century film

This chapter adopts a feminist critical position in exploring what is at stake in the discursive intersection of advanced ageing and deficient masculinity in a spate of films from the mid-2000s through the early 2010s, taking the position that the later-life friendships depicted operate as compensatory fantasies that redeem the failures of these characters to fulfil their social roles as fathers earlier in life. Whether due to loss, bereavement, trauma or bad life choices, these characters' masculinities are marked as problematic, which in each case is bound up with paternal failure or abjection. The failure to age 'well' into a paternal role must be reversed over the course of each narrative in order to restabilise their troubled ageing masculinities. The paternalisation of aged male characters in a spate of recent films that includes *Robot & Frank, Extremely Loud & Incredibly Close, Beginners, Up, Is Anybody There?* and *An Unfinished Life* – articulated through burgeoning and revitalising friendships with symbolically filial children – facilitate the paternally inflected recuperation of their derogated masculinities. This recuperation enhances the quality of their lived experiences of later life through what is presented as the rejuvenatory practice of surrogate fatherhood. In this way, they can be productively understood as examples of what Sadie Wearing foundationally theorises as ageing subjects of rejuvenation in postfeminist culture.[10] Wearing's concern is principally with the discourse of compulsory rejuvenation that she argues characterises postfeminist culture's policing of 'temporal impropriety' as it is marked on the ageing female body.[11] However, a similar discourse of rejuvenation underpins the considerations of ageing masculinities across all of the scholarly work outlined above. And as the following analyses illustrate, it is equally applicable to postfeminist culture's policing of temporal propriety where ageing masculinities are concerned. But it takes a highly different form, more concerned with the social dynamics of ageing than with its corporeal manifestation, indicative of the gendered double standards to which ageing masculinities and femininities are respectively held and with commensurately altered stakes for feminist interventions. It is significant that Wearing situates the discourse of rejuvenation that characterises cultural articulations of ageing explicitly in the context of a postfeminist culture that seeks to nullify the potential for feminist intervention. Part of what it reveals is that cultural meanings of ageing are mutable, contextually contingent, and always in a dialogic relationship with feminism, notwithstanding the ability of postfeminist culture to obfuscate that dialogue. Moreover, commenting upon the often cited and much discussed gendered double standard of cultural common sense norms surrounding ageing and the experience of later life foundationally hypothesised by Susan Sontag,[12] Patricia Mellencamp observes that in recent decades, 'our standard,' with respect to the cultural negotiation of this double standard, 'comes from the movies.'[13] She highlights that such standards are historically located, and thus necessarily subject to change over time, according to the concerns and proclivities of their respective moments.[14] It therefore stands to reason that such changes are observable in trends discernible in filmic depictions of ageing. The analyses that follow commence with brief sketches of how the paradigm plays out in some more minor entries in the cluster, culminating in lengthier discussions of higher profile films *Extremely Loud & Incredibly Close* and *Up*. The recuperation of deficient fatherhood through paternally surrogate grandfatherhood constitutes the narrative journey of Einar Gilkyson (Robert Redford) in present day western *An Unfinished Life*, setting the template for processes of rejuvenation and paternal renewal colouring narratives of later life masculinity in the films discussed hereafter. This film also underscores the political stakes of this paradigm with regard to both gender and race, when not only Einar's granddaughter but also his infirm African-American companion, Mitch (Morgan Freeman), serve as ciphers to facilitate his masculine redemption and negotiate the hegemony of the paternally signified white male. Einar has been estranged from his daughter-in-law, Jean (Jennifer Lopez), since the death, eleven years earlier, of his son Griffin in a car accident for which he blames her, harbouring deep embitterment and entrenched resentment born of paternal grief. When Jean turns up at his Wyoming ranch having fled from domestic violence, Einar learns of the existence of his granddaughter, Griff (Becca Gardner). Despite his initial rejection of her (refusing even to acknowledge her humanity, he refers to her as 'this' rather than 'she'), he gradually transforms from a misanthropic curmudgeon into a protective paternal-surrogate to the fatherless child. The effects of his ameliorating practice of paternal grandfatherhood enable him to transcend the abject state into which his masculinity descended following his son's death and redeem his patriarchal white masculinity. This is symptomatic of the ways in which this cycle of films recuperates what it otherwise configures as the abjection of later life, by situating grandfatherhood as a space in which to successfully re-enact fatherhood and thereby age 'well'. In this way, the symbolic re-centring of Einar as patriarch is successfully negotiated after he enacts protective paternalism on behalf of his daughter-in-law and granddaughter by physically dispatching the violent ex-boyfriend who follows them to Wyoming and harasses them on Einar's property. Having done so, his paternal recuperation is underwritten when he accepts his formerly estranged young family into his home for good.

In indie curiosity *Robot & Frank*, set in New York State in the nonspecific near future, retired jewel thief Frank Weld (Frank Langella) is struggling at home alone as his memory and ability to manage everyday life begin to succumb to worsening dementia. He is not wholly estranged from his adult children, Hunter (James Marsden) and Madison (Liv Tyler), but neither have much time or patience for him, which the film attributes to his failures as a father during their childhood – specifically, the extended absence from their lives that resulted from his long term incarceration, during which they grew up and distanced themselves from him physically and emotionally. Nonetheless, they remain tolerant of their ne'er-do-well father, even if Hunter can barely contain his contempt during weekly visits to check on the ailing Frank, and the more outwardly affectionate Madison can hardly find the time to make brief phone calls from far-flung international locations. The film was received by critics largely as an offbeat buddy movie, and the emergent relationship between Frank and his robot as a de facto friendship. However, consideration of the contrived scenario of ageing masculinity in relation to the cognate examples of later-life quasi-fatherhood under discussion here reveals a comparable dynamic to those that characterise the pseudo-father/child dyads showcased across the cluster. Similarly, closer scrutiny of the equivalent tropes by which the film narrates Frank's physical and mental decline alongside the temporary rejuvenation he experiences as an upshot of his partially recuperated fatherhood reveals clear paternal inflections to his interactions and rapport with the filially signified and physically diminutive robot.[15] The key scene in this regard sees Frank teach the robot to pick locks, while he ruminates on his failures as a father. This scene invites parallels between his failed attempts to bond with Hunter by teaching him practical skills earlier in life and his current easy rapport with the robot. After Hunter delegates his minimal care of Frank entirely to the robot, it becomes his compliant and biddable replacement son. Ultimately, the second chance at fatherhood afforded to Frank by the affectless robot, a blank slate upon whom Frank writes his partial paternal rehabilitation, facilitates a functioning if imperfect reunification with his largely estranged family, enabling some steps toward the redemption of his fatherhood in the eyes of his previously scornful and embittered son. The following section considers the second chance fatherhood afforded to the aged male leads of two much higher profile films: *Extremely Loud and Incredibly Close* and *Up*.

Extremely Loud & Incredibly Close depicts the germination of the incipient recuperation of the grossly excoriated absent fatherhood of Thomas Schell Sr (von Sydow), whose son, Thomas Jr (Tom Hanks), was killed in the 9/11 attacks never knowing his father. However, through his eventual re-acceptance into the dynamic of what remains of his tragically broken family and his embryonic friendship with his grandson Oskar, the film suggests that its project to redeem him will continue as it began, in small ways, to reconfigure his ageing masculinity in paternal terms. Information about the failure of Thomas Sr's fatherhood is drip fed via snippets of exchanges about him that take place in flashback between his son and grandson, as Oskar displays a child's curiosity about his unknown grandfather, and Thomas Jr matter-of-factly relates the little he knows. From one such exchange we learn that Thomas Sr absconded from his paternal responsibilities during his son's infancy, which is attributed to his postwar trauma as a survivor of the Dresden bombings of World War II. As Thomas Jr tells Oskar simply, 'He was from Dresden, which was in Germany, went through some really bad stuff, and decided he wasn't up to having a family.' His failure as a father earlier in life is juxtaposed in sharp contradistinction with the impossibly perfect fatherhood of Thomas Jr, which is only seen in flashback through Oskar's rose-tinted recollections, who cherishes his memories of Thomas to a degree commensurate both with the tragic circumstances in which he died and the narrative requirement to provide a paternal ideal against which Thomas Sr will fail to measure up. As Oskar later declares in an emotionally charged rejection of the flawed but ameliorating replacement fatherhood offered up by his grandfather, 'My dad was the greatest dad in the world.' The casting of Tom Hanks as the ideal father is significant here, given the role played by the earlier successes of *Sleepless in Seattle* (Nora Ephron, 1993) and *Saving Private Ryan* (Steven Spielberg, 1998) in cementing Hanks' dominant persona as the perfect paternal everyman.

Defying his grandmother's instructions to steer clear of Thomas Sr, Oskar wilfully befriends him, notwithstanding the old man's initial reluctance, curmudgeonly demeanour and clear trepidation about having contact with the boy. Having thus far refused to explain the story of his life to Oskar, Thomas Sr, in an apparent attempt to encourage the boy to transcend some of his fears and anxieties, coaxes him across a wooden bridge with the promise of answering his questions. He reveals pieces of information about his past, but he still does not reveal his true identity. Nonetheless, he and the boy have by now forged a bond strong enough that Oskar determines to retain the old man as his weekend companion. This development marks a breakthrough in their relationship, which thereafter is increasingly signified in terms of Thomas Sr's surrogate fatherhood. However, this halcyon bonding period is short lived, as when Thomas Sr is confronted with the painful and tragic reality of the failure of his own fatherhood, he reverts to his former behaviour and leaves. As his taxi drives away, this reversion is brought into clear focus by Oskar's anger as he verbally excoriates the failure of Thomas Sr's fatherhood, yelling after his grandfather: 'My dad was the greatest dad in the world because you were the worst!' Later though, having better come to terms with the death of his father, Oskar re-evaluates the relationship they built while they wandered the city together and writes to his grandfather asking him to come home. This both re-enables Thomas Sr's already partially attained paternal renewal and signifies his reacceptance into the family life he had twice abandoned. Here again, the abjection of an old-aged masculinity marked as deficient by paternal failure, is surmounted through a recuperative discourse of surrogate fatherhood. And it is one that over-determines the significance of this role, both in terms of its rejuvenatory possibilities for the masculine experience of later life and at the cost of the legibility of later-life femininity, as the significance of Oskar's mother and grandmother are given short shrift. All of these themes and tropes are revisited in *Up*.

Disney Pixar's box office mega hit, *Up*, is by far the most significant entry to date in this cluster of later-life fatherhood films in terms of its financial success and the manifest resonance with audiences of mainstream cinema that necessarily accompanies the level of popular cultural saturation that films from this studio typically attain. *Up* opened with a very wide release to become the fifth highest grossing film of 2009.[16] The montage sequence that closes the film's explanatory set up in the opening section became a cultural talking point in the film's popular and critical reception,[17] as it narrated the story of one couple's life together as an emotionally charged backstory explaining the present day abject solitude of senescent misanthrope Carl Fredericksen (Edward Asner). Unsurprisingly, given both the ownership of Pixar (The Walt Disney Company purchased Pixar Animation Studios in 2006)[18] and the family audience addressed by the film, of all the films under discussion here, *Up* contains the most gentle treatment of its senior character's paternal shortcomings. Moreover, of this group of derogated seniors who experience comparable paternal epiphanies towards the end of their lives, Carl is the most blameless for his failure at fatherhood as a younger man. It is thus important to the film's negotiation of Carl's childlessness and the hegemony of the (in this case easy) recuperation of his troubled later-life masculinity through paternal rehabilitation to note that Carl and his wife, Ellie, were not childless by choice. In a brief but affectively charged, dialogue-free segment within the aforementioned opening montage, it is made clear that Carl and Ellie are fully prepared to fulfil their social roles as an emblematically heteronormative couple by marrying and having children, but they are thwarted in their attempt to become parents, which is presented as a small but significant tragedy in the otherwise idyllic coupledom showcased in this expositional précis of their lives. Relaxing in the shade of a tree on a sunny day over a picnic during the early period of their married life, Carl and Ellie happily gaze up at cloud formations, which present themselves in the shape of a sky full of laughing babies. They look at one another meaningfully and smile before the scene ellipses forward to depict them purposefully decorating a nursery. Another forward ellipsis is this time accompanied by a melancholic key change in the heretofore upbeat and melodic score, as Carl and Ellie are revealed in the illuminated doorway of an otherwise silhouetted pregnancy clinic. Ellie's head is in her hands as she weeps, while Carl silently comforts her from behind with his hands on her shoulders as a doctor breaks bad news. As is the case in so many of contemporary popular cinema's postfeminist fictions of recuperated white masculinity, the solitary male protagonist's paternal epiphany is both enabled and negotiated by the convenient narrative elision of motherhood. Hence, Carl's expository montage necessarily ends with his loss of Ellie after a long and happy life together, but it is one in which they neither fulfilled the social function of their marriage to have children, nor achieved their lifelong ambition to travel to South America. Carl's abjectly aged and melancholic masculinity is thus primed for him to transcend this dual derogation. And in this way, through the combination of Carl's bereavement and reluctant childlessness, the film neatly evades postfeminist debates about reproductive choice and lifestyle parenting (i.e., the political stakes of the choice to remain child-free or not, the cultural imperatives to perform 'bravura' parenting, and the cultural politics of gendered specificities of parenting in postfeminism) to situate Carl in a melancholic position that enables him to sidestep and transcend these issues.

The film narrates the unlikely friendship that develops, ultimately growing into a de facto father/son dyad, between socially awkward, overweight and effectively fatherless boy-scout Russell (Jordan Nagai), and curmudgeonly (childless) widowed senior citizen Carl. Determined to win a badge for helping the elderly despite Carl's resistance to accepting help and his disinclination to receive visitors, Russell finds himself marooned on Carl's floating house, which lands the two of them in a remote part of South America. In a contretemps with a construction worker from a firm that is busy redeveloping the area surrounding Carl's home – the last edifice standing from the neighbourhood that previously occupied this space – Carl unintentionally injures the man. After this, Carl is branded a public menace and forced by court order and against his will out of his home and into a retirement community. So, in an attempt to push back against the fate of social disenfranchisement and enforced relocation to an Othered social space that has been determined for him by a youth-oriented society dismissive of his right to agency over his mode of existence, and to prevent the demolition of his lifelong home by property developers, Carl rigs the house to fly free of its foundations with a huge number of helium balloons (he had previously worked as a balloon seller in a zoo). From the moment he discovers the terrified Russell on the front porch of his house, now flying at a high altitude above the city, Carl reluctantly assumes pseudo-paternal responsibility of care for the hapless boy.

Over the course of the early exchanges between Russell and Carl, the boy makes repeated reference to his father, with loaded suggestions that point to his absence from his son's life and thereby to his paternal failings. Russell nonetheless conveys a son's devotion to his absent father, indicative of the extent to which he craves a paternal presence in his life and priming the audience to anticipate Carl's rejuvenation through his recuperative uptake of the paternal role that eluded him at the earlier, requisite point in his otherwise normative lifecycle. For example, on their first meeting, Russell explains that the motivation behind his ardent desire to become a 'Senior Wilderness Ranger' is the ceremony to mark his attainment of this status, at which the fathers of the rangers are expected to be present to witness their sons' rite of masculine passage. Later, once the house is aloft, Russell proudly and confidently assures Carl that during his nap he successfully steered them to South America using the GPS device gifted to him by his father. It comes out later, as Carl and Russell chat beside a campfire, and by way of explanation as to why Russell has never been camping and does not know how to assemble a tent: his father is actually a distant and intermittent presence in his life with little time or patience for his son. This explanation is one of the film's numerous attributions of Russell's deficient masculinity (he is overweight and lacking in practical skills and athleticism, showcased by his inability to climb ropes) to the absence of fatherhood. Thus realising the truth of Russell's de facto fatherlessness following this candid conversation, Carl's demeanour towards the boy softens noticeably. And put to the test in the series of trials and obstacles that he and Russell face in the wilderness thereafter, Carl is afforded the opportunity to recuperate both of their masculinities by taking up the paternal role via the enactment of a number of acts of protective paternalism. Commensurate with the discursive correlation of fatherhood and rejuvenation that is made in all of the narratives of later-life masculinity that comprise this cluster of films, Carl's fulfilment of the paternal role through the development of his relationship with Russell enables him to transcend some of the derogating physical and psychological effects of his ageing. Specifically, this transcendence is underscored towards the end of the film when, after having cemented his pseudo-paternal bond with Russell, he symbolically rejects his walking stick, a signifier of his aged masculinity to which he has thus far steadfastly clung. The beneficial effects of Carl's pseudo-fatherhood on Russell are similarly signified through the film's showcasing of Russell's newfound ability to climb a rope, suggestive of Carl's reparative paternal influence on the boy's otherwise jeopardised masculine normativity.

As revealed in the film's closing montage of still images, following their adventure and the paternal/filial dynamic of their friendship Carl has become Russell's principal father figure. This development in their relationship, too, is underscored at the end when Russell's actual father fails to turn up for the presentation of his 'Assisting the Elderly' award that marks his graduation to the status of 'Senior Wilderness Ranger' and thus constitutes a noteworthy rite of passage for his emergent masculinity – one for which his father ought to be present. It is of course Carl who steps up to fulfil this role, which he cements by replicating the father/son bonding ritual of ice-cream accompanied by a traffic spotting game, which Carl knows forms the core of Russell's fondest memories of spending time with his father, and which therefore symbolises his ascent to the status of the boy's surrogate father, to the mutual benefit of their respectively intersectional juvenile and aged masculinities. This ascent has the dual function of both plugging the paternal gap in the boy's life and salvaging the normativity of his masculinity (until now under threat from the absence of his father) and recuperating Carl's own masculinity that was previously marked as deficient by the dual derogation of his aged senescence and his inability to age 'successfully'.

Conclusion

In the case of all the aged male leads under discussion in this chapter, earlier failures to adhere to the requisite cultural script for successful, masculine, ageing fatherhood are recuperated, as each, towards the end of his life, is afforded the opportunity to redeem his troubled masculinity and to enhance the quality of his lived experience of old age manhood through paternal renewal in the practice of later-life surrogate fatherhood. It remains to be seen the extent to which this trope will continue to inflect, negotiate and shape the meanings of intersectional articulations of ageing masculinity, but the current status quo in contemporary popular cinema is suggestive. Symptomatic of the fact that the turn towards recuperative grandfatherhood in cultural representations of ageing masculinity remains not only a viable but also a lucrative means of negotiating this identity paradigm, at the time of writing the top grossing film at the US box-office, having displaced *Gravity* (Alfonso Cuarón, 2013), one of the year's most lauded and successful films, is candid camera road movie comedy of ameliorative (surrogate) paternal incompetence *Jackass Presents: Bad Grandpa* (Jeff Tremaine, 2013).[19] The abjectly derogated, grotesquely rendered and widowed single grandfatherhood of Johnny Knoxville's Irving Zisman is negotiated and recuperated over the course of a narrative in which he is charged with safely ferrying his grandson across America to his father, following the incarceration of the boy's mother (in keeping with the contrived and laboured narrative elision of motherhood that characterises so many of contemporary popular cinema's narratives of single fatherhood and paternal recuperation). Unsurprisingly, a paternal bond is formed over the course of their journey together, as the recuperative paternalisation of later-life masculinity continues to be negotiated across an ever wider and increasingly unlikely range of popular cinematic forms and genres.

Notes

1. 'A Growing Demographic – The Over-50 Moviegoer,' *The New York Times* (26 February 2011); Donna Peberdy, *Masculinity and Film Performance: Male Angst in Contemporary American Cinema* (Basingstoke and New York: Palgrave Macmillan, 2011), pp. 152–154.
2. Jaccques Mandelbaum, 'Alive and Kicking: The Changing View of Older People on the Silver Screen,' *The Guardian* (Accessed 30 July 2013).
3. Deborah Jermyn, 'Past Their Prime Time? Women, Ageing and Absence on British Factual Television,' *Critical Studies in Television*, 8:1 (2013), pp. 73–90; Deborah Jermyn, ed., *Female Celebrity and Ageing: Back in the Spotlight* (London and New York: Routledge, 2013); Josephine Dolan and Estella Tincknell, eds, *Aging Femininities: Troubling Representations* (Newcastle upon Tyne: Cambridge Scholars Publishing, 2012); Ros Jennings and Abigail Gardner, eds, *Rock On: Women, Ageing and Popular Music* (Farnham: Ashgate, 2012).
4. Chris Holmlund, *Impossible Bodies: Femininity and Masculinity at the Movies* (London and New York: Routledge, 2002), p. 153.
5. Peberdy, pp. 146–168.
6. Harvey O'Brien, *Action Movies: The Cinema of Striking Back* (London and New York: Wallflower, 2012), pp. 96–110. See also in this volume, Dominic Lennard, 'Too Old for This Shit?: On Ageing Tough Guys', pp. 93–107.
7. Hannah Hamad, *Postfeminism and Paternity in Contemporary U.S. Film: Framing Fatherhood* (New York and London: Routledge, 2014), pp. 70–90.
8. Hamad, pp. 1–26.
9. Hamad, pp. 18–19. *Kramer vs. Kramer* (Robert Benton, 1979) is the canonical early example, but contemporary instances include *The Descendants* (Alexander Payne, 2011), *That's My Boy* (Sean Anders, 2012) and *Delivery Man* (Ken Scott, 2013).

10. Sadie Wearing, 'Subjects of Rejuvenation: Aging in Postfeminist Culture,' in *Interrogating Postfeminism: Gender and the Politics of Popular Culture*, ed. Yvonne Tasker and Diane Negra (Durham: Duke University Press, 2007), p. 277.
11. Wearing, 'Subjects of Rejuvenation,' p. 278
12. Susan Sontag, 'The Double Standard of Aging,' *The Saturday Review of the Society* (23 September 1972).
13. Patricia Mellencamp, 'Crisis and Fear at the Movies and in Life, or On Being as Old as My Grandmother,' in *Screening Genders*, ed. Krin Gabbard and William Luhr (New Brunswick, NJ: Rutgers University Press, 2008), p. 87.
14. Ibid.
15. The robot's body is played by actress and dancer Rachael Ma who is 4 feet 11 inches tall (http://www.imdb.com/name/nm4567881/). The effect of the robot's diminutive physique is exacerbated when Ma acts alongside Frank Langella who is 6 feet 3 inches (http://www.imdb.com/name/nm0001449/bio), compounding the signification of the robot and Frank's filial/paternal dynamic.
16. '2009 Domestic Grosses,' *Box Office Mojo*, available at http://www.boxofficemojo.com/yearly/chart/?view=widedate&view2=domestic&yr=2009&p=.htm (Accessed 10 September 2013).
17. See for example Paul Gaita, 'Scene Dissection: "Up" Director Pete Docter on the Film's Emotional Opening Montage,' *The Los Angeles Times* (25 February 2010).
18. Laura M. Holson and Andrew Ross Sorkin, 'Disney Reaches Deal to Buy Pixar for $7.4 Billion in Stock', *The New York Times* (25 January 2006).
19. '*Jackass* Film *Bad Grandpa* Trumps at US Box Office,' *BBC News*, available at http://www.bbc.co.uk/news/entertainment-arts-24704034 (Accessed 28 October 2013).

6
Too Old for This Shit?: On Ageing Tough Guys

Dominic Lennard

'You've all seen the little things trying to make you feel less of a man because you're losing your hair,' Bruce Willis complained in a press conference for his film *16 Blocks* in 2006, 'but they can all suck my ... You know what I mean? I'm a man, and I will kick anybody's ass who tries to tell me that I'm not a man because my hair's thinning.'[1] Indeed, in the first decade of the 2000s, it seemed that such figures as Willis and fellow 1980s action icon Sylvester Stallone were never *more* manly. The return of Willis's heroic New York cop John McClane for a critically and commercially successful new instalment of the *Die Hard* series in 2007 (with another following in 2013), and the comeback of Stallone's beefcake icons Rocky Balboa and John Rambo punctuated a decade that seemed to swoon for the revival of traditional masculinities on film.

Hollywood's re-embrace of aggressive, action-defined masculinities can be linked to a period of national trauma and insecurity in the United States. In Susan Faludi's acclaimed analysis of the American cultural landscape in the aftermath of the terrorist attacks of 11 September 2001, she extensively demonstrates that the public response to 9/11 implied a necessary return to traditional gender roles, particularly an embracing of masculinities reminiscent of the 'tough' western heroes of the 1950s. She argues that women were erroneously constructed as the primary victims of the attacks, suggesting that the attacks were an assault on the domestic homes of America rather than on an urban workplace.[2] The salve for national trauma and feelings of sudden and terrible vulnerability was the heroism of strong manly men, men willing to do what it takes to combat such threats (real or imagined). Faludi documents a chorus of columnists who kissed goodbye to sensitive touchy-feely types, males 'pussified' under feminism, and underscored the importance of an older, tougher masculinity. Alternative ways of doing manhood certainly retained some commercial currency throughout the 2000s; 'bromance' comedies, such as *Superbad* (2007), *Knocked Up* (2007) and *Pineapple Express* (2008), often celebrated slobbish and unambitious masculinities, while *Superbad* star Michael Cera came to emblematise the under-confident and unimposing – yet thoroughly endearing – geek in films such as *Juno* (2007) and *Scott Pilgrim vs. the World* (2010). More broadly, though, a reversion to macho pleasures swept American media, and the 'tough' male's comeback was exemplified, as Faludi points out, in television programs like *The Shield*, *Prison Break* and *24*, as well as advertising and self-help guides that directed consumers on being a 'real' (i.e., macho, heterosexual) man.[3] Unsurprisingly then, the careers of a number of ageing male actors were reignited through the return of their iconic hard-men characters, in a mirroring of the process discussed at length by Susan Jeffords, in which the 'hard' male bodies of 1980s action cinema compensated for the political 'softness' of the Carter years: '[D]uring the Reagan era,' Jeffords writes, 'popular culture became the mechanism not simply for identifying but for establishing the relationship between the people and the State, through the articulation of that State as the unified national body of masculine character.'[4] As part of this tough-guy resurgence over the past decade, Sylvester Stallone (in his early 60s) flexed for *Rocky Balboa* (2006) and *Rambo* (2008); Bruce Willis returned (in his early 50s) as John McClane in *Die Hard 4.0* (released as *Live Free and Die Hard* in the US) in 2007. Stallone later regrouped with a veritable brigade of yesteryear's He-Men (including Willis, Arnold Schwarzenegger, and Dolph Lundgren) in *The Expendables* (2010) and *The Expendables 2* (2013), which gleefully added as many layers to the beefcake as possible, including newer tough-guy stars such as Jason Statham and Steve Austin.

The 'good-old' tough guy was back – but he was also older. Cultural understandings of age are, of course, powerfully gendered. Across nearly all media, fewer roles are offered to older women, whose ageing is seen to subtract from them the markers of desirable femininity. In Hollywood, scores of otherwise celebrated female performers seem to disappear once they do not so easily attract our adoring gaze. Few ageing male stars are so degradingly erased – and especially not ones associated with performances of rough and tumble masculinities. Yet Willis's irascible remark indicates the threat ageing poses to a masculinity defined by physical action, violence and endurance. The resurrection of particular types of masculinity is thus not merely a triumphal enterprise, but also a potentially dangerous one, which threatens to deflate the very 'macho' masculinity it showcases. Although by no means an exhaustive study of the phenomenon, this chapter identifies several key themes in the recent return of action cinema's tough guys. It argues that while using spectacular action feats to fortify masculinities perceived to be under threat from age, several of the films in question also acknowledge that the immense physical demands of this brand of masculinity cannot be re-performed indefinitely; consequently, they navigate for their stars alternative ways of maintaining tough-guy status. It also suggests that films featuring ageing tough guys anticipate critique of their archaic macho displays, adopting strategies to absolve our pleasure in the enactment of seemingly outdated masculinities.

Bringing back the beast: *Rocky Balboa*

In 2006 Sylvester Stallone directed and starred in the first *Rocky* film in fifteen years, which focussed on the Italian Stallion's comeback while well into his fifties. The resurrection of this tough guy participated in a broader, celebratory resurrection of physical and paternalistic manhoods, albeit in one of its cuddlier and more warmly nostalgic modes. As Rocky (Stallone) ambles around his Philadelphia neighbourhood, several flashbacks to *Rocky* (1976) draw on the audience's nostalgia for the original film, thus promoting viewers' nostalgia for the 'original', simplified and wholesome masculinity of its protagonist. Loveable old Rock does not flaunt his violent power but holds it in comforting paternal reserve. Demonstrating his fatherly care early in the film, he defends female bartender Marie (Geraldine Hughes) from a group of impudent hoods and provides her with a safe ride home, repeating a gesture from the original film, in which he forcibly ferried 'Little Marie' home, thereby saving her from a life on the street. In a neighbourhood that has sadly slipped from an idealised working-class past, now filled with posturing young homies, the Rocky of *Rocky Balboa* is the romantic stalwart of a 'genuine,' idealised, paternal (and powerful) masculinity.

The reason for Rocky's comeback in *Balboa* remains sufficiently unmoored for the film to work as a metaphor for any unresolved ambition. At the forefront, however, is the struggle for dignity and renewed self-image as one ages: the fight for upward mobility that characterised *Rocky* and *Rocky II* (1979) (where physical power counteracts social powerlessness) is transferred to a fight against feelings of obsolescence brought on by ageing. Rocky's wife (Talia Shire) has passed away from ovarian cancer between films, and the ageing former champ remains thoroughly fixated on the past. *Rocky Balboa* admirably confronts and dismisses the popular notion that reaching retirement age necessitates a cessation of individual aspirations. Yet boxing's role in illustrating this idea should not escape scrutiny. Rocky's desire to return to the ring does not merely demonstrate the ageing individual's lasting purpose; boxing's hypermasculine displays also mean that that purpose necessitates an impressive physical demonstration of the masculinity perceived to be under threat from age. When his irascible brother-in-law, Paulie (Burt Young), quizzes Rocky about the need for a comeback, Rocky articulates his sadness over his wife's passing, but he melds this sadness into the need to loosen some stifled inner power: 'Sometimes it's hard to breathe...I feel like there's this *beast* inside me.' 'This is who you are,' Marie earnestly advises him later on, 'Fighters fight.' The film thus depicts Rocky's reversal of the restrictions age seems to place on a violently active male body through suppression of its 'true' nature, a nature that Rocky must reengage to find purpose during his advancing years.

While *Rambo* (2008) did not explicitly thematise its hero's ageing as *Rocky Balboa* did, it attributed the return of the ageing tough guy to an ultimately irrepressible, mythic masculinity more directly – although with a more fatalistic and doom-laden touch. Prior to accepting his new mission (on which, as expected, he kills prolifically and spectacularly), John Rambo (also Stallone) wrangles with himself while forging a knife blade that doubles as a metaphor for his tortured, violent soul: 'You know what you are, what you're made of: war is in your blood. Don't fight it.' In both films the hero's masculinity is something that age aestheticises as immovable, dignifying the protagonist's understanding of himself as a combat machine. Whereas in *Rambo* this inner beast finds a sanctioned outlet in gory combat against a corrupt and brutal Burmese regime, its expression through boxing in *Rocky Balboa* allows it to be transformed into an inspirational tale of achieving one's potential. Most spectacular in *Rocky Balboa* is the transformation of the ageing Stallone's body to an impressible semblance of the rippled 1980s Rocky, which the film positions as material evidence that implausible dreams can be realised. The body here must, of course, be meticulously constructed, seemingly drawing attention to the *work* involved in performing masculinity;[5] yet it operates as a physical manifestation of Rocky's innermost and 'true' masculinity, which retirement has stiflingly concealed. More than cultural constrictions of age, what need to be overcome in *Rocky Balboa* are feelings that ageing has repressed and degraded a once-evident manhood – a manhood tied intrinsically to meaningful selfhood. The transformation of Rocky's ageing body demonstrates the hero's 'essential' beast triumphing over the restrictions of the physical.

But Rocky can hardly fight forever, or not competitively anyway; the body cannot persistently provide this awing 'evidence' of masculinity (and purpose). We note that the ageing champ's comeback strains credulity to the point that he narrowly loses against his young challenger, rather than emerging victorious (this narrow loss is taken as something of a victory in the spirit of the original *Rocky*). Consequently, *Rocky Balboa* also seeks to navigate a way for male prestige beyond what one's physical body can evidence through the transference of his masculinity and its associated heroism to others. At the start of *Rocky Balboa* the ageing slugger is estranged from his son, Robert (Milo Ventimiglia), who shirks his father's attempts at intimacy because his dad 'casts a big shadow', leaving him alienated from his father's heroic legacy. Instead, Robert is trying his hand with a rival patriarchy in the world of big business. Rocky and his son's sarcastic boss (Robert Michael Kelly) are juxtaposed as competing fathers when Rocky visits his son at work; the boss makes affable small talk as he poses for a photo with the former champ, Rocky's fist pressed playfully against his rival's cheek. After a pep talk from Rocky about self-respect, though, Robert pledges allegiance to his dad: Robert quits his job to help Rocky prepare his comeback, thereby rejecting the upper-middle-class hierarchy from which Rocky is alienated and enshrining his father as *the* totemic model of male selfhood and an explicit model of heroism.

The restoration of the ageing patriarch as the model for 'true' masculinity is dramatised more interestingly through Rocky's relationship with his younger opponent. Rocky mounts his return against Mason 'The Line' Dixon (Antonio Tarver), the smart-mouthed, undefeated, yet also unappreciated young champion, whose image will be improved, his agents feel, by an exhibition match for charity against an ageing legend. If Rocky's age means he must combat perceptions that his virile masculinity has been depleted, his young rival manifests his power too readily through systematic and effortless victories. Dixon does not suffer for his wins; his power is never imperilled, thus he never addresses and soothes a boxing audience's fear that masculinity might not be all-conquering. Consequently, in the dramaturgy of his fights, his character is without genuine sympathy or appeal. By comparison, in previous *Rocky* films, Rocky did not win until he had been utterly brutalised: transformed into an almost unwatchable vision of suffering that forced us to experience his thrashed, quivering, empurpled and thoroughly vulnerable male body. The suffering body in the action film frequently addresses anxieties about the true power of the muscular male body (still subject to pain, mortification and torture); it responds to the claim that the body is not, as its posturing ostensibly claims, invincible.[6] Rebounding from vulnerability accounts for the liabilities of masculinist ideology, demonstrating that vulnerability can be answered and suppressed by sheer willpower (by an 'essential' male spirit). In *Rocky Balboa* the ageing fighter's performance against Dixon convincingly resolves the feared liabilities of the ageing male body: Rocky loses – but only just, more than impressively demonstrating his competitiveness to the surprise of boxing pundits. Every bit as importantly, though, is the fact that he also pushes his opponent to the limit. Having injured his hand early in the fight, the untested Dixon is made to draw on interior reserves of 'true' power for once – that is, perform the wounded resurgence that characterises previous Rocky victories. In his narrow loss to Dixon, Rocky bestows on his young rival the capacity to suffer – the feature of a true champion. As well as demonstrating the triumph of one's most essential manly essence over the degradation of ageing, the ageing tough guy is positioned as the inspirational model of heroic masculinity.

The absence of Rocky's timid wife, Adrian, in *Rocky Balboa* leaves her as a mythic figure whom Rocky invokes and reveres as he ambles around Philadelphia; however, it also serves to centralise Rocky's parenthood. After he defends and befriends 'Little Marie', he politely rebuffs the possibility of a romantic connection, insisting that he remains devoted to his deceased wife. This devotion allows Rocky to remain the idealised father, indeed, the benevolent protector of 'Little Marie'. He also forms a relationship with her fatherless son, Steps (James Francis Kelly III), who joins his training camp, again suggesting Rocky as a guiding father. The ageing Rocky's apparently diminishing physical power is answered through his return to boxing; more than this, though, his legitimacy and prestige as a patriarch is restored – a 'family' reconstituted around this charismatic father. Consequently, the Rocky we see so inspirationally defying his age in *Rocky Balboa* is also confirming it: repositioned as an inspirational father who bequeaths the germ of masculinity to younger men.

Being 'that guy': *Die Hard 4.0* and *A Good Day to Die Hard*

Considerably more sardonic in its revival and celebration of tough-guy masculinity are new entrants into the *Die Hard* franchise, *Die Hard 4.0* and *A Good Day to Die Hard*. To an era in which President George W. Bush's 'tough' stance on terrorism was framed and appraised through cowboy references,[7] a new instalment of *Die Hard* (the first since 1995) was a fitting complement. *Die Hard* was always implicitly a cowboy film; the finale of the original (1988) mimicked the climax of *High Noon* (1952), while the protagonist's catchphrase, 'Yippee ki-yay, motherfucker', explicitly positioned him as a cowboy hero. To recap: New York cop McClane arrived grudgingly at the ritzy Nakatomi plaza in Los Angeles, as a guest at the Christmas party of his corporate-go-getter wife, Holly (Bonnie Bedelia), whose career had led to their separation. They greet and promptly bicker, and during that exchange McClane (whom we have already witnessed appraise an airline hostess and leggy airport patron) rebukes his estranged wife for merely using her maiden name. Terrorists strike the building, allowing McClane to prove his male worth while his wife plays the damsel in distress at the top of the tower. Holly's rescue by limping and blood-smeared McClane, as she screams and flails on the building's horrifying precipice, necessitates the relinquishing of her symbolic Rolex watch, a company gift proffered by her sleazy co-worker. Heist mastermind Hans Gruber (Alan Rickman) clings to Holly's wrist as he tumbles over the edge, threatening to drag Holly down with him; but his grip is fatally loosened when McClane swiftly unclasps the corporate status symbol. Rescue achieved, the tensions of the McClane marriage are resolved; McClane repaired the union not through correction of his deep insecurity with his wife's success, but through an awe-inspiring display of the working-class masculinity apparently under threat.

McClane was an ideal character to satisfy the desire for a heroism that underscored traditional gender roles. The disaster that calls upon McClane's heroics in *4.0* concerns a multivarious attack on US infra-structure via vulnerabilities in government computer software. Former CIA hacker Thomas Gabriel (Timothy Olyphant) exploits a weakness in the system to teach the US a lesson, manipulating it as a foreign threat might – but ultimately does not. Thus, the film engages with fears of terrorism while subtracting all real political content (content that might clutter the stage and cramp the style of triumphant macho action). *Die Hard 4.0* is dedicated to the apparently lost art of mascu-linity, which the returning hero embodies and ceaselessly demonstrates through stunts, fights, and a generally aggressive physicality. The affir-mation and celebration of the ageing McClane's masculinity is most trenchantly manifested in the suppression of the Others who challenge it. 'Playtime's over, sweetheart' he tells the villain's hacker/martial-arts girlfriend, Mai (Maggie Q), thus defining her role as unimportant, juve-nile, and trivial – while ensuring we recognise all these as characteristics of her gender. *Die Hard 4.0*'s sexism is on parade with most unashamed glee during McClane's fight with this same antagonist, who trounces him in a martial arts display reminiscent of the high-kicking heroines of

Charlie's Angels (2000), *Kill Bill* (2003) and TV's *Alias* (2001–2006). After this humiliatingly swift defeat, however, McClane hoists himself up, announcing, 'That's about enough of this kung fu shit.' The physicality central to McClane's power means his humiliation grants him licence to almost relentlessly brutalise his opponent – and grants the audience licence to enjoy every moment of it. McClane hurls Mai into a shelving unit, and his violence is affirmed and celebrated when he nonchalantly glances downward, alerting us that in his fist he still clutches a hank of this woman's long brown hair. When she somehow comes back for more, McClane's sadistic delight is further sanctioned: he drops Mai down an elevator shaft and celebrates his triumph with a primal roar. In such displays Willis's ageing body is reasserted over suspicions of physical deterioration; more than this, though, the vigour and power of youth, expertise and energy are translated into feminine frivolity inferior to the brutish authenticity of 'good old-fashioned' male muscularity.

McClane is paired with geeky twenty-something hacker Matt Farrell (Justin Long) so that the latter can cast into relief, and eventually introject, his senior's masculinity. Harvey O'Brien writes that 'Central to the "buddy" dynamic is the element of transference whereby ideas and values are exchanged through a shared experience.'[8] *Die Hard 4.0* offers all the superficial motions of this process. Matt advances the duo's quest through an impressive demonstration of his computer smarts and has a few amusing quips of his own to match the wise-cracking McClane. Yet the buddy dynamic consists primarily of Willis schooling his 'nerdy' young companion in hard knocks, assuming the firm paternal role. 'I just want to stop to take a breath!' Matt pants as the duo bound up a steel staircase; 'When I was young they had these things called gymnasiums,' McClane retorts; the smart-mouthed Matt is a sassy yet physically withering victim of modern masculinity that requires correction. In light of this mismatch of old and young, physical and technical, it is easy to see with which habitus the film invites us to identify. Early in the film, McClane tunes the duo's car radio to Creedence Clearwater Revival's 'Fortunate Son' as an American flag unfurls in lyrical slow motion outside to commemorate the Fourth of July. Back in the car, Matt derides McClane's taste, at odds with his own preference for noisy nu-metal demonstrated earlier in the film. The youngster's dismissal of the classic rock icons is annoying in its swift ignorance: 'It's *old* rock – doesn't make it classic. What sucked back then still sucks now,' and McClane rebuts this facile critique by turning the volume up, further centralising the song on the soundtrack. Thus the 'outdated' McClane is celebrated in nostalgic unison with the classic rock with which he identifies and with patriotic affection for the country that produced it. In this combination, the authenticity associated with classic rock[9] aids the construction of the 'authenticity' of an almost forgotten, masculinist ideology.

Philippa Gates observes the celebration of McClane's experience and physicality in the film, suggesting it counteracts our expectation that youth will be privileged; McClane proves that 'He may be older and not as up-to-date with the changing world, but he is still the muscle needed to dispose of America's most unwanted.'[10] Indeed, further than generously acknowledging McClane's experience and muscle, the film privileges it, repeatedly staging our delight in his tough-guy heroics. In deference to this 'needed' masculinity, Matt does transform in the end, proving his tough-guy worth and earning McClane's endorsement by shooting to death a bad guy who holds McClane's daughter, Lucy (Mary Elizabeth Winstead), hostage. Thus the film constructs the 'necessity' of Matt's transformation to meet imagined threats to the nation and its (female) citizens. We see Matt's capacity to be a male capable of dramatic violence – to adopt the kind of 'authentic' masculinity exemplified by McClane.

The imperilment of McClane's strong-willed daughter is crucial in *Die Hard 4.0*'s depiction of the paternalism of the ageing tough guy and its apparent necessity. At the start the film McClane 'rescues' his daughter, Lucy, in a car park from the unwanted advances of her boyfriend, a scene in which McClane's snappy wit ensures we delight in his fatherly good sense. His embarrassed daughter, whom we learn refuses to return his calls, is not so appreciative. No shrinking violet, Lucy rebukes Dad for his intrusion. Far from the narrative's acknowledging that her resistance was itself sufficient, it later places Lucy in the distressing custody of the film's main villain. With Lucy now gravely imperilled, we give thanks for the protective patriarch who will go to any means to retrieve her and the paternalistic violence he embodies – while Lucy boasts to her captor of her heroic father's pending intervention. The relationship between father and daughter, apparently damaged by McClane's veritably stalkerish paternalism, is repaired through an epic demonstration of that same control.

The reaffirmation (and celebration) of the ageing action star's masculinity demonstrated in *Die Hard 4.0* is taken further in the film's sequel, *A Good Day to Die Hard* (2013); yet here it also reaches a terminus where an alternative strategy for evidencing 'macho' masculinity must be negotiated. In this film, McClane's heroics are accompanied and doubled by those of his literal son, John 'Jack' McClane Jr (Jai Courtney), a CIA officer working undercover in Moscow, who bears both his father's name and – even amplified – all the signifiers of his virile heroism. Here is a buddy who has no deficit of the kind of masculinity that McClane coached into dithering Matt Farrell in the earlier film, having seemingly inherited it biologically. Yet despite their similarities, and for reasons only vaguely expounded, John Jr hates Dad's guts. For his own part, McClane senior derides his son's career, referring to his 'spy shit' as if it were no more than a juvenile fantasy. While John Jr is going through all the right macho motions, the film makes immediately clear that his violence is out of control; at the start of the film, he has been arrested in Russia for perpetrating an assassination, and is under threat from the henchmen of a corrupt and violent government official. John Jr's 'spy shit' is a classic over-identification with an aggressively masculinist system, performed in the absence of any actual father. While the son acts out an aggressive obedience to what Jacques Lacan called 'the name of the father,' the father himself is denied prestige. Thus, wrapped in *A Good Day to Die Hard*'s familiar plot of father-son disconnection is the threat that an ordinarily endorsed masculinist ideology might exceed and detach from the figures to whom it traditionally grants power and privilege – and figures whose age implies their increasing inability to embody that ideology.

Yet, as well as seeming to challenge his ageing father, the son also allows his father opportunity to negotiate his advancing years. Having been brutalised by baddies, the couple finally and predictably buddy up at the film's conclusion. The younger McClane, proud to share his father's macho legacy, embraces their shared name: 'It's hard to kill a McClane.' His father smugly points out that while their names are identical, his son is John McClane, *Jr*. 'That makes you a senior,' the son retorts. Yet, as strings swell nobly over the soundtrack, Dad has the final word, confirming his son's remark, not as a suggestion of obsolescence, but as proof of his venerability: 'That's right – and try not to forget it. I'm your father. Have some respect for your father.' The ageing McClane may not be able to convincingly compete with his son's heroics, but he can position himself as the ultimate 'cause' of them and seek reverence on that basis. One's inability to any longer manage the terrifying stunts that constitute a persuasive performance of macho masculinity can be negotiated by constructing oneself as that masculinity's origin and apotheosis. This gesture is made more complete at the film's very conclusion when father and son are joined by the worried daughter who served as the distressed (albeit tough-talking) damsel in the film's predecessor. The children's mother (having long-ago divorced her husband) is utterly forgotten: the ageing father is reinscribed as not merely family leader and model, but also the unquestioned originator, to be cherished and venerated.

In the tradition of toughness: *The Expendables*

Given the success of new *Rocky*, *Rambo* and *Die Hard* films, *The Expendables* (2010) sought to capitalise on the cultural soft spot for hard men by bringing most of them back at once. Written and directed by Stallone, *The Expendables* featured Sly, Dolph Lundgren, Bruce Willis, Mickey Rourke, Jet Li and (briefly) Arnold Schwarzenegger, as well as newer stars Jason Statham, Steve Austin and Randy Couture and plenty of explosions, fights and similarly spectacular evidence of the muscular masculinities on display. A sequel in 2012 included Jean-Claude Van Damme as the central antagonist, while Chuck Norris appears in a minor role, primarily to make one of the 'Chuck Norris jokes' that proliferated online from 2005 onward, celebrating the action star's tough-guy might. In the original instalment, Barney Ross (Stallone) heads a crew of elite, but in several cases ageing, mercenaries on a mission to overthrow a dictator, mercenaries who engage seemingly every signifier of macho masculinity: grim tattoos, motorcycles, martial arts abilities, weapons talk, knife-throwing and so on. As expected, *The Expendables* pays gleeful and exhausting tribute to outdated modes of 'doing' masculinity. Early in the film the team's mission coordinator, 'Tool' (Rourke), rides into their man-cave garage headquarters on a Harley-Davidson, on the back of which is perched a stiletto-heeled and Daisy Dukes–wearing young blonde. In accordance with this stylised sexism, Tool cannot remember this particular girl's name; he asks her, though, so he can most courteously instruct her to prepare him a drink (a martini, favourite of another idealised male, James Bond), before propelling her on her way with an encouraging spank on the ass. In such gestures, we see one of the film's many demonstrations of a process Sally Chivers has identified in the later films of Paul Newman, Clint Eastwood, and Jack Nicholson, whereby 'the older male figure...whose masculinity is perceived to be fading [is transformed into] a man whose masculinity is exaggerated and compensatory.'[11] A tattoo-artist, Tool works while Creedence's 'Keep on Chooglin' plays in the background, classic rock again used to signal 'classic' and 'authentic' masculinities. With its expended and frequent action sequences, the sheer excess of *The Expendables'* muscle-power cannot help but draw the film into self-consciousness, and the film and its sequel feature a number of jokes that reference its stars' iconic previous performances. This self-consciousness, however, does not transfer into a critique of the ideology of muscle power. As its protracted chase, fight and shooting sequences indicate, the film pays gleeful homage to tough-guy masculinity.

In this film, younger male action stars serve explicitly as recipients of the legacy of macho violence, most centrally Jason Statham as knife-throwing extraordinaire Lee Christmas. Statham made his screen debut in Guy Ritchie's *Lock, Stock and Two Smoking Barrels* (1998), the first of the director's lad-culture-inflected gangster films, and he more recently took over Charles Bronson's mantle in a 2011 remake of *The Mechanic* (1972). Whereas the most recent *Rocky* and *Die Hard* films prescriptively model manhood for younger men, *The Expendables* more conservatively indicates an unbroken continuum of tough guys, in which the presence of younger stars conveys the impression that macho masculinity is 'inherent' and naturally occurring rather than ideologically constructed.

Having returned from his mission for a romantic evening with his lover (Charisma Carpenter), Christmas finds her with another man. She substantiates her infidelity by complaining of his uncommunicativeness – after all, she doesn't even know what he does for a living. The wounded hardman sulks off, only to return to confront his girlfriend's new beau when he finds bruises on her face. After thrashing this miscreant and all his buddies – and wowing viewers – with his martial arts skill, Christmas reprimands his former lover: 'That's what I do for a living.' Although he seemed an unsatisfactory partner, Statham's paternalistic violence is offered in evidence of how satisfactory a man he truly is – how *manly*: shame on this whiny modern woman who presumed to expect openness, communication and more than periodic and swooping sexual interest. In this scene the film solemnly legitimises the excessive violence frivolously on display elsewhere in the film, making sure we understand the tough guy as not just a purely cinematic construction. Christmas's subplot moralistically legitimises evidences the masculinity of which Stallone and his contemporaries stand as weathered yet noble archetypes.

It's tough being tough: mourning the macho

While the form of masculinity articulated in yesteryear's action cinema and its ageing stars may have received a resurgence in popularity, many of these films also are canny enough to insulate their portrayals from feminist critique by tacitly apologising for the masculinities on display as well as celebrating them. Susan Jeffords has identified a shift in 1990s action cinema away from the hypermasculinity emblematised by Stallone and Schwarzenegger and toward the popularisation of more vulnerable male heroes.[12] Consequently, several of the new crop of tough-guy films sought to manage suspicions that the hero's brand of masculinity was outdated by asking the audience to deplore – even 'mourn' – his confinement to it, a strategy that absolves them of the pleasure they take in that masculinity's violent demonstration. In *The Expendables*, Tool sombrely recounts an anecdote of his desensitisation through years of violent work. Being tough is not glamorous, the film soberly reminds us; except that it is – a theme the vast majority of the film is dedicated to perpetuating. Similarly, Lee Christmas's subplot encourages our sympathy for the tough guy whose nobility, his very masculinity, means he has been left behind by his lover (who eventually reunites with him following his spectacular display). Just as veteran John Rambo of *Rambo* has chosen to remain behind in South East Asia, his masculinity is sutured to the past. In *Rambo*, militarised masculinity is something with which the hero is sadly yet irrevocably 'cursed'. John Rambo would do anything to escape his talent for war, but it constitutes his most essential self – as if the fact that this talent provides spectacular entertainment is not more than incidental.

In one of *Die Hard 4.0*'s few quiet moments, exhausted and overawed by his violent companion, Matt laments his alienation from the heroic masculinity that McClane represents: 'I'm not, that guy ... I'm not, like, heroic and everything – I'm not brave like you are.' McClane fobs off his adulation, indicating that his heroism has led to divorce and disconnection from his children: it's hard being hard. McClane's actions are merely responses to the necessities of the situation, responses that he self-sacrificingly enacts to his emotional detriment. Yet this apparent 'deglamourisation' gives the lie to the film's conventional aestheticisation of tough-guy heroics in moments too compulsive and numerous to properly catalogue here, and to the pleasure we are encouraged to take in them. Even nerdy Matt gets properly into the action spirit at the film's conclusion, gunning down the henchman who holds McClane's daughter hostage, proving himself capable of being 'that guy' (a mantle McClane later formally bestows). Despite McClane's veritably Oedipal policing of his daughter, the film implies the future romantic union of Matt and Lucy now that Matt has proven himself 'that guy' – or, we might say, '*a* guy', in the film's romanticised macho vein (and as he is driven to the hospital to the 'authentic' roots rumblings of 'Fortunate Son'). Being 'that guy' is scarcely the woeful condition the film earlier posited; it is what makes Matt a suitable match for McClane's self-possessed daughter. In the disingenuous mourning of the hero's toughness, we can see the construction of masculinity as something 'essential' and unchanging, an inner responsibility and not something subject to cultural flows or traditions. The adherence to an archaic masculinity seals a statement of either its necessity or one's tragic inability to change – a dignification that renders that brand of masculinity more venerable than adolescent.

Conclusion

Yvonne Tasker has postulated that 'the cinematic hero is in the business of performing manliness not only at the level of physique, incorporating as well as desire to embody authority, to play the figure of the father'.[13] Yet she notes that traditionally it is this authority that is denied the hero: he is neglected by, or himself neglects, patriarchal hierarchy, as in *Die Hard*, where McClane operates indifferent to and outside the approval of an inept police force. Yet the tough guy's return maneuverers him into a paternal role in which his authority is legitimised. In this new role, his authority is restated and romanticised, his masculinity enshrined as a mythic model for younger men. Although Indiana Jones (Harrison Ford) never partook of the same level of macho violence as a contemporary such as John McClane, his comeback in *Indiana Jones and the Kingdom of the Crystal Skull* (2007) also centralised the action star's transference of his tough-guy chops to his progeny. The consequence is that the hero's age works to 'confirm' and aestheticise what is 'essential', 'real' or insuppressible in gender terms. The resurrection of apparently archaic tough guys not only celebrates the masculinities they represent; it also suggests their power as contemporary paradigms, tracing them into the present.

Notes

1. Dan Feraci, 'Interview: Bruce Willis (*16 Blocks*),' *CHUD.com*, 2006, available at http://www.chud.com/5914/interview-bruce-willis-16-blocks/ (Accessed 30 August 2013).
2. Susan Faludi, *The Terror Dream: Fear and Fantasy in Post-9/11 America* (New York: Henry Holt, 2007), pp. 5–6.
3. Ibid., p. 139.
4. Susan Jeffords, *Hard Bodies: Hollywood Masculinity in the Reagan Era* (New Brunswick, NJ: Rutgers University Press, 1994), p. 13.
5. Richard Dyer, 'Don't Look Now,' *Screen*, 23:3–4 (1982), pp. 61–73; see also Yvonne Tasker, *Spectacular Bodies: Gender, Genre and the Action Cinema* (New York: Routledge, 1993), pp. 77–78.

6. See Jonathan Rutherford's psychoanalytic reading of *Rambo: First Blood Part II*, in which he argues that 'the spectacle of the male body in action is the central signifier of the attempted recuperation of a humiliated and defeated masculine identity,' in Jonathan Rutherford, *Men's Silences: Predicaments in Masculinity* (London and New York: Routledge, 1992), p. 187.

7. Faludi, pp. 78, 48, 148–164.

8. Harvey O'Brien, *Action Movies: The Cinema of Striking Back* (New York: Columbia UP, 2012), p. 52.

9. See Motti Regev, 'Producing Artistic Value: The Case of Rock Music,' *The Sociological Quarterly*, 35:1 (1994), pp. 85–102.

10. Philippa Gates, 'Acting His Age?: The Resurrection of the 80s Action Heroes and Their Aging Stars,' *Quarterly Review of Film and Video*, 27 (2010), p. 283.

11. Sally Chivers, *The Silvering Screen: Old Age and Disability in Cinema* (Toronto: University of Toronto Press, 2011), p. 99.

12. Susan Jeffords, 'The Big Switch: Hollywood Masculinity in the Nineties,' in *Film Theory Goes to the Movies*, ed. Jim Collins, Hilary Radner, and Ava Preacher Collins (New York: Routledge, 1993), pp. 196–208.

13. Yvonne Tasker, *Spectacular Bodies: Gender, Genre and the Action Cinema* (New York: Routledge, 1993), p. 128.

7

'The (un-Botoxed) Face of a Hollywood Revolution': Meryl Streep and the 'Greying' of Mainstream Cinema

Deborah Jermyn

In a January 2010 *Vanity Fair* profile of Meryl Streep, Leslie Bennetts proclaimed with some wonder that against all expectations in an industry seemingly preoccupied by youth, at 60 the star had become Hollywood's 'new box-office queen'.[1] With a record-breaking 18 Academy Award nominations (including three wins) under her belt and a film career dating back to 1977, Streep's CV might be considered exceptional by anyone's standards in terms of longevity and critical success. Yet as Bennetts noted, 'even her most ardent fans, until recently, wouldn't have linked her name with blockbuster receipts.'[2] Following the phenomenal success of *Mamma Mia!* (Phyllida Lloyd, 2008) and *Julie and Julia* (Nora Ephron, 2009), however, Streep has become box-office gold. Since it has long been received wisdom in the industry that studio executives and the highly sought after young male audience have little interest in films about women, and even less about older ones, Streep's reinvention was all the more remarkable; it was nothing short of 'a Hollywood revolution', in fact, as the subsequent success of rom-com *It's Complicated* (Nancy Meyers, 2010) underlined further still. Indeed, the box-office performance of all these films appears to point to changes in cinema-going demographics and the growing evidence that 'new' audiences, including groups of older women, are becoming increasingly important to the industry.

Since Bennetts was writing at the start of the decade, critical and scholarly attention to the perceived 'greying' of mainstream cinema has gathered momentum. Approaches to and reporting of this apparent shift are not always consistent, however, indicating the contentious nature of contemporary Hollywood's awkward relationship with mature audiences and, particularly, with older women stars. In May 2013, for example, *Slate* ran a piece by Sagit Maier-Schwartz called 'Hollywood

Abhors an Aging Woman. Too Bad For Hollywood', lamenting the fact that numerous television series were casting impossibly young women actors as mothers to co-stars unfeasibly close to their own age. The evident discomfort, even disgust, suggested by this reluctance to cast a breadth of older women, Maier-Schwartz contended, was 'just another example of Hollywood's insane ageism',[3] demonstrating how much there is still to be done to redress the imbalance of older women's enduring scarcity on screen. Yet that same month *The Hollywood Reporter* ran an article entitled 'Revenge of the Over-40 Actress', charting the remarkable number of current 'over-40 actresses whose careers aren't just thriving but dominating big castings in Hollywood',[4] suggesting a notable cultural and industrial change was underway. Significantly, Streep was identified as one of a handful of women stars (alongside fellow Oscar-winners Helen Mirren and Diane Keaton) whose longevity prefigured this shift.

In this chapter, I will examine how Streep has evolved as a key star in this apparent move towards the greying of contemporary cinema, a transformation evident at the level of both representation and audience, in Hollywood and beyond. In 2011 *The New York Times* noted that while the 50+ US cinema audience was still comparatively modest, it had nevertheless increased by 67 per cent since 1995,[5] while a survey in France by the National Centre for Cinema and Animation found that in the same year there, 'for the first time, seniors made up the biggest section of the audience.'[6] The stand-out box-office success of a series of films starring Streep in recent years has come to crystallise the sense that the industry is finally recognising that it has long underserved – and indeed from a business perspective rather foolishly left unexploited – the burgeoning 'baby-boomer' audience. While one must be cautious not to essentialise audience tastes, here, it might nevertheless be argued that within this demographic the popularity of these Streep films suggests that older *women* are often proving particularly key. Though the films noted here will clearly have been watched by other audiences, too, nevertheless they seem part of a trend which has seen women 'seniors' returning to the cinema not only for films which are female-protagonist led, but also very often for films within the 'women's genre' of what might broadly be called 'romances'.

This chapter explores these issues through analysis of three films – *Mamma Mia!*, *It's Complicated* and more briefly *Hope Springs* (David Frankel, 2012) – alongside discussion of their critical reception and Streep's star image. Reflecting on the implications of these films for feminist analysis of older women and cinema, I examine how in these texts Streep has contributed not just to a kind of reconfiguring of industry notions of what constitutes 'mainstream Hollywood', but also of who and what is addressed by 'romance' in popular film, bringing the knotty issue of ageing to bear on both. From a thematic concern with the neglected exploration of ageing and mother–daughter intimacy in the musical *Mamma Mia!*, and to the sexuality and desire of/for an older woman in *It's Complicated*, to the quotidian details of a faltering long-term marriage between an ageing couple in *Hope Springs*, Streep's films have instigated a re-articulation of what the mainstream audience, and popular romance, might look like reimagined in Hollywood. None of the synopses just proffered here speak to dominant conceptions of high-concept filmmaking or stories that would generally lend themselves to a mainstream 'pitch', scenarios which feminist film criticism has shown typically afford little space to older women stars in contemporary cinema. Yet *Mamma Mia!* went on to be the most successful film of all time in the UK at the point of its release;[7] *It's Complicated* grossed more than $112 million at US cinemas (imdb.com) and *Hope Springs* was greenlit via the industry cachet not just of Streep's star-power, but also the major box-office pedigree of director David Frankel (*Marley and Me* (2008); *The Devil Wears Prada* (2006)). What, then, might these films and Streep's recent rise to prominence as a kind of figurehead for the return of older women to Hollywood tell us about the industry's changing relationship with ageing stars and audiences?

'Capture every minute': *Mamma Mia!*, time and mother-daughter intimacy

When *Mamma Mia!* came to the big screen in 2008, it did so on the back of the phenomenal success of the musical stage production of the same name, a farce-like tale of the confusion that ensues when Sophie (Amanda Seyfried), a young woman about to be married, goes behind her mother's back to find out the identity of her unknown father. It is constructed around a series of songs by much loved 1970s pop group ABBA, and as a 'pre-sold property' could expect to have legions of fans already in place. Yet as Louise FitzGerald and Melanie Williams note, the trade press were initially rather lacklustre about the film's prospects,[8] indicating the low expectations that often come with films dismissively thought of as 'chick flicks', even if, like *Mamma Mia!*, they might actually very well appeal too to a larger family audience. Within months it would be quite a different story, however, as the film went on to be 'Universal's fourth-highest-grossing film of all time in the international market.'[9]

Indeed, speaking to this broader potential appeal, as the film opens it might seem initially that the story about to unfold will be Sophie's – it opens with *her* singing 'I Have A Dream', the preparation for *her* wedding to Sky (Dominic Cooper) and *her* plotting to find out who her father was – and thus *Mamma Mia!* looks set to shape up as a fairly familiar romantic comedy with a humorous investigative subplot. But the narrative soon shifts to become equally, at the very least, *Donna's* story, not merely in terms of finding out what she really got up to that summer 21 years earlier, but in terms of exploring at a rather broader level *her* subjectivity. In keeping with this perspective, I would argue that, rather than being driven predominantly by a heterosexual love story, the film privileges not only the pleasures of Donna's female friendships over her love life, but also presents the film's central 'romance' as being the relationship between mother and daughter, in Donna and Sophie's passage towards understanding. This play with romantic convention is highlighted crucially at the film's climactic wedding 'revelation' scene at the altar, where Sophie and Sky's happy ending, in quite progressive fashion, entails *not* marrying. Instead, against a backdrop of the paraphernalia of sanctified romantic union, Donna and Sophie embrace, declare love and forgive past misunderstandings, thereby plundering the potent cultural gravitas of this mise-en-scene and transposing it to the (so very often peripheral) mother–daughter relationship.

But the centrality of the mother-daughter 'love story' is importantly signalled earlier in the film with the performance of 'Slipping Through My Fingers', a sequence evidently highly cherished by women audiences,[10] which has been declared the film's real emotional highpoint and its 'money-shot'.[11] Donna is quietly delighted when Sophie asks her, and not her bridesmaids, to help her prepare for the ceremony, and it is in this context that she sings 'Slipping Through My Fingers' in Sophie's bedroom. The song movingly recounts a mother's experience of watching her daughter grow up and away from her. Significantly it is shot in such a way that the camera stays overwhelmingly with Streep, bringing the older star and Donna's subjectivity to the fore again, rather than focussing on the more obviously 'blockbuster' worthy (youthful, alluring) Seyfried, while the two also share moments of striking physical closeness and intimacy: Donna painting Sophie's toenails; kissing a cut on her leg better; drying her hair. The theme of the song is one rarely given weight or contemplation in blockbuster cinema, while father–son, and indeed father–daughter, relationships are widely threaded through all kinds of popular genres. Instead here, the words powerfully express Donna's sentiments, drawing on the language of romantic love – 'Slipping through my fingers all the time / I try to capture every minute / The feeling in it ... What happened to the wonderful adventures / The places I had planned for us to go' – signalling a sense of the overwhelming bonds of love and desire at stake between mother and daughter against a visual backdrop of romantic signifiers. Through all this runs a contemplative reflection on the ageing process, where female experience of growing older is neither buried nor made abject as it more typically is in popular culture, but is instead allowed meditative space. Though the song was written by a man, Björn Ulvaeus, its authorship as the audience perceives it 'moves' to the women that sing it in performance (here Donna, originally Ulvaeus' wife, Agnetha Fältskog). Much mainstream culture has largely disregarded or maligned mother–daughter relationships,[12] but here the 'low' (feminine) cultural forms drawn on by *Mamma Mia!* – musical, romantic-comedy, melodrama – provide a forum in which this relationship might move to the fore, and its centrality provides another explanation for the film's success being driven by older women audiences. Indeed the film's very title immediately foregrounds its maternal story, and the fact that this theme was arguably the central narrative drive in one of the biggest global cinematic hits of 2008[13] is nothing short of remarkable.

Streep's casting as Donna is inextricable from the film's success, and her critical reputation and cultural meaning, both as a mother herself and a highly esteemed actor who has aged in the public eye, are intricately imbricated in this performance. Widely regarded as the finest actor of her generation with 'an exceptional range and virtuosity'[14] that has seen her play a striking diversity of roles, her endorsement of the project immediately made it something potentially 'different' from, and thus a greater subject of interest than, most other musicals. So, too, is Streep's persona an interesting palimpsest in relation to representations of the maternal and mothering that predate *Mamma Mia!* across her oeuvre. First, Streep-as-mother exists at an extra-textual level, given that she is a mother of four and that, paradoxical though it may seem, her general reluctance to speak about her children publically has in some ways positioned her as a 'good mother'. In an age preoccupied with celebrity, where it has become commonplace and indeed expected that stars will offer up their private lives for discussion, her refusal to play this game signals her as a mother who values her children's privacy above her own stardom and indeed as a 'real' actor rather than a self-publicist. Second, at a textual level her role as Donna in *Mamma Mia!* is inevitably overladen with echoes of the other mothers she has played, often to great acclaim, including two of her three Oscars for titular roles dramatically situated as 'mother' characters (namely, Joanna Kramer in *Kramer vs. Kramer* (Robert Benton, 1979) and Sophie in *Sophie's Choice* (Alan J. Pakula, 1982)).

Both of these mothers were to different degrees tragic, troubled figures marked by heartbreak. So might one understand the maternal narrative in *Mamma Mia!* to be also about pain and loss at one level despite the film's 'feel-good' energy, since at its onset only child Sophie has chosen to marry at just 20, and the film is beset with fears that either Sophie will lose out on life's experiences by staying at home in order to cushion her mother from loneliness, or Donna will lose her daughter to life outside the island. The lyrics to 'Slipping Through My Fingers' make this clear, as Donna confesses to angst at time running away and 'that odd melancholy feeling' precipitated by the daughter leaving even momentarily. In this way, although the song was released in 1981, the performance of it in the film neatly projects the 'time anxiety' that Diane Negra has identified as central to postfeminism,[15] as well as the divisive theme of generationalism common to postfeminist discourse, where second-wave feminists/mothers 'lose' their daughters to the third-wave's disavowal of their politics. But *Mamma Mia!* crucially turns this around to become celebratory; in the utopian spirit of the musical genre, audiences are left not with the perception of loss, but a euphoric sense of Donna's vitality and future. The film resists dominant representations of ageing/older mothers as disenfranchised or spent. Instead, it endows Donna with an enduring and positive relationship with her offspring; and furthermore, as she rediscovers the pleasures both of her pop-star past and of having a romantic life, it imparts her with a dynamic subjectivity that both precedes and, by the end of the film, extends beyond her mother role.

Partly, and in conservative fashion, this is because the film very much situates Donna as *not* alone at the end despite her daughter's departure, when she finally marries her lost love Sam (Pierce Brosnan) and thereby evades the projected misery of remaining a single woman, a figure identified by Negra as abhorrent in postfeminist culture.[16] But at the same time, their reconciliation doesn't feel particularly like the film's dramatic climax, and our sense of Donna's ongoing zest for life lies more importantly in Streep's performance throughout; it is one of almost constant movement and energy, where Donna's/Streep's growing older is not in any sense marked by what Imelda Whelehan has called familiar 'narratives of decline',[17] but rather is played with a vivacity striking even by the musical's generic standards. Though it would be foolhardy to suggest the film's representation of ageing women is in any sense straightforwardly 'feminist' (cosmetic surgery gags abound at Tanya's (Christine Baranski) expense[18]), it is a film which evidently spoke to legions of older women, here presented with images of their 'on-screen selves' shown embracing life, behaving 'badly' and refusing to slope off into retirement quietly.

It's not complicated; it's a gerontocom

It can be assumed that many of the same women audiences returned to cinemas early in 2010 for the release of writer/director Nancy Meyers' *It's Complicated*. This romantic comedy cast Streep as professionally successful but romantically challenged divorcée Jane Adler, who unexpectedly embarks on an affair with her ex-husband, Jake (Alec Baldwin), following a drunken fling at their son's graduation while romance simultaneously begins to blossom with Adam (Steve Martin), the architect remodelling her kitchen. Just when empty nest syndrome might typically be expected to kick in, Jane is instead revitalised by a twin-pronged romantic revival. Elsewhere[19] I have borrowed the term 'gerontocom', coined by *Time Out* reviewer Anna Smith in her discussion of *It's Complicated* alongside Meyers' earlier Diane Keaton vehicle *Something's Gotta Give* (2003),[20] to point to the growing prevalence of this rom-com 'subgenre'. These films centre on (white, heterosexual) older/ageing protagonists embarking on love affairs, despite their advancing years, in a culture which typically colonises romance as the province of the young. Notwithstanding the growing visibility of such stories, it nevertheless says something about the enduring novelty of their premise that, having directed just two such films, Meyers has earned a reputation as something of an 'auteur' for the gerontocom, and she has been situated as a filmmaker whose work is particularly sensitive to the desires of older women, in terms of both representation and audience. Conversely, Daryl Wiggers has argued that Meyers' films are watched by, and appeal to, an audience very much consisting of *both* men and women.[21] Certainly, the cross-gender star appeal of Baldwin and Martin in *It's Complicated* should not be underestimated, with Baldwin in particular winning plaudits for his turn as a still charming, middle-aged rogue. Nevertheless, it is the female stars in both *Something's Gotta Give* and *It's Complicated* that have generated the most interest, and their roles that have been received as the most textured – in part, I would argue, because they have been continually positioned as emanating from Meyers' own experience of getting divorced and re-entering the dating scene after many years of marriage. Interestingly, Meyers has said, 'I don't want to be known as the one who makes movies for older people. I'm just making movies about relationships'[22] and indeed one might argue that the true sublimation of these films into the mainstream will have been achieved at the point at which they are understood just as 'romantic comedies' without the need for any sub-generic qualifiers.

Nevertheless, achieving a global box-office return of more than $219 million,[23] *It's Complicated* was crucial to Streep's shifting star persona in this period at the age of 60. Like *Mamma Mia!* with its energetic song-and-dance numbers, *It's Complicated*'s farcical comedy, featuring scenes of Jane getting stoned at a party on a date with Adam and vomiting into a bedside cabinet after a night of drunken sex with Jake, moved Streep further away again from the once prevalent vision of her as a doubtlessly gifted but somehow inherently 'serious' and overly sombre performer.[24] Here, as Jane she riotously embraces behaviour 'inappropriate' for her age, and the import of this should not be underestimated simply because it is done via scenes of comic frivolity; from a feminist perspective the film can be said precisely to use this comedy to challenge conservative cultural expectations that older women should withdraw quietly into respectability and invisibility. Karen Hollinger has noted how Streep had made a somewhat unsuccessful foray into comedy before in the late 1980s/early 1990s, with roles in films such as *She-Devil* (Susan Seidelman, 1989) and the 'disastrous[ly]' received *Death Becomes Her* (Robert Zemekis, 1992), a shift that was met as a 'definite downturn' in her career.[25] She observes that Streep's professional recalibration at that time was understood by some critics to be 'a deliberate attempt to lighten her image and demonstrate her acting range', but also that, significantly, this movement came about just as she turned 40 in 1989, a particularly loaded milestone in the life of a woman actor.[26] This apparently abortive attempt 20 years earlier to position herself as a diverse performer able to turn her hand to comedy has been understood in part, then, as a strategic response to 'her increasingly limited role choice as an older actress', which produced counterproductive consequences.[27] In contrast, two decades on Streep would be embraced as an actor possessing an admirable ability to not take herself too seriously and equally able to adroitly play comic roles, with much of the audience pleasure in *It's Complicated* coming from the unexpectedly risqué and absurd scenarios Jane finds herself in. The roles of Donna and Jane evidently did nothing to dent Streep's esteem if her subsequent 2011 Best Actress Oscar playing Margaret Thatcher in *The Iron Lady* (directed again by Phyllida Lloyd) was anything to go by, a trajectory that once more seemingly points to the richer field being opened up to women actors today by the recent greying of mainstream cinema.

As I have noted elsewhere, despite its box-office achievements (and in similar ways to *Mamma Mia!*) the critical reception of *It's Complicated* was often mixed at best,[28] with many commentators taking a predictable pleasure in lamenting the predictability of its rom-com formulae and the privileged milieu of Nancy Meyers' particular brand of 'lifestyle porn'.[29] The often strikingly contemptible digests of the film reveal much about the wall of preconceived disdain that regularly meets romantic comedy as a default position and indeed Meyers as one of its most successful, and, crucially, female, progenitors. Nevertheless, even in some of the more unfavourable reviews, Streep's performance was recurrently noted as a saving grace (as was Baldwin's), and indeed the film won her yet another Golden Globe nomination. 'Streep spins gold from straw', Tim Robey's *Telegraph* review declared in this vein, before grumbling about how 'the plot groans and creaks' and conceding that 'as an indulgent confection, it's more filling and less embarrassing than we had any right to expect'.[30] I would posit that a frequent thread in critics' professed agitation or glib dismissals of the film was their sense that this was a film that was overwhelmingly meant for, and would be most enjoyed by, 'women of a certain age on girls' nights out', as Todd McCarthy put it in *Variety*,[31] or 'gal pals taking a movie break after returning Christmas presents' as Roger Ebert observed[32] (neatly conflating two activities to project and bolster a habitual image of woman-as-consumer). Again, at the heart of this perceived appeal to the older female audience lay the rare image of a multidimensional, animated, yet meditative, ageing woman protagonist and Streep's engaging performance of her.

Mirroring the women audiences imagined by McCarthy and Ebert, *It's Complicated* contains scenes of Jane's joyful gatherings with her circle of girlfriends, and this spectacle of ageing women coming together and reaping great pleasure from company devoid of men is one that clearly holds much feminist potential and troubles patriarchal culture ('annoying girl-talk sessions' as David Germain's infantilising *LA Times* summary put it).[33] Manohla Dargis was another to suggest that Meyers' romances are 'pitched at a niche demographic, by which I mean women over 40.' But despite being troubled by the film's problematic premise that the male characters prompt Jane's later-life revival, Dargis goes on to trace how Streep 'takes this character and makes you love her'. Streep, she observes:

> [looks] sensational, but she and her crinkles also look close enough to her real age (60) to reassure you that she hasn't resorted to the knife. That may sound grotesque and petty. But in an industry in which actresses whittle themselves down to nothing so they can have a little

screen space only to fade away once they hit a certain age, there's nothing trivial about a movie that insists a middle-aged woman with actual breasts and hips and wrinkles can be beautiful and desirable while also fully desiring.[34]

Here Dargis underlines the powerful politics at stake in the film and its casting of Streep, in a movie that on superficial consideration may seem, like romantic comedy *per se*, to be capable of offering only amusing diversion. Instead, while Streep may be lovingly lit, the film also tackles the gendered politics of ageing, desire and sex head-on. Moments such as the exchange where Jane refuses to let Jake see her naked standing up ('things look different lying down') or the visit to the fertility clinic, which reveals the prevalence of older men struggling to make babies with much younger women, are captured with wry humour which still speak volumes about the absurdity and inequity of how men and women experience ageing differently in our culture. Furthermore, the film also seems to give a conscious (and approving) nod to Streep's well documented refusal to have cosmetic surgery, when Jane runs from a horrifying consultation with a cosmetic surgeon after learning what it will take to 'fix' her droopy eyelid. It is refreshing indeed to see a critic of Dargis' standing note that while Meyers' rom-coms may be 'fairy tales', this possibility does not mean they are therefore 'trivial'.[35]

'Hope springs' in later life

There is, however, an alternative critical position on all this romping which is unconvinced by its progressive potential and which asks instead whether by having the older protagonists of Hollywood's new grey cinema seemingly take on the romantic and sexual narrative preoccupations of Hollywood's younger protagonists and the apparently universal desire to reach fulfilment by finding 'the one', such films miss the opportunity to more fully explore the different experiences of later life stages. The films thereby come to inadvertently risk augmenting the very problem they appear to wish to address by seemingly venerating youth and representing what have been typically perceived to be youthful pursuits as enduring and cross-generational goals that must be continually aspired to. In this vein, writing on *The Guardian's* film blog site, David Cox called on cinema to 'explore the reality of [older people's] lives' and wrote of *It's Complicated* that '[the] film asks us to believe that maturity is much the same as youth...yet attempting to sprinkle romcom stardust on the predicament of older people does them few favours. It tells them that the preoccupations of only the young have value. Unless they try to ape them, their lives will be worthless'.[36] Cox does not expand on what the 'preoccupations' of older people, in contrast, might be. Nevertheless, his article prompts the question, what sort of issues might alternative, less sanguine representations of mature romantic relationships seek to contend with?

To reflect on this question, it is instructive to turn to Philip French's review of *It's Complicated* which, like Dargis', dared to entertain the notion that the film could be both 'a piece of wish-fulfilment' and something more substantial by invoking a high-art association and arguing:

> [its] central thrust is similar to Ingmar Bergman's deadly serious *Scenes From A Marriage*: wedlock can be the death of romance; love can be better the second time round (even with the same partner); the greatest challenge to a relationship is making that transition from midlife crisis to sensible middle age.[37]

I want to suggest that French's summary here provides a telling synopsis not just of *It's Complicated*, but also of Streep's next screen romance, *Hope Springs*; and to briefly explore how this latter, far darker (even if finally optimistic film) can in some ways be imagined as the alternate outcome to Jane and Jake's divorce a decade prior to the start of *It's Complicated*. What if they had not broken up? What if they had smoothed over the cracks and soldiered on? What happens when Kay (Streep) and Arnold (Tommy Lee Jones), an ageing couple with more than 30 years of marriage behind them, face up to the fact that their relationship has become tired, even toxic, devoid of sexual and emotional intimacy, and that without attention it may fold?

The marriage crises of the late middle-aged do not constitute the kind of territory that Hollywood typically seeks to bring to the big screen,[38] evidenced by the apparent struggle to 'anchor' the film that appears to have played out in the publicity for *Hope Springs*. This is a film which is predominantly made up of agonising scenes of domestic tedium and dialogue-heavy intensive couples' therapy, and as such at times it is a distinctly troubling melodrama. Yet it was oddly promoted as a 'romantic comedy', evidencing the useful elasticity of this generic category, as if the studio either did not know how else to pitch it or suspected it would never sell if more accurately pitched as a relationship drama. The poster's tagline proclaimed, 'Sometimes to keep the magic you have to learn a few tricks', with a picture of a mischievously smiling Streep looking aslant and somewhat suggestively holding her hand to her mouth. Its 'narrative image',[39] bolstered by the trailer, thereby implied that the film would be a light-hearted and slightly naughty romp with perhaps a thoughtful edge, and in this way very much capitalised on Streep's recently successful roles in *Mamma Mia!* and *It's Complicated.*

What audiences actually sat down to was an unusually unhurried depiction of the inertia and solitude that can develop in a long-term marriage and the difficult passage that comes with trying to save the couple's fading relationship after Kay, entirely out of character, insists that Arnold attends relationship counselling with her. In contrast to the feisty Jane, Kay is sweet but 'mousey', frumpily dressed and long suffering, not the owner of a thriving bakery but a retail assistant dominated by the recurrently fractious Arnold, and as such she is an even less viable older 'heroine' for mainstream cinema than Streep's earlier roles. Indeed, Frankel's film and Streep's performance of Kay take precisely the kind of inconsequential middle-aged woman our culture renders invisible and brings her centre stage. Where *It's Complicated* implied riotous and orgasmic (if discreetly edited) sex, *Hope Springs* charts the stumbling, humiliating efforts this couple undergo as they try to rekindle desire buried under years of celibacy and miscommunication. Arnold, we learn, cannot look at Kay during sex; Kay's fantasy of performing oral sex on Arnold in the cinema ends in her running away from him in tears. What might have been played for laughs (and indeed what through wily editing and up-tempo music enabled the sex-farce-meets-rom-com styled trailer) is instead deeply discomforting viewing, and it is significant that, having eschewed sex scenes in the early part of her career,[40] Streep gamely took these ones on at this time. Here, middle-aged bodies meet awkwardly and hesitantly in a series of frank sequences that dramatically underline how narrow the spectrum of sex offered by Hollywood typically is. Though the film's gender politics are complex, one should not underestimate the feminist potential of its willingness to show that this older, frumpy and seemingly submissive woman – one who is well outside a sexual economy which values and acknowledges only the bodies and sexuality of young girls and women – is actually still a desiring subject who finally finds the will to articulate her ('taboo') desire. Streep's 'dowdy' physical transformation as Kay offers a striking contrast to her appearance in the earlier two roles discussed and this central image of an 'ordinary' but sexual middle-aged woman arguably makes it the most challenging of these three texts; note that it was the least commercially successful of these movies. The film ultimately delivers a 'feel-good' (though clumsy) payoff as the couple do indeed rediscover love and sex and renew their wedding vows in sentimental romantic fashion on the beach. Nevertheless, in the 90 minutes preceding this scene, *Hope Springs* makes some brave and memorable inroads into meeting David Cox's call for greater exploration of 'the reality of [older people's] lives' and shows how finding romance can entail labour and resilience, not merely serendipity.

Meryl Streep at 60+: rewriting the ending

It can be argued that the 'feel-good' motifs uniting all three films and perhaps appealing to mature women audiences lie in their shared narratives of the 'triumph of the older woman'[41] and in their bestowing of the sense of a *future* on their ageing female protagonists. So, too, might one posit that these are the very attractions that Meryl Streep has come to embody. At a biological age when received wisdom would have it that Streep, as an older woman star, should be featuring in ever rarer roles, and fading from the public consciousness because of limited access to only the most constrained repertoire of character types, she has instead undergone a renaissance. As the female face of Hollywood's repositioning into an industry tentatively courting the grey dollar, Streep's metamorphosis sells the baby-boomer ideal that life can indeed remain rich, rewarding and surprising after middle age; that there might be adventures and experiences not yet had, not yet imagined, still ahead. The call to ongoing personal 'reinvention' has become one of the mainstays of neoliberal discourse, and as such it holds particularly problematic ramifications for women. But at the same time a drive to continually reimagine herself has long informed Streep's choice of dramatic characters as a star who in her sixth decade remains, in French's words, 'as indefatigable as she is versatile'.[42] From her 'worthy' place as the most lauded, most revered woman actor to have carved a Hollywood career, in these recent films she has 'let her guard down', as Nancy Meyers said of *It's Complicated*,[43] to star in roles requiring her more than ever to sing and dance; to enact the difficult, crass or awkward sex scenes she had eschewed earlier in her career; and to play slapstick and farce to unashamedly unruly effect. Asked by *Vanity Fair* in 2009 to explain why Streep was 'having such a moment right now', Meyers replied:

> With so many actors, it's the familiar that you look forward to, and with her it's the originality that you look forward to…I think the Meryl experience is that she's gonna take you somewhere. And it's going to be something new, and it isn't what you saw her do last year.[44]

And it is precisely in the life-affirming appeal of this aptitude for vitality in ageing, for reinvention rather than a slow-fade-to-grey, that Streep's success as 'the (un-Botoxed) face of a Hollywood revolution' lies.

Acknowledgements

With many thanks to Nathalie Weidhase for research assistance and Karen Randell for positivity.

Notes

1. Leslie Bennetts, 'Something about Meryl,' *Vanity Fair* (January 2011), available at http://www.vanityfair.com/hollywoodfeatures/2010/01/meryl-streep-201001 (Accessed 9 May 2013).
2. Ibid.
3. Sagit Maier-Schwartz, 'Hollywood Abhors an Aging Woman. Too Bad for Hollywood,' slate.com (7 May 2013), available at http://www.slate.com/blogs/xx_factor/2013/05/07/hollywood_is_allergic_to_aging_women_and_too_bad_for_them.html (Accessed 9 May 2013).
4. Tatiana Siegelo, 'Revenge of the Over-40 Actress,' *The Hollywood Reporter* (14 June 2013), available at http://www.hollywoodreporter.com/news/sandra-bullock-melissa-mccarthy-beyond-562530 (Accessed 18 June 2013).
5. Brooks Barnes and Michael Cieply, 'Graying Audience Returns to Movies,' *The New York Times* (25 February 2011), available at http://www.nytimes.com/2011/02/26/business/media/26moviegoers.html?pagewanted=all&_r=0 (Accessed 2 August 2013).
6. Jacques Mandelbaum, 'Alive and Kicking: The Changing View of Older People on the Silver Screen,' *Guardian Weekly* (30 July 2013), available at http://www.theguardian.com/film/2013/jul/30/film-cinema-age-older-people-france (Accessed 1 August 2013).
7. Louise FitzGerald and Melanie Williams, 'Facing our Waterloo: Evaluating *Mamma Mia! The Movie*', in *Exploring a Cultural Phenomenon: Mamma Mia! The Movie*, ed. Louise FitzGerald and Melanie Williams (London: I.B. Tauris, 2013), pp. 1–19, p. 3.
8. Ibid., p. 2.
9. Hy Hollinger, '"Mamma" moolah!,' TheHollywoodReporter.com (15 September 2008), available at http://www.hollywoodreporter.com/news/mamma-moolah-119162 (Accessed 29 May 2013).
10. See, for example, Louise FitzGerald's discussion of the scene's reception in 'What Does Your Mother Know? *Mamma Mia!*'s Mediation of Lone Motherhood,' in FitzGerald and Williams (2013), pp. 205–222, 205–206.
11. Ibid, p. 205.
12. Classical Hollywood's 'maternal melodrama' films are a prominent exception to this, though not without their own ideological difficulties.
13. The film ranked fifth globally in 2008, grossing almost $610 million, according to boxofficemojo, available at http://boxofficemojo.com/yearly/chart/?view2=worldwide&yr=2008 (Accessed 30 July 2013).

14. Linda Mizejewski, 'Meryl Streep: Feminism and Femininity in the Era of Backlash,' in *Acting for America: Movie Stars of the 1980s*, ed. Robert Eberwein (Rutgers University Press, 2010), pp. 201–222, p. 203. See also Kirsty Fairclough's chapter in this collection.

15. Negra, Diane, *What a Girl Wants?: Fantasizing the Reclamation of Self in Postfeminism* (London: Routledge, 2009).

16. Ibid.

17. Imelda Whelehan, 'Ageing Appropriately: Postfeminist Discourses of Ageing in Contemporary Hollywood,' in *Postfeminism and Contemporary Hollywood Cinema*, ed. Joel Gwynne and Nadine Muller (Basingstoke, Palgrave Macmillan, 2013), pp. 78–94, p. 83.

18. See also Claire Jenkins on the film's early infantilisation of Donna, and eventual recuperation of her into a more conventional family structure, in 'Not Too Old for Sex? *Mamma Mia!* and the "Older Bird" Chick Flick,' in FitzGerald and Williams (2013), pp. 163–176.

19. Deborah Jermyn, 'Unlikely Heroines?: Women of a "Certain Age" and Romantic Comedy,' *CineAction*, 85 (2011), pp. 26–33.

20. Anna Smith, review of *It's Complicated*, *Time Out London* (5 January 2010), available at http://www.timeout.com/london/film/its-complicated (Accessed 15 August 2013).

21. Darryl Wiggers, 'Enough Already: The Wonderful, Horrible Reception of Nancy Meyers,' *CineAction*, 81 (2010), pp. 65–72.

22. Nancy Meyers, 'The Ex Files; Nancy Meyers on Making a Grown-up Rom-com,' *The Times*, (8 May 2010), p. 13.

23. Figures at http://www.boxofficemojo.com/movies/?page=intl&country=UK &id=itscomplicated.htm (Accessed 20 August 2013).

24. See Mellamphy (2013) on Streep's highbrow roles and 'serious' star persona, p. 61. "See that girl, watch that scene': notes on the star persona and presence of Meryl Streep in *Mamma Mia!*' in FitzGerald and Williams (2013), pp. 60–75.

25. Karen Hollinger, p. 78. It should be noted nevertheless that *Death Becomes Her* was successful at the box office, and earned a Golden Globe nomination for Streep. *The Actress: Hollywood Acting and the Female Star*, London: Routledge, 2006.

26. Ibid.

27. Ibid.

28. Jermyn, pp. 31–32.

29. Julian Sancton, 'Q&A: Nancy Meyers on *It's Complicated*,' *Vanity Fair* (23 December 2009), available at http://www.vanityfair.com/online/oscars/2009/12/ qa-nancy-meyers-on-its-complicated (Accessed 6 August 2013).

30. Tim Robey, review of *It's Complicated* (7 January 2010), *The Telegraph*, available at http://www.telegraph.co.uk/culture/film/filmreviews/6946761/ Its-Complicated-review.html (Accessed 16 May 2013).

31. Todd McCarthy, 'Rich People, Not-so-rich Comedy in "Complicated".' (14–20 December 2009), *Variety*, p. 29.

32. Roger Ebert, review of *It's Complicated* (23 December 2009), available at http:// www.rogerebert.com/reviews/its-complicated-2009 (Accessed 16 May 2013).

33. David Germain, *It's Complicated*, in *LA Times* (23 December 2009), available at http://www.latimes.com/topic/zap-review-its-complicated-sns-ap,0,6 159650.story (Accessed 28 May 2013). Similar patterns of distaste and

discomfort at scenes of women-only socialising can be found in the critical reception of *Mamma Mia!*

34. Manohla Dargis, 'A September-September Romance,' *The New York Times* (24 December 2009), available at http://movies.nytimes.com/2009/12/25/movies/25complicated.html?pagewanted=all&_r=0 (Accessed 16 May 2013).

35. Ibid.

36. David Cox, 'It's Complicated When Hollywood Tries to Celebrate Greying Passion' (11 January 2010), available at http://www.theguardian.com/film/filmblog/2010/jan/11/its-complicated-meryl-streep-alec-baldwin (Accessed 24 May 2013).

37. Philip French, review of *It's Complicated*, in *The Observer* (10 January 2010), available at http://www.theguardian.com/film/2010/jan/10/its-complicated-meryl-streep (Accessed 16 May 2013).

38. Though one might note here that two of Streep's earlier melodramas cast her as a wife in a dull marriage unexpectedly caught up in an extra-marital love affair, namely *Falling in Love* (Ulu Grosbard, 1984) and *The Bridges of Madison County* (Clint Eastwood, 1995).

39. John Ellis, *Visible Fictions: Cinema, Television, Video* (London: Routledge, 1982).

40. Hollinger, p. 74.

41. Whelehan, p. 87.

42. French (2010).

43. Sancton (2009).

44. Ibid.

8
Grown Up Girls: Newspaper Reviews of Ageing Women in Pop

Lynne Hibberd

Introduction

Pop music is the most youthful of music genres: conservative in style and form, produced on a massive scale, dominated by young pop stars and designed to appeal as widely as possible. Its apparently simple and repetitive musical styling, coupled with its commercial intentions, makes pop appear for the large part depoliticised and benign. In a society that claims to place a high value on protecting the presumed innocence of youth, these factors make it perfect for a younger audience who likes to bounce around to it, buy stuff associated with it and belong to its associated popular subcultural groups. Seemingly superficial and immediate, pop is as much about the visual style of belonging, conformity and the adoption of fashions as it is about musical prowess. The appearance of youthfulness is therefore crucial in pop as it delineates its form, stars, target audience and market.

If youth has always been central to pop, it is also symptomatic of postfeminist culture in which the goal of 'looking good' is framed as a desirable and acceptable aspiration as well as an expected norm for the empowered woman, a counterpoint to the 'letting oneself go' that constitutes accepting the ageing process as, when and how it transpires. Postfeminist discourses position the successful woman as one who is able to control and halt the ageing process through shrewd consumer choices, worth increasing amounts of expenditure 'because we're worth it'.[1]

This normalisation of a simple parallel between youth and beauty, and the relatively affordable availability of cosmetic surgeries, diets, body sculpting underwear and hormone treatments, mean that within our ever-ageing population the boundaries of what counts as old appear to be constantly shifting. To the middle-class, affluent and aspirational demographic targeted by neoliberalism, visible signs of age (for women and often for men) are positioned as something that should be neither tolerated nor embraced. Instead, successful ageing is dependent on the consumption of goods and services for adornment and distraction, a 'leisure' activity that takes considerable work, time and effort.[2] Whether postfeminism is defined as an extension of, or reaction to, feminism, its scholarship is overwhelmingly dominated by a focus on the experiences of young women. The figure of the ageing woman occupies marginal ground in both pop music and the discourse of postfeminism, and academic investigation of women in pop has tended to reflect this youth-centred state, focussing for the large part on fandom and media representations of female pop stars.[3] As ageing studies have come to the fore, there has been recognition that older women enjoy and partake in pop culture on many levels.[4] These studies emphasise that for women the ability to perform pop is governed by unspoken rules that delineate appropriate areas of participation. As the 'value' of women is intrinsically tied up, if not with being young then at least the successful illusion of it,[5] there are limited career options available to ageing female pop performers. These include replaying past successes to appeal to the nostalgia market, changing career to remain in the public eye, and – most problematically – maintaining a career with ongoing chart success.[6] This chapter sets out to explore the extent to which commentary on the careers of Girls Aloud, The Spice Girls, Kylie Minogue and Madonna replay these scenarios. Now in their 20s, 30s, 40s and 50s, each of these performers has achieved global success and has a career spanning at least ten years, a near eternity in pop terms. The thesis is that for an older woman in pop, the judgement of a successful performance is reliant both on musical style and showmanship as well as on the successful obfuscation of age. In other words, it is anticipated that central to a credible pop performance will be a subtext: that it does not matter that these performers are getting older as long as they are able simultaneously (and paradoxically) to act their age appropriately and not look like they are ageing at all. This essay sets out to explore how this enigmatic position is reflected in newspaper reviews of live performances of ageing female pop stars over the course of 2012 and 2013.

Although the news press is neither the primary nor the most popular site for reviews of live pop performances or the best barometer of pop superstardom, there are good reasons for exploring discourses of ageing within this medium. The news press offers an intriguing archive for analysis because it is evident that the papers are an influential and legitimate medium whose readership consists of a sizeable older audience, particularly so in the case of the British broadsheets.[7] Existing as a small part of a wider news and magazine remit, pop reviews in the papers are more often chanced upon rather than sought out by fans or music aficionados. My interest in considering how a selection of newspapers present women ageing in pop is to reflect on this casual, authenticated discourse which is often the site for older people's engagement with music reviews. In this chapter I examine some of the key motifs that characterise pop reviews of these performers in both the tabloid and the broadsheet press. Although the print media exists as something of a marginalised and neglected area within a much wider maelstrom of information about pop, sidestepping online media altogether in this analysis is a deliberate strategy. Online papers target a slightly younger demographic and utilise different journalistic conventions to accommodate this audience. Pop reviews in print are generally informal and discursive, drawing attention to the reviewer's personality and preferences almost as much as they attempt to provide a map for the reader to interrogate, understand and appreciate pop performances. For the large part the Internet requires users to pull information from it by searching specific terms: it does not appear to be 'just there' as the papers do. As I argue below, the active searching required by audiences to locate information seemingly liberates online reviewers from the chummy, familiar and familial style of press reviews and tends to illicit a more caustic and critical mode of address from reporters. An analysis of a Twitter feed would reflect less of the 'chance' encounter of press reviews, though no doubt a more animated and discursive engagement with pop and celebrity, and it would yield different results if discussions about the same performers were tracked. Later on in the chapter I briefly consider the significance of this targeted online engagement with older women in pop.

Queens, princesses and commoners: establishing a popular hierarchy

There is a clear hierarchy in pop music culture in which the canonical status of Madonna makes a comparison with Girls Aloud akin to comparing *The Godfather* with *Glee*. Even without subjecting them to sustained quantitative analysis, this pecking order is immediately evident both in the number of newspaper reviews and in the manner in which stars are discussed. This hierarchy is established, maintained and affirmed through references to longevity, age, gender, class and global recognition as a brand, all of which are utilised to various degrees to connote differing levels of power and relevance. While it is not possible here to fully articulate the ways in which this hierarchy is played out, a brief background of the stars under scrutiny highlights some of the disparities and anomalies in the ways that these defining terms are used in the press.

Madonna's MDNA tour was the highest grossing live performance of 2012.[8] Commencing in Israel and with a stopover appearance at the NFL Super Bowl intermission, it was always designed to have a high public profile. There are far more reviews of Madonna's MDNA tour than there are reviews of the other bands, and this global tour was often (inexplicably) reviewed in the UK press even when the actual performances took place much further afield.[9] Madonna is the subject of frequent derision in the celebrity press where she is positioned as an ageing figure who performs sexuality beyond 'the age of appropriacy [*sic*]'.[10] In the papers, however, her reign as Queen of Pop is reverentially upheld by her reviewers and her status as a cultural icon is acknowledged in all press accounts. While all of the performers under discussion here have proved of interest to feminist scholars working in the field of popular cultural studies, Madonna is easily the most over-determined figure. The most studied, critically acclaimed, derided and analysed of the performers, Madonna's career and personal life has been the subject of much scrutiny and the site and subject of an entire field of media and cultural studies during the 1990s.[11] Following her emergence as a pop star in her mid-20s Madonna has achieved considerable global success as a singer, actor, producer, fashion designer, director, writer and media owner. Over the course of the 1980s and 1990s her expertise in attracting and maintaining the attention of the world's media helped to redefine the nature of celebrity and blur the boundaries between public and private star personas.[12] Judging by the citations she receives from almost every female pop star, she remains the single biggest female influence on the nature and style of pop music over the course of the late twentieth century. Now in her 50s, Madonna – as celebrity, performer, mother, role model and icon – is the site of both critical debate and academic study, much of which perpetuates its own form of ageism. She is widely considered to have defined the discursive space for examining female popular music performers over the last 30 years and has continued to dominate recent academic debate about the role of ageing women in pop.[13] Madonna is, then, the archetypal postfeminist pop icon, and it is hard to imagine that Kylie Minogue could have existed without her as a forerunner.

Indeed, although Kylie has also achieved a mononymic global status she has always occupied something of a difficult position as the Princess of Pop in relation to Madonna's 'Queen', where (like Lady Gaga) she has often been accused of emulating Madonna's career too closely without establishing a definitive style of her own. With an early career as a daytime soap star, Kylie has closely manufactured and maintained a girl-next-door appeal despite manifest changes in style, often geared to appeal to specific niche audiences and attract a cult following. Kylie's 'nice' appeal generally dominates coverage of her in official press junkets as well as celebrity gossip, and her pliant, accessible and curvy version of feminine sexuality receives little of the vitriol which is so liberally and ruthlessly applied to Madonna, whose sexuality is often framed as androgynous, masculine or threatening (see below). Similarly, her acting is generally commended even when the films and television series that she has appeared in have been critically derided. Inexplicably, although Kylie performed live several times throughout the year in a number of guises including Proms in the Park, her own K25 Tour and the Diamond Jubilee Concert, her shows received very little journalistic attention. So few in fact that this chapter makes scant reference to them, and those that do remain are more to point out her absence than because they offer any particular commentary on her as an ageing star. It is difficult to say with any certainty what this dearth of reviews may indicate, but I reflect briefly on this absence in the conclusion.

Just as Madonna's success helped to create a way of understanding Kylie, so too did their individual successes pave the way for the creation of the next two bands under discussion. Although female groups have been around since pre-pop days, The Spice Girls were one of the most popular bands of the 1990s, globally successful, clearly branded and responsible for both establishing the Girl Power phenomenon and promoting this ethos through marketing, tours, music and most crucially merchandising.[14] The Spice Girls' one-off reunion for the London 2012 Olympics Closing Ceremony was not formally reviewed as much as it was commented on, and these observations reflect the more personal and often more hostile terminology of the celebrity press which features comments about physical appearance to much greater effect. While in the 1990s it seemed as though The Spice Girls' influence would be unquestionable, fifteen years later this influence is harder to pinpoint, and their iconic status is equally questionable. As a now-defunct pop group, the impact of The Spice Girls as a band has undoubtedly weakened, though the influence of Victoria Beckham alone as a phenomenon of girl power is surely global.

Girls Aloud were born of an era in which the convergence of real and celebrity lifestyles had become the norm. Established in 2002 as a result of TV talent contest *Popstars: The Rivals*, the members of Girls Aloud are ultimately known as much for their appearances, associations and acrimonious alliances as they are for their music. In 2012 they were reunited for a comeback tour which eventually transpired to be a farewell tour. As manufactured bands that were shrewdly stage-managed with a keen eye on their potential markets, both bands have posed something of a problem for those determined to measure exactly how much power and control they can be perceived to have. Central to this critique is the way that they are made up of particular 'types' of girl, with strategic appeal to different demographics of sexuality, race, and region. Both groups are imbued with ordinary, working-class connotations which are echoed in their press coverage: the broadsheets are dominated by coverage of Madonna, Kylie, The Spice Girls and Girls Aloud in that order while the tabloids operate a broad reversal of this; a clear indication of the target audience for respective papers. In the broadsheets the Girls Aloud show is accused of having 'high art pretensions' which jar with their 'Saturday night/tottering girl-next-door' appeal played out in relation to northernness...while 'the live band sound like they're playing in a working men's club in Preston.'[15] *The Independent's* reviewer comments that 'everyone here looks amazing...on the terms of their own Geordie Glam aesthetic [of] microskirts, spray tan and massive hair',[16] while the *Guardian* describes Girls Aloud member Nadine as 'a brave and resourceful woman – just the kind who'd use her money to open a pub'.[17]

The reviews under examination here frequently acknowledge the cultural hierarchy of pop and the intergenerational baton-passing which takes place in it. Hence, Girls Aloud are discussed as having 'almost the Spice Girls' level of ubiquity',[18] and giving a performance which incorporates 'a bit of Kylie sparkle [and] a soupçon of Madonna's on-trend choreography'.[19] In this way, the cultural and critical hierarchy of pop is established, maintained and affirmed. The disparity in the quantity of reports indicates that for a number of reasons, some types of pop performances are legitimised over and above others. This absence should not be seen as indicative of pop stars' current popularity but rather as a way of managing the 'threat' that is posed by the image of the powerful woman.[20] In this sample of newspapers at least, it is notable that the middle-aged performers receive less coverage than the older or younger stars.

Letting the girls grow up

Press reviews feature the rhetoric of ageing explicitly in all accounts of pop stardom as they have the generic convention of referring to the star's age as standard practice regardless of gender. This convention is another way in which pop is signified as young – it is normal for children to use their age as a way of describing who they are, but it is not common for adults to do this. Nor does this practice apply to reports of other music cultures – rock, indie and classical stars are not referred to by their age as a matter of course; similarly, other entertainment reviews, such as those for film and theatre, do not use this convention. Age is invariably included as part of any celebrity commentary regardless of how a star has become known.[21] The convention of reporting age makes the age of the performers explicit at the same time that it normalises pop as naturally young. A complication to this naturalisation is that age is not referred to in discussions of pop groups, most probably because it would make for clumsy copy to refer to multiple members by name and age. In the examples drawn on here it is the names of the groups that insist that their members are recognised in relation to age, as 'girls'. Consequently, describing them appropriately involves either an equally clumsy phrase: 'the women of Girls Aloud' or attributing a gender-neutral term: 'the members of The Spice Girls'. In this manner the linguistic discourse of the girl groups, in which being young is the very thing that defines them, makes it impossible to articulate any understanding of ageing within them and so the process of ageing is rendered invisible, gender neutral, and by default sexless. The rhetoric of youth is so firmly established in the groups that commentators also use childish terms in their descriptions, such as: 'now Cheryl, Nadine, Sarah, Nicola and Kimberly are *all grown up*'.[22]

As the generic conventions of pop reviews establish, repeat and reaffirm that pop is young, the ageing of these performers is most often framed in relation to their longevity in a young field. It is rare for any successful pop performer to remain in the limelight and retain global visibility into their 30s and beyond. These women are consequently given respect for enduring: 'When Girls Aloud were formed ten years ago...few would have rated their long-term chances'[23] and are teased for the same: 'Girls Aloud have kept going long enough practically to become a heritage act'.[24] Madonna's career is again exceptional in this regard. Achieving many of her bigger hits later in life, retaining a youthful vitality to her musical style and collaborating with younger performers to ensure her edge and new musical directions, Madonna's longevity in the pop world is an 'ever-present subtext' which underscores all reviews.[25]

Age is also signalled by noting the temporality of the performers in relation to their audience. The implication is that if pop is young, so is its audience, and if stars grow older in this career, they are required to take their same audience with them, moving and changing alongside them as they grow. Hence, Kylie 'is still with us, glimmering and ironic as ever.'[26] Reviews consider the performers in relation to their audience, so Girls Aloud perform 'In front of a packed crowd of women, straight men of a certain age...and a good quota of the pink pound brigade';[27] Madonna's audience '[come] alive for some of the older hits',[28] and the Girls Aloud reunion tour 'gives the screaming crowd exactly what they want: 20 consecutive top 10 smashes, including four No 1s, in near-chronological order.'[29] This temporality is disturbed if pop stars' current focus is perceived to be different to that of their implied 'true' audience of those people of a contemporary age. Thus Madonna is criticised for embracing a new audience with the claim that 'she's trying too hard to keep up with the kids.'[30]

As a band The Spice Girls do not exist anymore so their one-off show situated as part of the pageantry of the London 2012 Olympics Closing Ceremony was always going to be more a celebration of *an* age than it was of *their* age. In this instance it was framed as a celebration of the BritPop phenomenon that they were part of, a peculiarly laddish culture which celebrated the possibility of raucous, fun loving, sexually liberated, attractive women.[31] The images of The Spice Girls as different types of girls who were united in a collective embrace of friendship and fun was as perfect for the Olympics as it was for operation Cool Britannia – a celebration of national unity which simultaneously championed elitism in an international arena. This was a necessary looking back on national effort, achievement and production rather than a concerted attempt to look forward. Reviews of The Spice Girls' role in this show reflected this nostalgia and attempted to inscribe their performance with meaning and agency. These reviews highlighted the clumsiness of trying to grow up in an ethos which puts girliness central to empowerment:

> 'they are most certainly the best possible pin-ups for Middle Aged Woman Power. And that is a force to be reckoned with. Between them they've had the highs and lows of most women their age in the country. And they're still standing, looking great and being strong. Now that's Woman Power.'[32]

But there is a clear problem with this: the term 'middle age' has inherent negative connotations. Steadying, mundane and settled, it is the antithesis of all that pop, for all its formulaic features, should be. As such, the ageing of The Spice Girls was predominantly framed in negative discourse which emphasised both the impossibility of women acting

younger than they are and the ridiculousness of this being a requirement: 'The Spice Girls clambered out of...black cabs like five middle-
aged women arriving at a Daniel O'Donnell concert'.[33] Interestingly, in
order to make this jibe, the *Daily Record's* reviewer draws on an image
of an older male performer as indicative of something that middle-aged
women may 'justifiably' enjoy, even as he undermines the validity of
middle-aged women having fun by painting a clumsy and caricatured
image of what this might look like. In other instances the idea of The
Spice Girls ageing at all, much less appropriately – was dismissed by the
suggestion that they were older than they are – surely the height of all
insults. For example, referring to the steel frame on top of the London
black cabs on which they were dancing, one reviewer comments that
'Victoria nearly fell off the roof of a taxi – even though a Zimmer frame
had helpfully been provided.'[34] The emphasis here by the *Daily Mail*,
singling out Victoria Beckham as someone who has bypassed middle age
altogether, is something of an oddity which draws much more heavily on
the style of the celebrity press than it does on the address of pop reviews.
It perhaps indicates that Gerri Halliwell, the most frequent subject of
media sneering about age during The Spice Girls' heyday, has now 'aged
successfully', not least by maintaining a relatively low public profile in
comparison with the more public and very successful Victoria Beckham.
As I have stated earlier, the odd nature of these reviews – somewhere
between review and comment in which The Spice Girls' performance
was acknowledged as one small component of a ceremonial mega-event
of entertainment – perhaps allows for a more easy reliance on the norms
of celebrity gossip.

Remember when ...

Unlike The Spice Girls, Madonna's continuing pop career means that
her contemporary live performances necessarily include her earlier
successes as well as her current catalogue. While an audience of her
contemporaries might expect to hear songs from her back catalogue,
critical responses to the changes in her seminal *Like a Virgin* were mixed:
for the *Telegraph's* reviewer this mix made up one of the most poignant
parts of the show,[35] while the *Guardian* considered it to have been inef-
fectively 'faffed about with in a way that speaks less of a brilliant reinvention than an innate misunderstanding of [its original strengths].'[36]
Regardless of the critical reception of reformulating known songs, any
current show of an ageing active performer must contain old material. Deviations from this inclusion are poorly tolerated by reviewers as

when someone notes that MDNA contains 'too many unknown (new) songs'.[37] In contrast, as a defunct group, The Spice Girls are actively not required to breathe new life into *Spice Up Your Life*: its relevance lies in its repetition as what it was. The role of reminiscence takes a key role in reviewers' accounts of performances where it is claimed that watching Girls Aloud 'take[s] us back to a time when Gareth Gates was a household name, we'd never heard of Facebook and nobody moaned about the economy.'[38] As I have stated earlier, the more personal reflections of the print room allow for an intimate, journalistic feel, which often draws attention to the reviewer's own experiences: 'I was 18 when Girls Aloud won ITV's *Popstars: the Rivals* and I have been singing and dancing along to their songs ever since';[39] and are used to solder the reviewer's preferences with that of their imagined reader, as when Kate Wills claims that Kylie's songs played live sound '(almost) as good as when you'd made up dance routines to them on cassette in your bedroom.'[40] It is often clear that reviewers want the performance that had resonance for them in a particular era: 'would it have been so hard [for Kylie] to slip in *Spinning Around*?';[41] similarly, Madonna's performance of Vogue is 'proof of her musical majesty',[42] because it harks back to an era when she had more relevance for her critic. A reviewer for the *Daily Mirror* implicates the gendered nature of these re-imaginings, advising prospective audiences of Girls Aloud to 'grab your girlfriends, your mother, your aunt or even your mother-in law because it is definitely going to be the ultimate girls' night out where you too can reminisce about the past ten years.'[43] The nostalgic nature of these reflections suggests that things were intrinsically better in a former era and a younger time, and it acknowledges that the process of ageing involves reflecting on how the self compares to others. Thus, Kylie Minogue asks 'a sea of teary forty-somethings, drunk on nostalgia and mulled cider' how long they'd been waiting for her reunion with Jason Donovan and a reviewer concludes that, ultimately, 'She's Kylie. And he's that bloke off the Iceland ad.'[44]

Nostalgia

Nostalgic reviews reinforce the sense that youth is preferable to age, placing higher value on the past rather than the present. Examining discourses of ageing in these performers reveals as much about sociopolitical and technological ages as it does about age as an absolute. Madonna's fame was built in part on her ability to court controversy as a highly sexualised figure – a controversy made possible because it drew attention to the sexually volatile socio-political climate of the

1980s in which the struggles for gay liberation were played out against a conservative agenda keen to position equal rights as a threat to family values and public health. In an Internet age sexual images are ubiquitous to the point of boredom and censorship as silly as it is futile, or so we might believe were it not for the fact that responses to Madonna's performances show the massive limitations on what is still deemed acceptable sexual behaviour for women. While the newsprint reviews are relatively conservative, in an online environment, reactions to the ageing sexual body are casually caustic and brutally offensive.[45] This vitriolic discourse does not take place solely in the social media, but it also exists in legitimised news blogs where the most damning vilifications often come from women journalists and bloggers. The *Telegraph's* online review, for example, which is not available in print, claims that 'at 50-something, Madonna's no longer titillating, but embarrassing, a cougar whose biggest victim is her dignity...[her] mutton-dressed-as-lamb act is painfully, wincingly humiliating.'[46] The news blogs then reveal much about the roles and norms of online communication in which the virtual space of the blog exists as a part documentary, part gossip account ungoverned by editorial discretion.

The level of hostility directed at Madonna may be related to age, but it has always been evident in discussions in which her pursuit of success is seen as having all the qualities of a military operation conducted with relentless, ruthless strategic precision.[47] This demonising trend continues in contemporary pop reviews which use age and experience as a further threatening feature of her performance, suppressing her autonomous sexuality through mockery and sneers: 'it is hard to deny that aggression suits her [as she] stomps around the set in black leather like an ageing dominatrix.'[48] If Madonna is presented as an over-empowered, masculinised threat, an altogether different version of sexual empowerment emerges in reviews of Girls Aloud. Here, they are objectified to the point of inanimation, presented as 'one of Simon Cowell's early experiments...impossibly glamorous, totally unavailable robot women';[49] 'perfectly calibrated, with the threat of malfunction, like Austin Powers' fembots';[50] and 'five fully posable Girls standing doll-like on top of a sparkling podium bearing their name'.[51] Their ability to be in control is clearly indicated by their ability to display themselves to best effect rather than being read as indicative of real political, economic or social empowerment.[52] Lacking Madonna's agency, 'Girls Aloud are a fantastic pop band because they understand what is expected of them.'[53] While Madonna's star image is a site of contradiction that both subverts images of male dominance and reproduces dominant ideas about consumer culture and capitalism,[54] Girls Aloud's performance offers a paucity of meanings which are more rigidly defined, contained and controlled. Critical reviews of pop performances attempt to situate real pop as though it is a natural and exuberant phenomenon which glosses over age as a performance. Hence: Girls Aloud are 'pure pop...frothy and youthful...perfect: bright, perky and extremely camp'.[55] Not-ageing is positioned as a natural and spontaneous reality in contrast with the deliberately constructed, robotic, controlled performance of their show with the claim that it is 'during the bits where [they] are just bouncing up and down that the arena seems to be exploding with joy'.[56] Girlishness then is innocent, youthful, vital: a wobbling, bouncing, teetering display of natural gender which is at odds with Madonna's honed, buffed, ripped physical prowess, a body 'starved to perfection'[57] and presented as unnatural. The strict regime that Madonna undergoes to maintain her look is commended at the same time that it is also made clear that not *even* Madonna, the foremost example of extreme health and beauty discipline, is 'immune' to ageing and that this is a 'sad' but inevitable state.[58] This narrative of pop simplicity clouds the effort of not-ageing and presents fame as something attainable to everyone, regardless of ability or class.[59] Instead, it is something that can be bought ready-made; 'a transformation happens when these five normal women get together, utilise quality styling products and become pop superstars.'[60]

Conclusion

The modern celebrity lifestyle, coupled with a consumer focus, proves something of a problem when it comes to defining age: success, wealth and esteem are no longer as clearly associated with having been earned over a period of time. While Madonna consciously crafted her image to appeal to a mass audience and used the media to deliberately blur the boundaries between her real and star personas, reality TV has offered the chance of fleeting celebrity to everyone, and social media gives the impression that celebrities are barely mediated at all. Celebrity women above all others hold a voyeuristic fascination, and in an age where being a celebrity can be solely about being seen, looks are crucial. When reviewers acknowledge the non-ageing of performers – 'Ahh Kylie – age cannot wither her (or is it the Botox?)'[61] – it draws attention to a successful performance. Accepting age remains the ultimate sign of failure, which signals a lack of relevance and an unwillingness to play the game. The performance of not-ageing is one of the ways in which the performance of gender is still most closely controlled and monitored. Not-ageing involves buying and consumption, overt displays of wealth that signal the wholesale adoption and endorsement of lifestyle choices. Not-ageing is the most convincing way for privileged women to fashion their identities. Not-ageing can be sold in a way that ageing simply cannot; ageing can be done naturally and without a market. Consequently, it has little place in pop.

The beginning of this chapter noted that much of the discussion that goes on about popular music takes place on Twitter and other social networking sites, and a brief scan of these suggests that the discourses of ageing are far more vitriolic, damning and unforgiving than those in the traditional published media. These diatribes are worrying, suggesting as they do that new media does not count or leave a footprint, that we have grown so accustomed to seeing the artifice of not-ageing, and that seeing the lack of it is both noteworthy in the first instance and repulsive in the second. And it demonstrates the casual misogyny of attitudes to ageing more generally. At the risk of taking too essentialist a view of gender, it is clear that the most damning vilifications of all of the performers came from women journalists and bloggers. Consequently, I find it all the more encouraging that the press, even under pressure to be increasingly inter-active with its audience, does not indulge in these damning discourses too readily. A tentative hypothesis though – and one which may explain Kylie's relative absence – is that it is more difficult for a woman to be represented in the media if she is middle aged than it is if she is more clearly identifiable as 'old'. As I said at the outset, while the boundaries of this term are poorly defined, constantly shifting and frequently mean-ingless, in this instance the popular dismissal of age in pop music may in and of itself be liberating. To be 'old' is to be in a position in which one is allowed to be distinguished, dignified, decorous or daring, while to be in one's 40s is to be neither young nor old, invisible by convincingly faking youth or embarrassingly visible by poorly forging it.

Notes

1. Deborah Jermyn, '"Get a Life, Ladies. Your Old One Is Not Coming Back"; Ageing, Ageism and the Lifespan of Female Celebrity,' *Celebrity Studies*, 3:1 (2012), pp. 1–12.
2. Hilary Radner, *Neo-Feminist Cinema: Girly Films, Chick Flicks and Consumer Culture* (London and New York: Routledge, 2010).
3. See *The Adoring Audience: Fan Culture and Popular Media*, ed. Lisa A. Lewis (London: Routledge, 1992); Virginia W. Cooper, 'Women in Popular Music: A Quantitative Analysis of Feminine Images over Time,' *Sex Roles*, 13:9–10 (1985), pp. 499–506; Lisa L. Rhodes, *Electric Ladyland: Women and Rock Culture* (Philadelphia, PA: University of Pennsylvania Press, 2005).

4. *'Rock On': Women, Ageing and Popular Music*, ed. Ros Jennings and Abigail Gardiner (Farnham: Ashgate, 2012).
5. Simon Biggs, 'Age, Gender, Narratives, and Masquerades,' *Journal of Aging Studies*, 18 (2004), pp. 45–58.
6. Paul Watson and Diane Railton, 'Rebel without a Pause: The Continuity of Controversy in Madonna's Contemporary Music Videos,' in *Jennings and Gardiner*, pp. 139–154.
7. 'National Readership Survey', available at http://www.nrs.co.uk/top-line-readership/ (Accessed 02 August 2013).
8. Amy Gladwell, 'Madonna Tops List of Highest Earning Tours for 2012,' *BBC News* (17 December 2012), available at http://www.bbc.co.uk/newsbeat/20754852 (Accessed 19 April 2013).
9. 'Global' stars sometimes have their international shows acknowledged as part of the 'light' news commentary on world affairs, but a pop review of a show outside the UK is very unusual.
10. For a full discussion see Kirsty Fairclough, 'Nothing Less Than Perfect: Female Celebrity, Ageing and Hyper-Scrutiny in the Gossip Industry,' *Celebrity Studies*, 3:1 (2012), pp. 90–103. Jennings and Gardiner identify themselves as women enjoying pop music despite being beyond the unspoken but clearly defined 'age of appropriacy' for involvement in it, p. 3.
11. John Fiske, *Reading the Popular* (London: Unwin Hyman, 1989); John Fiske, *Understanding Popular Culture* (London: Unwin Hyman, 1989); Douglas Kellner, *Media Culture: Cultural Studies, Identity and Politics between the Modern and the Postmodern* (London: Routledge, 1995); *The Madonna Connection: Representational Politics, Subcultural Identities, and Cultural Theory*, ed. Cathy Schwichtenberg (Boulder; San Francisco; Oxford: Westview Press, 1993).
12. Ellis Cashmore, *Celebrity/Culture* (Abingdon; New York: Routledge, 2006).
13. Jennings and Gardiner, p. 3.
14. Imelda Whelehan, *Overloaded: Popular Culture and the Future of Feminism* (London: The Women's Press Ltd., 2000).
15. Dave Simpson, 'Pop Supremos Deliver the Ultimate Girls' Night Out,' *The Guardian* (23 February 2013), p. 48.
16. Simon Price, 'It's Been Emotional, Says Cheryl. Forget That – It's Been Fab,' *The Independent* (24 February 2013).
17. Kate Mossman, 'I Think We've Split up Now: Girls Aloud Remain a Pretty Formidable Pop Outfit – but Just Try Getting Them to Agree on Whether This Really Is the End…,' *The Observer* (24 February 2013), p. 36.
18. Simpson, p. 48.
19. Fiona Shepherd, 'Review: Girls Aloud,' *The Scotsman* (12 March 2013), p. 20.
20. Erin Hatton & Mary Nell Trautner, 'Images of Powerful Women in the Age of "Choice Feminism"', *Journal of Gender Studies*, 22:1 (2013), pp. 65–78.
21. Fairclough, pp. 92–93.
22. Alice Finegan, 'Girls Fulfilling Promise,' *Daily Mirror*, The Beat (8 March 2013), pp. 2–3.
23. Shepherd, p. 20.
24. Will Hodgkinson, 'Pop,' *The Times*, T2 (4 March 2013), p. 10.
25. Neil McCormick, 'Madonna's Still a Sure Shot: Pop,' *Daily Telegraph* (19 July 2012), p. 24.

26. Caroline Sullivan, 'Kylie without the Hits? Charming and Chirrupy – but a Long Two Hours: Kylie Minogue Hammersmith Apollo, London,' *Guardian* (5 April 2012), p. 41.
27. Joe Mott, 'Good-Time Girls Still on Top,' *Daily Star Sunday* (3 March 2013), p. 41.
28. Harriet Walker, 'Madonna Delivers Everything Fans Want (except Full-on Moral Outrage),' *Independent* (18 July 2012), p. 22.
29. Simpson, p. 48.
30. McCormick, p. 24.
31. Sheila Whiteley, *Women and Popular Music: Sexuality, Identity and Subjectivity* (London and New York: Routledge, 2000), pp. 214–217.
32. Alison Phillips, 'Spices Still Hot...,' *Daily Mirror* (15 August 2012), p. 21.
33. Tam Cowan, 'Olympics Opening and Closing Ceremonies Were Brill – Shame About the Dull Bit in the Middle,' *Daily Record* (15 August 2012), p. 13.
34. Polly Hudson, 'Spice Reunion Is True Legacy of the Games,' *Daily Mirror* (14 August 2012), p. 9.
35. Neil McCormick, 'Star Power Burns Off Younger Rivals,' *Daily Telegraph* (18 July 2012), p. 25.
36. Alexis Petridis, 'Madonna Busts a Gut – but the Grinches Steal Her Volume: Madonna Hyde Park, London,' *Guardian* (19 July 2012), p. 31.
37. Hodgkinson, p. 10.
38. Daisy Wyatt, 'A Plea to Girls Aloud: Don't Split Up', *Telegraph* (21 March 2013).
39. Lizzie Anderson, 'Girls Aloud Newcastle Metroradio Arena,' *The Northern Echo* (25 February 2013).
40. Kate Wills, 'IoS Pop Review 2: The Hit Factory Live, O2, London; All Hail Chart Royalty and One-Hit Wonders,' *Independent* (23 December 2012).
41. Sullivan, p. 41.
42. Walker, p. 22.
43. Finegan, p. 3.
44. Wills, p. 22.
45. Kristyn Gorton and Joanne Garde-Hansen, 'From Old Media Whore to New Media Troll,' *Feminist Media Studies,* 13:2 (2012), pp. 288–302.
46. Cristina Odone, 'Madonna, Stop Embarrassing Yourself!' *Telegraph. co.uk Blog* (18 July 2012), available at http://blogs.telegraph.co.uk/news/cristinaodone/100171544/madonna-stop-embarrassing-yourself/ (Accessed 10 June 2013).
47. Cashmore, pp. 42–50.
48. McCormick, p. 24.
49. Hodgkinson, p. 10.
50. Mossman, p. 36.
51. Shepherd, p. 20.
52. Whelehan, p. 4.
53. Hodgkinson, p. 10.
54. Nick Stevenson, 'Audiences and celebrity,' in *Understanding Media: Inside Celebrity*, ed. Evans and Hesmondhalgh (Maidenhead: Open University Press, 2005).
55. Ibid., p. 10.
56. Mossman, p. 36.

57. Hodgkinson, p. 10.
58. Fairclough, pp. 95–96.
59. Valerie Walkerdine, *Daddy's Girl: Young Girls and Popular Culture* (Basingstoke: Macmillan, 1997).
60. Hodgkinson, p. 10.
61. Wills, p. 22.

9
Mature Meryl and Hot Helen: Hollywood, Gossip and the 'Appropriately' Ageing Actress

Kirsty Fairclough-Isaacs

In a 2009 article from the UK *Guardian*, Vanessa Thorpe writes,

> When a film star seduces someone 20 or 30 years their junior on screen, the audience doesn't bat an eyelid. In fact, it is an established cinema convention. If the older star is a woman, however, public reaction is harder to predict. But now Hollywood, so long accused of sexism because of the way it treats female talent, finally seems prepared to tackle a subject once regarded as beyond the pale: sex and the sixty-something woman.[1]

Somewhat surprisingly, Thorpe implies that one of Hollywood's enduring battles has been won. What prompted this article was the success of Meryl Streep in *It's Complicated* (2009), the romantic comedy written and directed by Nancy Meyers and starring Streep as Jane Adler, a woman well into middle age who finds herself romantically pursued by her ex-husband who is finding life with his much younger 'trophy wife' stressful and unfulfilling. Whilst Streep's enduring star power and performance in this film is noteworthy, it is quite a leap to suggest that Hollywood has cast off its long-standing regressive attitude towards its older female stars and is now squarely addressing the issue of middle-aged female sexuality.

However, in recent years, there has been an increase in the number of films aimed at and starring older women in major, often romantic roles in Hollywood. The benchmark of the trend was arguably set in 2006 with *The Devil Wears Prada* (Frankel, 2006). This continued with *Sex and The City* and *Sex and The City 2* (King, 2008, 2010), *Mamma Mia!* (Lloyd, 2008), *Julie and Julia* (Ephron, 2008), *It's Complicated* (Meyers,

2009), *The Best Exotic Marigold Hotel* (Madden, 2011) *A Song for Marion* (Williams, 2012) and *Hope Springs* (Frankel, 2012), which all not only alerted Hollywood to the financial benefits of aiming films at a lucrative older demographic, but also portrayed older women on screen in major roles where the narrative is actually centred around them.

Streep is not the only older actress who is an exception to the rule of Hollywood's ageism. Helen Mirren and Judi Dench have both enjoyed high-profile careers in Hollywood in recent years. Dench's relative youthful 'plainness' has worked in her favour as she has aged with recent roles in *The Best Exotic Marigold Hotel* and *Skyfall* (Mendes, 2012). Dench's look and classical theatre training have proved an alluring combination for Hollywood, and along with Mirren (who will be discussed in detail in this chapter) she has managed to secure major film roles well into her sixth decade, a feat almost unheard of in Hollywood.

These actresses are clearly exceptions. Older female stars in Hollywood remain consistently linked with ageing narratives, in part due to the rapid acceleration of discourses of celebrity gossip, largely circulating online. The age narrative is *the* central trope in celebrity gossip discourses where the perpetual discussion of the age of female stars and whether their behaviour, lifestyle and look is 'age appropriate' feeds an increasingly dichotomised account of ageing femininity. Discourses in popular culture surrounding the majority of older female Hollywood stars are first and foremost framed in terms of narratives of ageing, which are always structured in terms of how well the actress is 'managing' her ageing process. It would appear that discourse surrounding the female star's face and body are the principal ways in which they are now both represented and consumed in the media. It is discourse about a star's ageing face and body that becomes the locus for discussion in the media. These women are still revered at one level, but they are also exposed, examined and scrutinised in order to reveal their corporeal construction and to somehow make visible the artificial nature of their identities.

In the context of a mass media that scrutinises every aspect of the ageing star, this chapter will consider the star images of Meryl Streep and Helen Mirren, two of the most successful older female actresses in Hollywood. Streep and Mirren are interesting examples as they are often perceived as examples of 'growing old gracefully'. Both have been central to the perceived recent recognition of older women on screen in Hollywood and how it may appear that, through their success, the maturing female star is now beginning to be revered rather than rejected in popular culture. This chapter will examine how despite the perceived positive nature of these shifts, this acceptance appears possible only when it is also linked to the legitimacy of the 'craft' of acting, where certain actresses are spared unremitting scrutiny of their ageing process and are allowed to mature on screen because they are considered 'authentic' talents and therefore more 'acceptable' as ageing women. Both Mirren and Streep are considered substantial talents. Evidenced by their numerous nominations and awards worldwide from the Academy Awards to the BAFTAs. Therefore, their appearances seem less important to their star image and indeed their ageing, yet they both actually conform to a rather narrow standard of beauty that Hollywood espouses. Also, this chapter will address the construction of the ageing female celebrity and the state of endless transformation, which appears to be so prized in postfeminist culture and will explore how these actresses are 'allowed' to age. Evidently, others have a much more problematic relationship with Hollywood, celebrity and indeed their own ageing narratives, such as Kelly Le Brock, Cher, Melanie Griffith and Kathleen Turner. To conclude, the chapter asks what might these contradictory themes tell us about ageing and Hollywood in the twenty-first century that might be different from previous eras?

Ageing in the spotlight

In an article from *The Hollywood Reporter* in 2013, Tatiana Siegel suggests,

> Planned obsolescence used to be the norm, where fresh young faces eventually obliterate the existing reigning class. But the new premium on concept over casting has upended a nearly 100-year-old star system. The March 2013 *Performer Q Study*, which measures both how well-known and how well-liked a celebrity is, found Sandra Bullock statistically tied with Tom Hanks, 56, for the film star top spot among U.S. survey respondents over 18. 'Her movie roles have been so diverse, from comedies to serious, that she's tracking younger and older, male and female. She cuts across the spectrum.'[2]

Siegel suggests that a previous industry norm – where older actresses, typically over 40, would be replaced by younger stars – seems to have undergone a shift. Those stars that were at the top of their industry a decade ago, such as Sandra Bullock, Nicole Kidman and Cameron Diaz, are still there. Siegel argues that they are just as able to attract audiences as they once were. If this is the case, it is a seismic shift in thinking from an industry that has long mistreated its older female stars. In fact, there remains an endemic attitude to older female stars that they may appear on screen, but they should never look their age, unless it is a key element of the narrative of the film.

Rosalind Gill suggests that postfeminism privileges 'Femininity as a bodily property; the shift from objectification to subjectification; an emphasis upon self-surveillance, monitoring and self-discipline; a focus on individualism, choice and empowerment; the dominance of a makeover paradigm; and a resurgence of ideas about natural sexual difference.'[3] Indeed, the popular media embodies postfeminism in such a way that suggests women must always look younger than their years. They are routinely instructed to maintain a slender body, engage in exercise and diet regimes and participate in carefully chosen 'appropriate' surgical and nonsurgical interventions to extend middle age for as long as possible. Those that are perceived to 'fail' the navigation of these boundaries are widely denigrated in the popular press and online gossip discourse. At this juncture, it is important to examine some of these issues and address why some older female actresses in Hollywood appear to escape the unremitting scrutiny of their faces and bodies and are instead revered as quintessential examples of how to grow old 'gracefully'. These stars are often deemed acceptable due to their moderate use of cosmetic surgery. A precarious balance exists in that stars such as Mirren and Streep are celebrated because they appear to eschew cosmetic surgery, whilst others are scrutinised for either a lack of attention to their ageing faces, as in the cases of Kathleen Turner and Brigitte Bardot or the overuse of cosmetic surgery such as Meg Ryan and Melanie Griffith.

Indeed, in the popular media, the older female face and body is regularly deemed ugly unless it has been modified 'correctly' by cosmetic surgery or is considered hyper-feminine and associated with glamour narratives from the bygone Studio System era. Ageing in the spotlight has long been couched in these terms, where the fact of ageing is considered something that must be fought rather than accepted or embraced. There are now huge contradictions in evidence in celebrity culture when discussing the representations of cosmetic surgery. Virginia Blum argues that there is a strong connection between celebrity culture and cosmetic surgery, and that the star system has actually worked to create a beauty norm that has led to the widespread adoption of cosmetic surgery. She states,

Of course, stardom can happen only in the context of a large audience that converges in the celebration of the iconic actor. Consider how necessary this institutionalisation of star culture has been to the creation of a culture of cosmetic surgery. In order for cosmetic surgery to be appealing, not to mention a viable professional solution, enough of us have to agree on standards of beauty... the star is both the standard and an instrument of standardization.[4]

These repeated narratives and images have now led to a culture where cosmetic surgery is not just accepted, but also embraced as an essential part of the fight against ageing, and not only in the entertainment industry.

In gossip discourses, ageing stars are often configured in terms of disintegration and invisibility. Ageing is rarely represented in the media in terms of a woman's growth and development of knowledge. Ways to maintain youthful beauty are espoused continually, often through the careful use of cosmetic surgery. Representations of cosmetic surgery when linked to stars and ageing are steeped in contradictions. Female stars are both vilified as extreme versions of abject plasticity and routinely praised for 'fighting the battle' with age by embracing the surgical technologies available to them and conversely revered for growing old naturally. Hollywood actress Melanie Griffith provides an interesting example. Griffith is a product of Hollywood. She is the daughter of actress Tippi Hedren, has been working since she was nine months old, has had a career of highs and lows and was most notable for her widely lauded performance in Mike Nichol's *Working Girl* (1988), which gained her an Academy Award nomination. She has fought widely publicised battles with alcohol and painkillers and has been tabloid fodder for many years, particularly since her marriage to Antonio Banderas in 1996.

Much of the discourse surrounding Griffith is now focussed on her inability to age well. There is very little positive coverage of her: she is perceived as a woman whose failure to use cosmetic surgery 'correctly' has resulted in limiting her ability to gain work. In 2007, *The Daily Mail* showbiz section reporter Kristina Perdersen wrote,

> When Melanie Griffith arrived at a film premiere last weekend, it was her plump lips and line-free forehead which drew all the attention. But a few days later on a shopping trip, the focus moved down a few feet – to her wrinkly knees. Although the actress does not turn 50 until August, the area exposed by her white cut-off jeans could have belonged to a woman of far more advanced years.[5]

Indeed, this and similarly negative coverage on a plethora of gossip sites surrounding Griffith is linked to her supposed failure to understand that the processes of age management must be barely visible for a woman. Her infamous 'trout pout' lip filler in the 1990s still remains the most talked about aspect of her star image. The *Celebrity Cosmetic Surgery* website stated in 2013:

> If you speak to her current husband, Antonio Banderas, the answer may be clear. When asked about his wife having plastic surgery, he said, *'This lust for beauty is a terrible thing. I've forbidden her from ever going to a cosmetic surgeon again. It is something we have agreed to for the sake of our marriage.'* Perhaps Banderas is afraid his wife will eventually go down the path of awful celebrity plastic surgery with the likes of former Playmate Shannon Tweed, Mickey Rourke or 'The Cat Lady' Jocelyn Wildenstein.[6]

It would appear that according to the popular media ageing women who do not manage the ageing process correctly in effect deserve the negative coverage and subsequently gain little work in the latter stages of their careers.

Despite this widespread negativity, some Hollywood stars who have managed to circumvent these discourses and have become synonymous with the recent shift in the acceptability of visible ageing in Hollywood. Those stars who are characterised as not engaging in cosmetic surgery are represented as 'brave' as they choose to 'grow old gracefully'. There are also those such as Mirren and Streep who are considered so talented that their looks are not the main focus of their star image. Such women are singled out as bringing something unique to their craft. This appears to be linked to their backgrounds as classically trained actors and the idea that they bring a sense of gravitas to projects that they appear in.

Helen Mirren: ageing and the 'hot' body

As Imelda Whelehan suggests in her analysis of postfeminist discourses of ageing in Hollywood cinema, 'Producers and consumers of popular culture have reached a bizarrely schizophrenic impasse in which older women rarely pass scrutiny because there are no positive meanings that reconcile postmenopausal women to the body; the numerical fact of their age generally renders them not fit to be seen.'[7] Indeed, Whelehan is correct to suggest that older women who discuss or display their bodies or their sexuality are most often treated with disdain. The older woman's body is rarely seen in Hollywood cinema, and is almost never discussed beyond a framework of decay. Postmenopausal women are mostly invisible in Hollywood. This invisibility is why some journalists heralded a sea-change in Hollywood based on the success of *It's Complicated*, because it was simply so unusual for Hollywood to address female mid-life sexuality in this way. Indeed if this film had starred another older Hollywood actress, it may not have gained such widespread attention. Meryl Streep and Helen Mirren are two of the few examples of a new kind of acceptability; they have managed to age in front of the camera and be highly visible in celebrity culture without facing the vitriol and lack of roles that many other actresses are confronted with as they age. This new kind of acceptability highlights the deeply schizophrenic discourse of ageing where some women are 'allowed' to age and others are continually disparaged for their supposed inability to manage their ageing.

Helen Mirren is often considered evidenced by her recognition by organisations such as BAFTA, The Critics Circle, The Emmys, The Academy Awards, The Golden Globes amongst others and the longevity of her career in film, on stage and in television. She has been the recipient of numerous awards from the major industry awarding bodies and organisations, including an Academy Award, four BAFTAS, three Golden Globes and four Emmys to date. As a classically trained actress who worked extensively with The Royal Shakespeare Company early in her career, Mirren's willingness to perform semi-nude and nude scenes in a variety of her film and stage roles developed a persona associated with sex and sensuality that has become her trademark. In an industry that is notoriously insecure in terms of employment, Mirren has worked consistently. Her reputation as a 'serious' actress was secured early in stage roles such as *Cleopatra* (1965) and further cemented in popular culture with her roles in classic television dramas such as *Prime Suspect* (1991–2006). She has also embraced more experimental work in Peter Greenaway's *The Cook, The Thief, his Wife and Her Lover* (1989). Mirren's persona was established alongside the relaxation of stage censorship in the 1960s and broader sexual liberalisation in society more widely. As she has aged, Mirren's star persona has continued to be shaped by associations with sex and sensuality. Yet, due to the cultural value that is associated with serious theatre, Mirren has been virtually exempt from negative criticism in the media regarding her looks because she conforms to a version of tasteful ageing that is celebrated in the mass media.

When Mirren was photographed by the paparazzi in a bikini at the age of 62 on holiday in 2008, the image went viral. It was discussed, debated and dissected across the world, largely praised as an example of sexy yet tasteful ageing. Mirren has subsequently been associated with sexual allure, confidence and beauty. What is interesting is that she is seen as a figure of transgression, in that she speaks to a narrative of rebellion. Older women are not supposed to wear bikinis and flaunt their ageing bodies; they are not supposed to dye their hair pink and appear at film premieres flirting with younger actors as Mirren has. Indeed, she is able to circumvent the discourses of disdain that are normally associated with ageing women. However, it seems that the image went viral because Mirren conforms to traditional notions of body image and youthful physical standards, and because of this image, Mirren is now held up as the role model for feminine ageing. As Sadie Wearing suggests, 'Ageing in postfeminist culture seems marked by both a gesturing toward utopian desires to transcend time and chronology evident in makeover paradigms and a concurrent tendency to emphasise time, chronology and generational (and sexual) difference'.[8] In this context, it is the uncovering of an essentialist version of femininity that lies at the heart of celebrity culture and that Mirren represents. In her article on performing age and gender, Kathleen Woodward points to this overriding negative association with ageing in western culture. Woodward explores what she terms 'the youthful structure of the look', which exhorts us to pass for younger once we reach a certain age. She explains:

> In our mass-mediated society, age and gender structure each other in a complex set of reverberating feedback loops, conspiring to render the older female body paradoxically both hyper-visible and invisible. It would seem that the wish of our visual culture is to erase the older female body from view. The logic of the disappearing female body would seem to be this: first we see it, and then we don't.[9]

Indeed, Mirren is one of the few exceptions in an industry that is youth-obsessed and she is singled out as bringing something unique to her craft. She is perceived as a slightly eccentric, yet authentic, glamorous example of how to not go under the knife and still 'age well'. What is interesting about Mirren is that she performs youthfulness very successfully and attempts to galvanise positive media debates about the older female body and face. From her red carpet appearances to interviews, there is a sense that she is keenly aware that she is being judged as an older woman and appears to play around with this idea in the way that she dresses and carries herself. Sarina Lewis from Australia's *Sunday Morning Herald* suggests, 'At 65, Dame Helen Mirren is more sexually charged goddess than cardigan-clad nanna, and she's at the vanguard of a new breed of 60-somethings for whom age is little more than a number. This group of women, previously consigned to the garbage bin of cultural irrelevance, are redefining long-held stereotypes and successfully battling society's youth focus to become a powerful new authority.'[10]

Lewis clearly suggests that there is a binary opposition at work in both the cultural stereotype of the older woman as a 'cardigan-clad' 'nanna' and the idea of a female Hollywood film star as a 'sexually charged goddess'. It would appear that according to Lewis, there is little in between, but that this is being challenged by stars such as Mirren. Lewis argues that there has been a shift in the way that older women are perceived and in the way that they are perceiving themselves through the women that are currently representing their demographic in the popular media. However, the dichotomy remains that women such as Streep and Mirren are deemed acceptable, even attractive, because they do not display 'normal' signs of ageing. These ascriptions are couched in a rhetoric of femininity, whereby because they look younger and very feminine, therefore they are still worthy of positive media attention. If Mirren had displayed an ageing body that is closer to the majority of 'normal' women's bodies with the usual signs of ageing – wrinkles, weight gain, varicose veins, sagging breasts and cellulite – it is unlikely she would be considered a 'sexually charged goddess'.

Meryl Streep: re-defining ageing in the spotlight?

For nearly 40 years Meryl Streep has been considered one of the greatest actors of her generation. Streep studied at Yale Drama School and then worked in New York on Shakespeare Festival productions and on Broadway. Like Mirren, this 'classical' theatre training affords Streep an identity linked to authenticity, true talent and legitimacy. These characteristics operate through these women's ability to immerse themselves within a role. This ability is an important part of Streep's persona and reputation and the meticulous method that is often associated with her. Streep's 'method' is constructed similarly to some male contemporaries, yet Streep's performances are often considered as more measured and careful without the extremes associated with other method actors in the industry, such Robert De Niro, Christian Bale and Daniel Day-Lewis.

Since the release of *Mamma Mia!* in 2008, her most commercially successful film to date, Streep has become synonymous with the perceived new visibility of the mature woman in Hollywood and has also been a vocal critic against ageism in the film industry. In a 2012 interview in *Vogue* magazine Streep stated, 'Once women passed childbearing age they could only be seen as grotesque on some level.'[11] At the 2009 premiere of *Doubt* (John Patrick Shanley), when asked whether she had come up against discrimination in her career, she said: 'Yes, of course there is ageism in the film industry. There's discrimination in every profession. Look around the room. There are a lot of young women here who are journalists, but do you see any women my age? No. And if you look into the corporate corners of your company, there aren't a lot of women there either. But we're fighting that, and we're making inroads against discrimination.'[12] Streep is able to voice this viewpoint with little criticism because she is perceived as Hollywood royalty, having earned the right to express her opinions. More recently, Streep gained huge mainstream commercial success with *The Devil Wears Prada* and *It's Complicated* and has since become synonymous with a version of ageing that has been configured as acceptable, relatable and sexy, far from the usual malicious discourse reserved for the majority of ageing women in Hollywood.

Theories about Streep's durability in a harsh industry tend to run along two related lines: her talent and her choice of roles. Critics and scholars alike cite Streep's acting reputation as the main reason for her longevity, such as Karen Hollinger's idea that 'her success in receiving Oscar nominations is perhaps the single most important factor in the development of her career, stimulating it in its initial stages and buttressing it during a midcareer decline'.[13] In gossip discourses, both in the popular press and online, it is interesting to note that Streep barely appears in any gossip blogs or magazines in anything but a positive light. Streep's case may be a tentative sign that there has been a minor shift in terms of positive attitudes towards ageing in the spotlight, but she is a rare example in the midst of a maelstrom of negative coverage of ageing women. Typical discourse in the gossip industry and blogs in particular, generally place female stars into ageing categories, most often linked to their use, or not of cosmetic surgery and which are generally couched in terminology that is based around being 'gruesome' or 'desperate'. These terms tend to outline the flow of discourse that pervades gossip in relation to female celebrities, which is then often integrated into their star images and those images become part of the circulation of discourse in relation to their star status. The culture of hyper-scrutiny that exists within the gossip industry is explicit and contradictory. There are websites such as awfulplasticsurgery.com and famousplastic.com that track celebrities' surgery in minute detail and allow readers to view detailed images. Such sites present categories such as *Bad Brow Lift*, *Bad Cheekbone Implants* and *Awful Plastic Surgery Victims* and simultaneously deride and revere the processes of surgical transformation, mocking the celebrity but offering the reader advice and guidance on how to undergo surgical procedures correctly and where to gain sound advice. Sites such as these present their versions of appropriate and inappropriate age-maintenance with sections that feature examples of 'bad' surgery and sections that congratulate celebrities for getting their surgery right. These sites tend to define these good examples as 'invisible' and those that 'enhance' rather than change the celebrity's face. Websites such as these also punish the celebrity for attempting to transcend time or, more pertinently, for making visible the signs of labour involved in maintaining a youthful look. Many of these sites present a difficult and aggressive negotiation about what is and what is not acceptable in terms of cosmetic surgery. The gossip industry thrives on waiting for and sometimes provoking the female celebrity to 'fall from grace', as if it is always only a matter of time before age will catch up with them.

Molly Haskell suggests, 'An anti-star mystique seems to govern her life and her roles, a convergence, perhaps of her seriousness as a performer and the inhibitions of a well-bred Protestant.'[14] It is this anti-stardom that allows her to be accepted as she ages. Publically disdaining celebrity culture, but presenting a star image that is based on openness and honesty, Streep appears to avoid such scrutiny. Instead, she is widely praised for what is usually described as her 'grace, warmth, wit and talent', rather than her physical appearance, undoubtedly an unusual treatment of an older female star in popular culture. Indeed, Hollywood is beginning to recognise women's acting talent and that this may well supersede physical attractiveness. Early in her career, Streep was often associated with a sense of over-calculation and a lack of sex appeal, both of which seem to be currently working in her favour. Whereas Mirren's success was linked directly to her sexuality, Streep's inhibitions led her to be represented as cold and serious. It is Hollinger's contention that 'Meryl Streep's image is composed of two distinct image clusters centered on her renown as a great actress and her reputation as a devoted wife and mother' (79). These facets of Streep's star image as both career woman and family woman have allowed her to circumvent the typical negative treatment of an ageing Hollywood star. It is this notion of the presentation of a sense of authenticity in both career and image that have allowed her to manoeuvre around the discourses of disdain.

Streep's star identity is a complex mixture of everywoman, star, feminist and traditional family woman. She has openly discussed her allegiance to feminism throughout her career, taking on roles that often represent figures of female authority, but none that pose any kind of significant threat to other women, at least not up to this point. Streep's reputation, which has always been based on her talent and not her looks, may in fact position her as a progressive figure in female stardom in Hollywood, in that her focus on female-centred stories, her avoidance of graphic sex scenes and her ability to influence the direction of her characters have paved the way for other actresses.

Yet the majority of her films have been squarely mainstream, and their narratives have essentially reinforced hegemonic ideas about femininity, family and career choices. Many of her films, such as *The Bridges of Madison County* (Clint Eastwood 1995), *Marvin's Room* (Jerry Zaks 1996), *Dancing at Lughnasa* (Pat O'Connor 1998) and *One True Thing* (*Carl Franklin* 1998), are unabashedly female-focussed tearjerkers that stereotypically associate femininity with uncontrolled emotional expression and often maudlin sentimentality. Hollinger suggests, 'a number of extremely traditional aspects of Streep's star persona render her a very safe female role model for contemporary women and recuperate her progressivity for the patriarchal status quo' (95). Indeed her middle-class educated background further renders her particular brand of ageing Hollywood stardom a veritably safe one. Streep represents a version of ageing sexuality that is deemed appropriate and acceptable. Her image is one of the 'everywoman'. It is traditional, safe and not completely unattainable, and it embodies a version of middle-aged motherhood that is still 'sexy' and yet mature enough not to be deemed controversial – hence her mass appeal to both men and women. It would appear that traditional values – marriage, motherhood and conformity to a largely traditional beauty ideal – have been reconfigured in the star image of Streep as something fresh and inspirational.

Many of Streep's contemporaries have disappeared into the abyss of few and limited roles for women beyond their mid-40s. Stars such as Susan Sarandon, Diane Keaton and Sissy Spacek have as film critic Jonathan Romney suggests, 'fallen by the wayside, suffered patchy careers, or bowed out, weary of sub-par roles'.[15] Keaton, for instance, has been unable to capitalise on the success of *Something's Gotta Give* (Meyers 2003) and of the few projects she has appeared in since, many were flops, such as *Mama's Boy* (Hamilton 2007) and *Mad Money* (Khouri 2008). However, Streep has managed to navigate these trends that normally disadvantage ageing actresses. Indeed, discourses about her physical appearance have taken an interesting turn, with media commentary tending to bolster her 'desirability' as an attractive older woman: 'There's a glow, a sensuality and a radiance about Streep these days. Put simply, she's looking great.' Also, she possesses a relatable kind of beauty that makes her seem more like one of 'us.'[16]

The overriding meta-textual theme circulating around Streep is her refusal to undergo cosmetic surgery. Streep has openly stated she is anti-cosmetic surgery; whether this is actually the case is up for debate, but it remains an important aspect of her relatable star image. This is another facet of Streep's stardom that has worked in her favour, as despite the cultural pressures on famous women to remain 'youthful', the use and overuse of cosmetic surgery has harmed the careers of a number of high-profile actresses and who have become labelled as gruesome or grotesque, such as Meg Ryan, Cher and Melanie Griffith. Streep has successfully avoided these discourses and her acting ability, rather than her looks, has become the primary marker of her star image. Her ageing is accepted because she is somehow considered 'authentically attractive' and possesses a relatability that renders the malicious discourses redundant.

This judgement may well be in part due to her versatility and her ability to disappear into a character so that the audience is unable to associate her with a particular look or sense of 'Streepness' as is possible with other stars of her generation, such as Goldie Hawn. Hawn's star persona as the blonde, ditzy and cute all-American girl is present within all of her roles. Whereas Streep's acting talent means that the audience is able to forget that they are watching Meryl Streep, and her star persona becomes largely subsumed by the character she is playing. Indeed, Streep's ability to play such a range of characters never allows the audience to form a firm relationship with a core 'image', such as that exhibited by Hawn. Of Streep's contemporaries, many have core traits around which particular themes gather; for example, Diane Keaton and Sally Field seem girlish, engaging and all-American, and Jessica Lange is often characterised as having a fragile sex appeal. Yet in Streep's case, there is no set of predictable characteristics. The irony is that all of those characteristics once considered limitations in her star image appear now to be her strengths. As Streep has never worked within the confines of her image being based on sex appeal, she has no need to live up to an image that can be dismantled as she ages. Her decision to talk openly about nudity in her films has categorised her as a rebellious, sexy, older woman who has both talent and looks. Streep's star image has certainly been 'rebooted' (the commercial strategy term that reframes a franchise, comic book, character, etc. in order to revive it and profit from it) in recent years. This reboot is a useful way to situate the recent resurgence of Meryl Streep's career. By moving away from her characteristic intensity and dramatic works into lighter, more comedic roles, Streep has shifted her star image in recent years. While it is not completely uncommon for long-career trajectories to function cyclically, which emulates the way that genre often functions in Hollywood, her ability to consistently work and still find success should not be understood in terms of merely the projects she is offered or the commercial success that may or may not follow. Indeed, Streep provides a complex and contradictory example of the newly acceptable ageing woman on screen, only acceptable because she ticks many of Hollywood's normative boxes in terms of her physicality in that she is slim and toned and conforms to western standards of female attractiveness. Thus, this acceptability is always within narrowly defined boundaries, and those that do not conform to these very limited ideals will often find themselves unable to secure major roles in mainstream cinema.

The axis of talent and beauty

In conclusion, both Meryl Streep and Helen Mirren represent unusual examples of ageing in Hollywood, whereas many of their peers have been unable to keep working continually in film and/or gave moved to television to find more complex roles or indeed roles at all. From this analysis, it is clear that Streep is revered for her talent and her refusal to display her body, whereas Mirren is revered for her talent and for displaying her body. Whether or not their success is truly indicative of a new acceptability of a woman ageing 'naturally' in Hollywood remains to be seen, but Streep's and Mirren's respective acceptability presents a more positive representation of the ageing female Hollywood star on screen. Indeed, there appears to be a link between the ways in which talent is configured in relation to beauty in Hollywood and in the media in general. Those actresses whose ageing is not received in a positive way are also not critically acclaimed for their work or are considered 'past their prime'. For some, the success of their performances in their youth can never be recaptured as they are unable to retain the essence of their looks that went with that performance, emphasising the complicated ways in which gender imbues performance for women in film. There are notable exceptions, one of which is Judi Dench, whose career in film has been enhanced as she has aged. Yet, representations of ageing women in postfeminist celebrity culture and the gossip industry reinforce the need for reinvention to avoid the pressure of the ageing process. Celebrity culture and postfeminism offer ways to transcend time: postfeminism suggests that meticulous management of the ageing process will somehow provide the means to rescue the self. Women, famous or otherwise, are taught to internalise temporal constraints; only through a variety of given techniques will they be able to defy time. Cosmetic surgery provides the means to achieve these temporal problems. Ageing in celebrity culture and in Hollywood in particular emphasises continual engagement with corporeal intervention. Only by fighting age correctly, being subject to hyper-scrutiny and passing internalised tests will the celebrity or star become accepted as an ideal model of selfhood and achieve that transient state of perfection that Streep and Mirren appear to have achieved.

Notes

1. Vanessa Thorpe (2009), available at http://www.theguardian.com/film/2009/dec/20/hollywood-sex-older-woman-weaver (Accessed 12 October 2013).
2. Tatiana Siegel (2013), 'Revenge of the Over-40 Actress,' available at http://www.hollywoodreporter.com/news/sandra-bullock-melissa-mccarthy-beyond-562530 (Accessed 6 May 2013).
3. Rosalind Gill, 'Post feminist media culture: Elements of a sensibility,' *European Journal of Cultural Studies*, 10:2 (May 2007), pp. 147–166.
4. Virginia Blum, *Flesh Wounds: The Culture of Cosmetic Surgery* (Berkeley: University of California Press, 2003).
5. http://www.dailymail.co.uk/tvshowbiz/article-453826/Melanie-Griffith-fights-losing-battle-signs-ageing.html (Accessed 30 December 2013).
6. http://www.celebrityplasticsurgery24.com/melanie-griffith-plastic-surgery/#
7. Imelda Whelehan. 'Ageing Appropriately: Postfeminist Discourses of Ageing in Contemporary Hollywood,' in *Postfeminism and Contemporary Hollywood Cinema*, ed. Joel Gwynne and Nadine Muller (Basingstoke: Palgrave Macmillan, 2013), pp. 78–96.
8. Sadie Wearing, 'Subjects of Rejuvenation: Aging in Postfeminist Culture,' in *Interrogating Postfeminism; Gender and the Politics of Popular Culture*, ed. Yvonne Tasker and Diane Negra (Durham: Duke University Press, 2007), pp. 277–310.
9. Kathleen Woodward, 'Performing Age, Performing Gender,' *NWSA Journal*, 18.1 (2006).
10. Lewis, available at http://www.smh.com.au/lifestyle/beauty/helen-mirren-and-the-art-of-ageing-gracefully-20101018–16pmj.html (Accessed 12 February 2013).
11. Vicki Woods, 'Meryl Streep: Force of Nature,' *Vogue* (January 2012), http://www.vogue.com/magazine/article/meryl-streep-force-of-nature/#1   qccshttp://www.vogue.com/magazine/article/meryl-streep-force-of-nature/#1 (Accessed 12 October 2013).
12. http://www.telegraph.co.uk/news/celebritynews/4274528/Meryl-Streep-attacks-film-industry-ageism.html
13. Karen Hollinger, *Hollywood Acting and the Female Star* (New York: Routledge, 2006).
14. Molly Haskell 'Finding Herself,' *Film Comment* (March/April 2008), p. 32.
15. Jonathan Romney, 'The Streep Effect: Why Economists Love Her,' *Independent*, 16 (August 2009).
16. David Gritten, available at http://www.telegraph.co.uk/culture/film/6937328/Meryl-Streep-60-and-never-sexier.html.

10
Funny Old Girls: Representing Older Women in British Television Comedy

Rosie White

Feminist academics have noted how age – like race, sexuality and class – offers a double discrimination with regard to gender. As Simone de Beauvoir writes: 'If old people show the same desires, the same feelings and the same requirements as the young, the world looks upon them with disgust: in them love and jealousy seem revolting and absurd, sexuality repulsive and violence ludicrous.'[1] Ruth Shade lists the pejorative tendencies of jokes about older women as trivial, invisible, forgetful, mean-spirited, intimidating, toxic, embarrassing, over-talkative, unattractive, sexually frustrated, undesirable, and – paradoxically – both sexually predatory and sexually moribund.[2] On network television older women have tended to inhabit the margins of mainstream programming as widows, grandmothers or eccentric spinsters. While soap opera and sitcom have traditionally harboured visible numbers of older female characters, they have often been stereotyped as gossipy, asexual spinsters or as battle-axe figures feared by their husbands. Vera Duckworth in long-running British soap *Coronation Street* embodied the latter, her marriage a seaside postcard caricature of a wife who wants to keep the romance going, while her husband would rather tend to his pigeons. Such narratives repeat dominant ideologies about ageing women as fearsome, abject or pathetic. This chapter examines representations of older women in television comedy, arguing that television sitcoms and sketch shows provide a space in which ageing femininity can literally embody its contradictions, as both derogation and celebration. From Peggy Mount to *The Golden Girls* television comedy has offered an arena for older women to behave badly; more important, it has allowed them to be the focus of the story, if not the hero. This chapter also addresses the British tradition, founded in music hall and pantomime, of drag performances as older women, arguing that such representations can work to confirm *and* to explode stereotypes about age, gender and sexuality. In the work of Les Dawson, Harry Enfield, Catherine Tate and Brendan O'Carroll, funny old girls confront western attitudes to older women who are violent and sexual figures.

Patricia Mellencamp notes that because 'television is a medium of extended families and generational families' it has offered a space for older women to be seen: 'Since its inception in the late 1940s, television has been the stomping ground for middle-aged women.'[3] A number of British programmes have made that stomping ground a forum for older men and women by basing comedies in an old people's home. In these sitcoms the elderly are presented as comic figures but take centre stage and, inevitably, such programmes address questions of *how* one should age, usually through the comedy inherent in older people behaving in age-inappropriate ways. By focussing on transgressive behaviour, *You're Only Young Twice* (1977–1981) and *Waiting For God* (1990–1994) offer a celebration of ageing; the mischievous activities of older protagonists in these comedy series represent a more positive model of ageing than is often apparent in serious dramas. Sally Wainwright's *Last Tango in Halifax* (2012–) deployed this strategy to critical acclaim, basing a BAFTA-winning comedy drama around the late-life romance of two widowed pensioners and eliciting comparisons with *Gavin and Stacey* (2007–2010) when the first series was broadcast on PBS in 2013.[4] In the United States, *The Golden Girls* (1984–1992) put women front and centre, and allowed them emotional and sexual lives. These 'girls' are, however, the 'young-old' – women of pensionable age who are still healthy and active – rather than the 'old-old' – women whose health is failing and who have become dependent on carers for support.[5] In these terms *The Golden Girls* offers a rather tidy account of growing old; death rarely makes a showing and Estelle Getty as Sophia Petrillo, the oldest of the 'girls', is clearly a younger woman in a wig. In *The Golden Girls* much of the comedy again centres on proper and improper behaviour for women in late middle age, such as Blanche Deveraux's sexuality, or Sophia's age-inappropriate language.

These active, eccentric examples of older female character roles are swimming against more prevalent representations of the older woman as marginal, more sedate, secondary characters. Margaret Meldrew (Annette Crosbie) in *One Foot in the Grave* (1990–2000) embodies a sitcom stereotype – the long-suffering wife as foil to a central male protagonist. While this British sitcom broke new ground by addressing ageing and death with dark humour, it stuck to the traditional gender dynamic of the suburban comedy by placing the middle-class wife in a secondary, reactive role.[6] *Last of the Summer Wine* (1973–2010) is a notable example of this formula, and a candidate for the longest-running sitcom on British television, recently topping a poll for the most repeated British comedy series.[7] The show focusses on the eccentric adventures of three elderly men, but it also features a number of older women – such as Ivy (Jane Freeman) and Norah Batty (Kathy Staff) – relegated to the role of humourless battleaxe:

> Over the course of a series, male stereotypes become vivid and human, as we pick up little items of information about them. ... With female figures, however, it is difficult for this transformation to happen; the available stereotypes are strictly limited to the nag, the spinster and the dumb sex object. All of these define, rather than transgress, the 'norm', since they all relate at bottom to the invisible ideal of the family against which male eccentrics pull.[8]

Although older characters are given transgressive roles, the gender dynamic of many series still falls into stereotypical patterns as older women are aligned with a repressive domestic regime. Shows such as those listed above indicate the appetite for comedic material about ageing and the elderly; whether this serves a growing demographic, in an era where the white middle class are living longer and baby boomers are more visible and wealthy than preceding generations of pensioners, is debatable. Older characters may also embody the fears and desires of younger, middle-aged viewers, regarding the demands of caring for the older generation or regarding their own ageing in a future where social services are cut to the bone. Popular television comedy offers a space in which the question of *how* to grow old is debated. The statistical capacity of women to outlive men would seem to logically require a boom in female-centred comedy, or at least a comedy in which older women are more visible than their younger counterparts, but most mainstream shows since *The Golden Girls* have tended to focus on elderly male protagonists.

Transvestite figures

One television format in particular has traditionally offered a strangely reflexive account of ageing women: British sketch comedy. Transvestite representations of older women in British comedy sketch shows unpick some of the anxieties and contradictions of ageing femininities. Just as Judith Halberstam proposes that women cross-dressing as men, or 'female masculinity', foregrounds contradictions inherent in hegemonic masculinity, so here younger performers who cross-dress as older women expose contradictions inherent in popular representations of ageing femininity.[9] The cross-dressed figure of men or young women as older women follows a British and American theatrical tradition of comic transformations; it is logically situated in the format of the sketch sequence with its heritage in burlesque, music hall, theatrical revue, variety and vaudeville.[10] Sketch comedy tends to rely more heavily on caricature than sitcom, offering an often stereotypical shorthand performance style which carries political weight. The antirealist style of sketch comedy performance thus offers a means of articulating anxieties and fears about age and ageing. Margaret Montgomerie, for example, proposes David Walliams' controversial role as the elderly incontinent Mrs Emery in *Little Britain* as ambivalently invoking both the 'ultimate image of the abject' and 'a critique of British manners and taboos'.[11] The format is embedded in British broadcasting:

> Sketch shows are usually half an hour in length, minus advertisements on commercial channels or station identification and trailers on BBC. Sketches on social, sexual, political or current mores last for up to four minutes; shorter sketches, usually 10–15 seconds, known as quickies, usually connect the sketches to each other.[12]

British sketch shows follow two broad comedy traditions. The older, working-class sketch shows, often based around named comedians such as Benny Hill and Dick Emery, are now associated with an outdated comedy style from the 1970s inspired by a theatrical tradition of burlesque and variety shows. This outdated style has largely been replaced on British television by middle-class sketch shows, such as *Monty Python's Flying Circus* (1969–1974) and *Not the Nine O'Clock News* (1979–1982), fuelled by performers from Cambridge University's Footlights Society or from comedy revues at the Edinburgh Festival. Sketch series are usually written by the actors who perform in them, unlike sitcom which tends to have a separate writer or writing team.[13]

A number of female performers cross-dress as men in their sketch shows; most notably *French and Saunders* (1987–2005) and more recently *The Morgana Show* (2010), but the dominant tradition is for male comedians to perform as older women. In Geoff King's examination of American film comedy he notes: 'The female is the marked term, designated as more specific, more problematic and more visible, requiring a seemingly more active process of transformation: all those montage sequences in which make-up, wigs, foundation garments and other accessories are applied.'[14] Where female protagonists have cross-dressed as men in films such as *Sylvia Scarlett* (George Cukor, 1935) or *Yentl* (Barbra Streisand, 1983) they appear to need little more than a pair of trousers and a haircut. This suggests that men cross-dressing as women is hard to divorce from its fetishistic and sexually transgressive implications, but also that it is somehow 'easier' for men to cross-dress because of all the equipment associated with heterofemininity.[15] Cross dressing, in this figuration, shores up the binary illusions of heteronormativity; yet at the same time, the prevalence of men cross-dressing as women implies that ageing femininity is unrepresentable in comedy except by impersonation.[16] In her examination of transgendered fantasy film in the 1980s and 1990s, Elizabeth Abele observes that transgender representation 'simultaneously critiques, celebrates, reforms and reinforces traditional constructions of heterosexual masculinity and femininity.'[17] Such arguments reiterate Judith Halberstam's claim that women cross-dressing as men trouble the 'natural' facade of heteronormative identity, because it exposes the extent to which masculinity, too, is reliant on prosthetic accessories.

Much contemporary debate about cross-dressing references Marjorie Garber's work, *Vested Interests* (1992), where she argues:

> The transvestite is both a signifier and that which signifies the undecidability of signification. ... The transvestite is a sign of the category crisis of the immigrant, between nations, forced out of one role that no longer fits ... and into another role, that of a stranger in a strange land.[18]

While Garber addresses gender, class and race, the category of age may equally be understood as interpellating the 'category crisis' which cross-dressing embodies. Many male performers who dress as older women expose the heteronormative limits of patriarchal discourse via their comic discussions of gynaecological issues (or 'women's trouble') and also mark the limitations ascribed to the older woman by embodying the grotesque, excessive ageing body.[19] The 'category crisis' of male to female cross-dressing in television comedy does not automatically entail a radical or liberatory transgression; it can also reiterate the binary understanding of gender that positions women as more subject to the vicissitudes of their natural bodies than men. Men cross-dressing as older women may thus be understood as both an exposé of the taboos which adhere to ageing femininity *and* as misogyny in action.

Laraine Porter comments on the ambiguous dynamic of such performances:

> On one level, these representations can be understood as a celebration of female solidarity and survival. They illustrate a fixation with aspects of femininity which are unknowable to men: dropped wombs, large bosoms and hot flushes.[20]

Porter maps the history of British comic female impersonators, proposing that they fall into two groups; from the 'glamorous if over-determined drag' of performers such as Danny La Rue and Edna Everage to the 'harridan, the older woman with coarse facial features, voice and body' such as 'Dick Emery's parodies of inelegant 1970s womanhood, [and] Les Dawson's celebrated Ada Sidebottom', the latter played as a double act with Roy Barraclough as 'Sissy' in sketches on Dawson's comedy shows (1974–1980).[21] Such performances are also differentiated by their class identities; La Rue is glamorously bourgeois, while Everage is an aspirational Australian housewife-turned-celebrity.[22] Emery, Dawson and Barraclough perform ageing women who are marked by their accent and costume as emphatically working-class and thus doubly 'inappropriate' in their feminine performance.[23]

'The Lovely Wobbly Randy Old Ladies'

Cross-dressing in British television comedy thus has an extensive genealogy which informs more recent examples, such as *Harry Enfield and Chums* (1994–1997), *The Catherine Tate Show* (2004–2009) and *Mrs Brown's Boys* (2011–). Harry Enfield and Kathy Burke's performances as 'The Lovely Wobbly Randy Old Ladies' from *Harry Enfield and Chums* demonstrate the complexities which representations of elderly women continue to expose.[24] 'The Lovely Wobbly Randy Old Ladies', always introduced onscreen by a title card which presents them in these terms, appeared in only four episodes of *Harry Enfield and Chums* in 1994 and only two episodes in 1997 but have had an afterlife on fan sites, on YouTube and via their catchphrase 'Young *man!*' The Ladies' generic name encapsulates the sketch content; in a variety of situations Hilda (Burke) and Gladys (Enfield) harass a younger man, reading sexual innuendo into his conversation and finally assaulting him. The scenarios invert the normative dynamic of masculinity/youth/activity and femininity/age/passivity for comic effect. In their second appearance on *Harry Enfield and Chums*, Hilda and Gladys are shown in their living room, facing the camera in a pair of armchairs. The doorbell rings and Gladys gets up to answer it, saying 'That will be the lovely young gas man' and asking Hilda how she looks, to which Hilda responds: 'Gorgeous!' As Gladys leaves the room, Hilda sprays herself with perfume, lifting her skirt to spray between her legs. Both women move slowly, shuffling in their slippers and displaying the 'wobbly' tremors of advanced years. Gladys is clearly not 'gorgeous' and their evident infirmity is deployed throughout in comic contrast with their monstrous desire for younger flesh. While Hilda and Gladys are dressed as cosy old ladies their dialogue and devious plotting give them a disturbingly vampiric quality – they uncannily enact fears about the elderly not 'acting their age'. Their first exchange with the gas man (Simon Greenall) introduces their catchphrase:

Hilda: Cooeee!

Gasman: Hello ladies; have I come too early?

Gladys: [with delight] Young *MAN*!

Hilda: You wash your mouth out with soap and water, you naughty young man!

Gladys: Young *man*!

Hilda: Where's the lovely dark boy that was here yesterday?

Gasman: [disconcerted] Er, he begged me to come today. So where's the gas leak this time?

Gladys: You're a lovely young man too, you know, young man. Do you know, we think you're the spitting image of a young Lester Piggott!

Gasman: Right. Well, if you could just show me wh...

Hilda: [grabbing his arm] Go on, show us your muscles!

Gasman: [distinctly unnerved] Yeah... if you could just show me where you smelt the gas, eh?

Gladys: Oh! You saucy devil! It's in the bedroom this time. Follow us!

The sketch continues in this manner and concludes with Gladys and Hilda wrestling the gas man to the floor; Gladys straddles his crotch and holds his legs down while Hilda throws herself across his torso and secures his arms. Gladys finally looks into the camera, saying: 'Don't you just love being in control?', while behind her Hilda gives a thumbs up to the camera with a big grin (*Harry Enfield and Chums*, 1:2).[25]

How are we to understand this sequence? On the one hand, it seems to confirm de Beauvoir's statement that sexuality and violence in the elderly are perceived as ludicrous. The repeated 'Young *man*!' emphasises the difference in age between the ladies and their victims; the sketches also feature Gladys and Hilda chanting 'At my age!', 'At your age!', in response to any misconstrued advance from the 'young man'. We are constantly reminded that these are not golden *girls* but characters in their 70s or 80s. The sketches play upon what Mary Russo calls the 'scandal of anachronism': 'Not acting one's age ... is not only inappropriate but dangerous, exposing the female subject, especially, to ridicule, contempt, pity and scorn – the scandal of anachronism.'[26] Hilda and Gladys are anachronistic; they are not 'acting their age' – they confound the stereotype of the weak and passive old lady by asserting their hypersexual desires both linguistically, through constant innuendo, and physically, by assaulting the young men they encounter.

The sketch does not, however, position its audience unequivocally in ridiculing the old ladies. We are invited to laugh at their antics, but also to laugh with them, as in the final moment where Kathy Burke as Hilda looks into the camera and gives a triumphant thumbs up. This is a complex and contradictory account of elderly women – the old ladies are laughable but also 'in control'. They induce hilarity but also a potential for identification. In Russo's essay she argues against the scandal of anachronism, proposing that one must risk anachronism as one gets older – particularly as a woman. She writes, 'In my view, anachronism is a risk which is both necessary and inevitable as a *sign of life*.'[27] In these terms the comic anachronism that Hilda and Gladys represent is a necessary risk, as it opens up the possibility of truly living, rather than merely existing. Russo states that 'Acting one's age, in a certain sense, can be understood as a caution against risk-taking, with higher and higher stakes associated with advanced chronological age until finally acting one's age means to die.'[28] Hilda and Gladys represent a mischievous refusal to lie down and die.

Queer transactions

Clearly, this representation of old women is not simple or singular; we are aware of the performers beneath the wigs and floral dresses throughout. Burke and Enfield are dressed and padded to look like old ladies, but they are not heavily made up; they are not trying to 'pass' as old. Nelly Quemener addresses this disjunction in her examination of cross-dressed characters in sketch comedy on French talk shows, arguing that they 'rely on actorly embodiment' rather than visual artifice, so that the sketch character becomes a fluid apparition rather than a concrete persona.[29] Quemener proposes that discrepancies between appearance and behaviour in comedy sketches offer a queer transaction between performers and their audiences and that when women take on discrepant performances they open up a space 'on a scale from female femininity to female masculinity.'[30] At the same time, Quemener is aware of the provisionality of comedy television performance and the dangers of assuming a singular or predictable reaction from its viewers:

> The mainstream target of the performances and the entertainment contract with the viewer nevertheless produce performances that rely on a double speak mechanism. ... In other words, they usually contain elements both of ambivalence and of reflexivity that either open up possibilities of destabilization or can be seen as elements of resistance.[31]

This is how I understand Hilda and Gladys; not as unequivocal queer resistance, but just for a moment undercutting cultural norms of gender and age, not least through the evident discrepancies between the performance and the identities of the actors. Old age is mobilised in these sketches as a space of opportunity where it is possible for women to behave badly – to be inappropriate and not be punished for doing so.

It is worth noting here the queer trajectory of Kathy Burke's career as an actor. From her roles as rough-diamond magazine editor Magda in *Absolutely Fabulous* (BBC 1992–2012), to the delusional Linda La Hughes in *Gimme Gimme Gimme* (BBC 1999–2001), she has performed aberrant versions of heterofemininity, often based on working-class personae that undercut white, middle-class respectability.[32] As Hilda, too, Burke (and Enfield as Gladys) is marked as old and *working class*. Beverley Skeggs argues that in the nineteenth century, 'Working-class women – both Black and White – were coded as the sexual and deviant other against which [middle class or "proper"] femininity was defined.'[33] In these sketches with Harry Enfield ageing femininity is queered; it is performed as a space of play and desire where violence is tolerated and whimsical. Their male victims are disconcerted and embarrassed, but not apparently hurt. The aberrant behaviour of women in these sketches is made safe by their age. They are so evidently weak and incapable of 'real' violence that it is less their actions that lead to their triumph over the young men than their victims' inability to resist them, either through embarrassment, shock or a gentlemanly unwillingness to hurt the older women. These old ladies thus take the disadvantages of age and deploy them as guerrilla tactics; the surprise of the attack, the incongruity of the attackers. Who would think that these 'lovely' old ladies would have such desires or would act upon them?

In an essay on *Privilege*, Yvonne Rainer's 1990 film about ageing and the menopause, Gwen Raaberg comments:

> Although they express a range of responses to aging, a number of the women report experiencing themselves as more spontaneous, freer – 'off the hook,' as one woman says, 'free from needing to please other people in all kinds of ways.' And many report aging as a positive experience: feeling more focussed and less controlled by psychological and emotional forces; being more open, less judgemental of different perspectives, and more willing to act outside prescribed gender, class, ethnic, and sexual norms.[34]

Rainer's film addresses menopause as a means of examining how getting older is experienced differently by women of different races, classes and sexualities, according to their privileged positions. *Privilege* demonstrates the complex intersectionality of identity and the even more complex effects of such intersections on the experience of ageing. It also addresses wider issues of privilege, in particular the privilege assigned to white people in American society. Rainer's film and performance work is informed by avant-garde practices of art cinema and radical politics, which make an odd juxtaposition with the 'everyday' medium of popular television. Yet the Lovely Wobbly Randy Old Ladies, Hilda and Gladys, also challenge our views of older women. They too 'confound in a certain way'[35] by poking fun at our assumptions about what old women want; what they *should* be and what they *can* do.

Catherine Tate's 'Nan'

In the early 2000s *The Catherine Tate Show* also featured a transgressive older character; Nan (Catherine Tate) is an East End cockney grandmother whose politically incorrect opinions and bad language are suffered by her grandson Jamie (Mathew Horne).[36] Nan is usually depicted in her flat, often sitting with legs akimbo, ranting about the 'fucking state' of friends, relations, the country and so on. Nan is *not* a 'lovely' old lady; she is an irascible character, occasionally breaking into song to illustrate her point of view. In the third series she is joined by the famous British actor Sheila Hancock as her sister, Auntie Junie:

> *Auntie Junie*: [of Jamie] Ain't he handsome? Ain't he handsome? I mean, he's gonna break some hearts.... Have you got a job darling?

Jamie: Oh, no, I'm at university.
Auntie Junie: You at university?
Jamie: Yeah.
Auntie Junie: You at *university*?
Jamie: Yeah!
AuntieJunie: [Turning to Nan] Fucking poof!
[Nan and Auntie June cackle uproariously]
Nan: Here June, have a look at these old pictures. Remember when that one was taken? That's Frankie and Nelly Butty's wedding.
Auntie Junie: They went to Great Yarmouth for their honeymoon.
Nan: That's right. And then Frankie turned over the guesthouse and spent the next four years inside. [Nan and June cackle]
Jamie: What? He went to prison?
Nan: Oh yeah, he was in and out of the nick all his life. But then they were the first people in their street to get colour TV so you got to weigh it all up, ain't you?

(The Catherine Tate Show, 3:6)

This sequence offers an interesting juxtaposition with Tate, then 38, cross-dressed as a much older woman and Hancock, at 73, very much playing her age. Like Burke and Enfield's Lovely Wobbly Randy Old Ladies, Catherine Tate's Nan sketches mine the discomfort of a young man when faced with the transgressive behaviour of old women. Once again, youth and masculinity are the 'norm' in contrast to the queer excesses of ageing working-class femininity. Nan is not nice; indeed, in this sequence she and Junie reminisce over a series of horrific crimes by East End gangsters they knew in their youth, to the horror of her grandson:

Nan: Look, it was different years ago, son. I mean, yes, they boiled people alive in vats of burning oil; yes, they sent people to their death in concrete slippers; yes, they'd cut your head off for eating one of their biscuits; BUT, they were very good to their mothers and you could leave your back door wide open. [Pause] Not that you'd want to with that fucking mob running about!

Nan confounds the stereotype of the cosy old lady with fond memories of a golden past. Her past was clearly less than idyllic, and she revels in her ability to control the present by playing up to stereotypes of the nice old dear and then berating people behind their backs. Jamie, her grandson, is the middle-class avatar, expressing horror at her language, her behaviour and, in this sketch, her memories. Above all Nan is an angry old woman who refuses to be quiet and discreet.

In *The Catherine Tate Show Christmas Special* (2007), Kathy Burke appears as Nan's daughter, a younger woman who clearly follows her mother's lead, teasing Jamie about his sexuality and launching into a tirade when Nan leaves the room. Her mother's daughter, she only pretends to perform filial fondness when in fact she is seething with anger at perceived slights. This sketch caricatures the tensions inherent in mother-daughter relationships, puncturing the fantasy of a happy family Christmas, just as Nan, and Hilda and Gladys, take the wind out of the stereotype of the lovely old lady. When the daughter's boyfriend arrives Nan asks if she looks alright – to which Burke's character replies 'Gorgeous' in a direct quotation of Burke's role as Hilda a decade earlier. Such tidy continuity between generations of comedy performance should not obscure the uncomfortable issues these sketches address. While Hilda and Gladys and Nan offer a celebratory (and hilarious) deconstructions of the patronising view often afforded older women in popular media, they also carry the weight of contemporary fears about ageing. As in the list of pejorative jokes about older women I cited at the beginning of this chapter, Hilda and Gladys and Nan are, indeed, intimidating, embarrassing, over-talkative, unattractive and (in Hilda and Gladys' case) sexually predatory. Their strength as comedy characters, and as representations of older women, is that they are unconcerned by the social opprobrium around them. They are unafraid of ageing and refuse to be cowed or controlled by their younger relations or by any 'young man'.

Mrs Brown's Boys

A more muddied account of ageing femininity is visible in Brendan O'Carroll's hit show, *Mrs Brown's Boys*. O'Carroll's performance as Mrs Brown depicts a postmenopausal Irish working-class mammy in a shapeless cardigan and curled wig. Like Les Dawson's Ada Sidebottom, O'Carroll deploys Agnes Brown as a trickster figure who transgresses gendered boundaries, through physical clowning, gynaecological reference, and age-inappropriate language and behaviour. In one sequence Mrs Brown hides her son's mobile phone in her underwear because she thinks it is stolen; she is sitting at her kitchen table with two priests when her son's friend rings his mobile, and she is given an orgasm by its vibrations (3:5). *Mrs Browne's Boys* is a ratings success on British and Irish television, but it has been slammed by critics for returning to the retrograde working-class comedy of the 1970s.[37] Agnes Brown is closer to Dick Emery than to Catherine Tate. Yet *Mrs Brown's Boys* revels in its postmodern disregard for the fourth wall; the camera reveals the audience and the studio set at the beginning and end of the show; Mrs Brown opens with a monologue to camera and cast members frequently fluff their lines or visibly 'corpse'. Instead of erasing these 'bloopers' in the edit (and preserving them for the DVD box set), the show embraces the 'liveness' of such mistakes as part of an authentically chaotic aesthetic.

This carnivalesque style is evident in Mrs Brown, herself; a sweary, working-class matriarch, Agnes Brown is allegedly based on Brendan O'Carroll's mother, a Dubliner who had eleven children, became a Labour member of the Irish Parliament in the 1950s and established a shelter for victims of domestic violence. As with the odd juxtaposition of clunky jokes and postmodern aesthetic, however, this version of the ageing woman is an uncomfortable one. It is unclear whether we are to laugh with Mrs Brown or at her; O'Carroll as Agnes Brown is a rubber figure, unbreakable and unbelievable. While the Lovely Wobbly Randy Old Ladies and Nan are made vulnerable and given a darker aspect, Mrs Brown is all surface. In one sense, of course, this corresponds to the idea of gender as performative, and the unruly woman as a grotesque. At root, however, Mrs Brown and her boys ventriloquise a series of tics and tropes that play heavily on established stereotypes about class, race, sexuality and gender. *Mrs Brown's* disturbing juxtapositions are evident in 'Mammy's Valentine' (3:4); when Agnes is let down by a Valentine date acquired via an Internet dating site, she insists all her children go and have a good time with their partners, finally revealing that she has hired a 'Dial A Dick' gigolo by letting him out of the cupboard under the stairs. The gigolo character wears a G-string, leather chaps, a cowboy hat and a large moustache, coding him as gay, and is chased up the stairs by a frisky Mrs Brown as the credits roll. This confusion of gender and sexual identities opens an unreadable realm of signification. The 'Dick' emerging from the cupboard implies a 'coming out' process while Agnes Brown's avid sexuality in this scene sits oddly with her otherwise asexual characterisation.

How can we understand such a conglomeration of effects? Mrs Brown's unruly desires are figured as a confused layering of sexualities and genders, which have little to do with the desires of ageing women. In this sequence a mature woman's desire is, indeed, ridiculous because it appears to be unimaginable. While Quemener argues that the ambivalence and reflexivity embodied in transvestite performances entail 'possibilities of destabilization or ... elements of resistance', Brendan O'Carroll as Agnes Brown demonstrates that this is not always the case. Mrs Brown's performative palimpsest of genders and sexual signifiers renders the older woman merely ridiculous; it is hard to read resistance in a show which so determinedly evokes homophobic and sexist stereotypes. *Mrs Brown's Boys* demonstrates the limits of transvestite representations of ageing femininity. While the slippage of identities within British sketch comedy may demonstrate the 'possibilities of destabilization', siting that performance within a traditional sitcom (albeit one with avant-garde leanings) tells a very different story. Agnes Brown takes the representation of ageing femininity back to the misogynies of the pantomime dame and nineteenth-century music hall; a palace of complex negotiations for its time but a context that appears strangely anachronistic on twenty-first-century television.[38] The success of O'Carroll's Mrs Brown indicates the endurance of cultural taboos regarding age, femininity and sexuality. This funny old girl registers a warning for younger women; that to become old is to inhabit Ruth Shade's list of pejorative categories in jokes about older women – to become embarrassing, unattractive and sexually moribund.

As *Mrs Brown's Boys* beats *Downton Abbey* in the Christmas 2013 ratings, Agnes Brown serves as a reminder that, however transgressive and subversive cross-dressing comedic performances may appear, they can also demonstrate how ageing femininities continue to be policed within popular culture. Recent research commissioned by Channel 4 sampled 386 hours of primetime television on the five British terrestrial broadcasters and Sky 1, concluding that 'in light entertainment, comedy and drama [women] make up just four in every 10 participants' and that 'only four in every 10 women on screen are aged over 40'.[39] This offers a formula for older women on prime time television across all genres: 4/10 < 4/10. You do the math. Such fractional visibility on network television underlines the work that continues to be necessary in producing, watching, analysing and critiquing representations of older women in popular culture. More to the point, it is still necessary to seek out those few representations of older and aged women that confront, expose and deploy the 'scandal of anachronism' rather than merely reiterating misogynist discourses regarding what older women can be or do. Mrs Brown, for all her clownish antics, is anchored to the conventions of propriety and family, always already interred in her wig and cardigan. However, more optimistically, Hilda and Gladys, Nan and Auntie Junie deploy their aberrant behaviours to queer normative regimes of youth and masculinity, demonstrating that *living*, even at their age, is still possible.

Notes

An earlier version of this chapter was presented at *Console-ing Passions: International Conference on Television, Audio, Video, New Media and Feminism* (19–20 July 2012), Suffolk University, Boston.

1. Simone de Beauvoir, *Old Age* (London: Penguin, 1972), p. 10.
2. Ruth Shade, 'Take My Mother-in-Law: "Old Bags", Comedy and the Sociocultural Construction of the Older Woman,' *Comedy Studies*, 1:1 (2010), pp. 71–83.
3. Patricia Mellencamp, 'From Anxiety to Equanimity: Crisis and Generational Continuity on TV, at the Movies, in Life, in Death,' in *Figuring Age: Women, Bodies Generations*, ed. Kathleen Woodward (Bloomington and Indianapolis: Indiana University Press, 1999), p. 316; see also Patricia Mellencamp, *High Anxiety: Catastrophe, Scandal, Age, and Comedy* (Bloomington and Indianapolis: Indiana University Press, 1992), pp. 279–309.
4. Brian Lowry, 'An Enchanting Six-part Series about Lost Love, Missed Opportunities and Second Chances,' *Variety* (4 September 2013), available at http://variety.com/2013/tv/reviews/tv-review-last-tango-in-halifax-1200597888/ (Accessed 6 September 2013).
5. Andrew Blaikie, *Aging and Popular Culture* (Cambridge: Cambridge University Press, 1999), p. 97.
6. The final episode of the series appeared to acknowledge this; after Victor Meldrew's death his wife Margaret seems to take on some of his outrage, implying that she has now become a protagonist in her own comedy drama.
7. Jasper Copping, '*Last of the Summer Wine* Tops Repeat Charts with Ten Days of Television,' *Daily Telegraph* (6 April 2013), available at http://www.telegraph.co.uk/culture/tvandradio/9976718/Last-of-the-Summer-Wine-tops-repeats-chart-with-ten-days-of-television.html (Accessed 10th June 2013).
8. Frances Gray, *Women and Laughter* (Charlottesville: University Press of Virginia, 1994), pp. 85–86.
9. Judith Halberstam, *Female Masculinity* (Durham and London: Duke University Press, 1998).
10. See Robert C Allen, *Horrible Prettiness: Burlesque and American Culture* (Chapel Hill and London: University of North Carolina Press, 1991), pp. 165–178; Henry Jenkins, *What Made Pistachio Nuts: Early Sound Comedy and the Vaudeville Aesthetic* (New York: Columbia University Press, 1992), pp. 59–95; Oliver Double, *Britain Had Talent: A History of Variety Theatre* (London: Palgrave Macmillan, 2012).
11. Margaret Montgomerie, '"Mischief and Monstrosity": *Little Britain* and Disability,' in *Reading Little Britain: Comedy Matters on Contemporary Television*, ed. Sharon Lockyer (London: I B Tauris, 2010), p. 124.
12. Ian Mowatt, 'Analysing *Little Britain* as a Sketch Show,' in *Reading Little Britain: Comedy Matters on Contemporary Television*, ed. Sharon Lockyer (London: I.B. Tauris, 2010), p. 20.
13. Mowatt, pp. 20–21.
14. Geoff King, *Film Comedy* (London and New York: Wallflower Press, 2002), p. 141.

15. See Carole-Ann Tyler, 'Boys Will Be Girls: Drag and Transvestic Fetishism,' in *Camp: Queer Aesthetics and the Performing Subject – A Reader*, ed. Fabio Cleto (Edinburgh: Edinburgh University Press, 1999), pp. 367–392.

16. I am grateful to Imelda Whelehan for this acute observation.

17. Elizabeth Abele, 'Becoming a Better Man as a Woman: The Transgendered Fantasy in 1980–1990s Popular Films,' *Scope: An Online Journal of Film Studies*, 21 (October 2011), p. 4.

18. Marjorie Garber, *Vested Interests: Cross-Dressing and Cultural Anxiety* (London: Penguin, 1992), p. 37, p. 79.

19. For an overview of transvestism and the grotesque in British comedy see Peter Hutchings, 'Welcome to Royston Vasey: Grotesque Bodies and the Horror of Comedy in *The League of Gentlemen*,' *Intensities*, 4 (December 2007), available at http://intensities.org/Issues/Intensities_four.htm (Accessed 10th June 2013).

20. Laraine Porter, 'Tarts, Tampons and Tyrants: Women and Representation in British Comedy,' in *Because I Tell a Joke or Two: Comedy, Politics and Social Difference*, ed. Stephen Wagg (London: Routledge, 1998), p. 90.

21. Ibid., pp. 88–89.

22. Danny La Rue is the odd one out in this list as his long career on stage and television involved 'passing' as a glamorous woman in a drag act that became normalised as family entertainment on British television; although his performance referenced comedy it more closely adhered to the tradition of female showstoppers such as Judy Garland, whom he impersonated as part of his act. A regular on the annual *Royal Variety Performance*, La Rue was an outstanding example of a drag artiste; his closest contemporary equivalent is the American drag queen RuPaul.

23. See Beverley Skeggs' account of femininity as implicitly white, middle class and heterosexual, in *Formations of Class and Gender* (London: Sage, 1997).

24. Both Enfield and Burke have tended to play grotesques throughout their comedy work. A character sketch called 'Little Brother' from *Harry Enfield's Television Programme* (BBC, 1990–1992) was elaborated for *Harry Enfield and Chums* into the Kevin and Perry sketches with Enfield as spotty, sulky teenager Kevin and Kathy Burke cross-dressing as his sidekick Perry. Burke also partnered Enfield in the long-running Wayne and Waynetta Slob character sketch, which depicted a 'white trash' working-class couple. All of these character sketches satirize British society, working through categories of class, gender and age.

25. 'Don't you just love being in control?' was the catchphrase of a series of commercials for British Gas in the 1990s featuring British celebrities, including Enfield; this sketch with a gas man appears to directly parody that role.

26. Mary Russo, 'Aging and the Scandal of Anachronism,' in *Figuring Age: Women, Bodies Generations*, ed. Kathleen Woodward (Bloomington and Indianapolis: Indiana University Press, 1999), p. 21.

27. Ibid., p. 21.

28. Ibid., p. 27.

29. Nelly Quemener, 'Mockery or Fantasy? Transvestite Characters, Cross-dressing and Subaltern Sexualities in Sketches in French Talk Shows,' *Sexualities*, 15:1 (2011), p. 86.

30. Ibid., p. 85.
31. Ibid., p. 88.
32. Roberta Mock argues that Burke embodies 'heteroqueerness' in *Gimme Gimme Gimme* in her essay 'Heteroqueer Ladies: Some Performative Transactions between Gay Men and Heterosexual Women,' *Feminist Review*, 75 (2003), p. 32.
33. Skeggs, p. 99.
34. Gwen Raaberg, 'Views from "The Other Side": Theorizing Age and Difference in Yvonne Rainer's *Privilege*,' *Women's Studies Quarterly*, 30:1–2 (Spring 2002), p. 124.
35. Yvonne Rainer, referring to her film work, cited in Erin Brannigan, 'Great Directors: Yvonne Rainer,' *Senses of Cinema*, 27 (July 2003), available at http://sensesofcinema.com/2003/great-directors/rainer/#b1 (Accessed 10th June 2013).
36. Tate's Nan character has more recently been revived for an appearance in the BBC's *Comic Relief* (2013) and a new sitcom series, *Catherine Tate's Nan* (BBC 2014).
37. The show has been an overnight success with a lengthy gestation; O'Carroll's Mrs Brown was the basis for a comedy series on Irish national radio in the early 1990s, as well as novels, straight to DVD films and a series of stage shows, before being commissioned by the BBC in 2009. In September 2013 a *Mrs Brown's Boys* movie was being filmed in Dublin. See Donal O'Donaghue, 'The Life of Brown,' *RTE Guide* (21 December 2013–3 January 2014), pp. 30–31.
38. See Gray, chapter 4, 'On the Halls: Ms/Readings and Negotiations,' pp. 115–132.
39. Cited in Deborah Jermyn, 'Past Their Prime Time?: Women, Ageing and Absence on British Factual Television,' *Critical Studies in Television*, 8:1 (Spring 2013), p. 76.

11
Silence Isn't Golden, Girls: The Cross-Generational Comedy of 'America's Grandma', Betty White

Elizabeth Rawitsch

'I have a grandma', declare seven young men and women in a series of direct addresses to the camera. 'How', they ask, 'would *you* feel if your grandma was forced against her will to work at 88?' The grandchildren repeat the age '88' four times for emphasis. 'It's happening today, and you're condoning it, America', they chide. Produced in September 2010 and widely circulated on the Internet,[1] the mock public service announcement comically campaigned to 'stop unfair labour practices against Betty White', the then-octogenarian actress best known for appearing as Sue Ann Nivens in the *Mary Tyler Moore Show* (1970–1977) and Rose Nylund in *The Golden Girls* (1985–1992). White had recently enjoyed a late-career resurgence of popularity: between 2009 and 2010 alone, she earned praise for her performance in *The Proposal* (Fletcher, 2009),[2] appeared in what *USA Today* named as the most popular advertisement of Super Bowl 2010,[3] became the oldest person to ever host the sketch comedy show *Saturday Night Live* (1975–), costarred in TV Land's first original sitcom *Hot in Cleveland* (2010–), and made numerous cameo appearances on shows ranging from *30 Rock* (2006–2013) to *The Middle* (2009–) to *Community* (2009–). 'Leave Betty White alone', the representative grandchildren plead to America. 'She's gonna break a hip'.

The viral video is a comedic love letter to one of America's cultural icons, a performer with, it would seem, uniquely cross-generational appeal: White can be read as the grandmother in the repeated declaration 'I have a grandma': a cross section of America's youth has implicitly adopted her. Yet both her late-career comeback and her embrace by a younger audience are surprising given the supposed 'girling' of popular culture that was identified in postfeminist discourse at the very moment when White once again entered the public eye.[4] White's recent resurgence seems to imply that tweens and teens venerate their

172

elders – or at least some of their elders – even if that admiration is masked in irony.

While generational tension may be a hallmark of postfeminism (as the next section will explore), cross-generational respect has a more complicated relationship with contemporary feminism. Using White as a case study, this chapter interrogates the ways in which White sought to foster a cross-generational address in her late-career star persona, particularly her participation in – and intentional slippage between – traditional and contemporary grandmother archetypes. I will attempt to identify why White's popularity resurged at that particular moment in history – 2010 – by examining how the global economic recession of 2008 affected generational politics. This chapter explores the extent to which audiences are invited to laugh with White and the extent they are invited to laugh at her in order to ask: 'Can the figure of the eternally young older person ever be taken seriously?'

Down with the kids? Postfeminism and generational conflict

Defining postfeminism in 2007, Yvonne Tasker and Diane Negra argued that popular culture was distinctly preoccupied with the temporal: 'Women's lives are regularly conceived of as time starved; women themselves are overworked, rushed, harassed, subjected to their "biological clocks" and so on to such a degree that female adulthood is defined as a state of chronic temporal crisis.'[5] Youth consequently becomes fetishised to the point that, 'To some extent, girlhood is imagined within postfeminist culture as being for everyone; that is, girlhood offers a fantasy of transcendence and evasion, a respite from other areas of experience.'[6] The 'girling' of popular culture supposedly meant that old age disappeared into the background, losing visibility. As Sadie Wearing put it, 'It seems too obvious to state, but younger women are not encouraged in these discourses to "aspire" to age. To put this slightly differently, if chronological boundaries are indeed blurring, this happens in only one direction.'[7]

A distinct separation between generations of women occurs, because 'as postfeminism has raised the premium on youthfulness, it has installed an image of feminism as "old" (and by extension moribund)'.[8] Postfeminism imagines – and thereby creates – a conflict between the contemporary and feminism. As Negra argues, 'By caricaturing, distorting, and (often willfully) misunderstanding the political and social goals of feminism as rigid, serious, anti-sex and romance, difficult and extremist, in contrast, postfeminism offers the pleasure and comfort of (re)claiming an identity uncomplicated by gender politics, postmodernism, or institutional critique.'[9] This reclamation leads to the rejection of feminism and, by implication, the previous generation of women who championed it. Young women are encouraged to distance and distinguish themselves from their elders.

Yet Negra was already beginning to revise her position on postfeminism by 2009: 'In recent years an aggressively postfeminist representational culture has intensified the sexual visibility of midlife women. Grandmothers can now be attributed with "grey glamour", romantic comedy heroines are played by females in their late 30s and early 40s, and...a variety of slang terms have emerged in popular speech to designate sexually desirable mothers.'[10] Joel Gwynne and Sharron Hinchliff further document this increased sexualisation of ageing bodies in their respective chapters in this volume. Yet the phrase 'grey glamour' has never been used to describe White, whose character in *Hot in Cleveland* sports a new bedazzled tracksuit every episode. Why, therefore, did America turn (or return) to her? And does it suggest that comedy allows for a wider range of representations of older women?

Playing the generation game: Betty White's evolving star persona

There is a good deal of precedent within American popular culture for the late-career star persona of the actress who became 'America's Grandma'. While the representation of grandmotherhood in film and television has varied by genre and over time, it tends to fall within a spectrum between traditional grandmother figures, whose primary purpose in life is showering affection, advice, and material goods on those closest to them, and youthful granny figures who stubbornly refuse to act their age. Esther Walton in *The Waltons* (1972–1981) is a traditional (and nostalgic) grandmother figure, selflessly attending to the needs of her small community's younger generations during the Great Depression and World War II. Youthful granny figures, on the other hand, like Rosie in *The Wedding Singer* (Coraci, 1998), put their agency to their own benefit, boldly and crassly speaking as they please. However, the youthful granny's participation in popular culture tends to win her the respect of the younger generation. Performing the song 'Rapper's Delight' at her anniversary party, Rosie 'the rapping granny' quickly draws an audience of dancing youngsters who clap along with her to the rhythm. As the *Los Angeles Times* laments, making the elderly 'talk about sex or swear, or take drugs, or use language they're the wrong age to use is an easy laugh that contemporary comedy writers do not seem to be able to resist or improve upon, or think up alternatives to. (In an earlier generation, it was hilarious enough just to put them on a motorcycle or a surfboard.)'[11] These grandmother archetypes thereby reinforce ideas of age-appropriate behaviour and patriarchally acceptable constructions of womanhood even as they are transgressed, once again raising the question of whether these figures are being laughed with or laughed at. Yet elderly characters rarely fall into one category exclusively. For example, Queen Clarisse Renaldi, the uptight regal grandmother in *The Princess Diaries* (Marshall, 2001) and *The Princess Diaries 2: The Royal Engagement* (Marshall, 2004), learns over the course of the films to embrace her granddaughter's culture – including slang phrases such as 'shut up' – as she learns to embrace her granddaughter. Age defers to youth, while youth seems to defer to only the eternally young.

A tension between the traditional and the contemporary has been a part of White's star persona from the very beginning. In *The Mary Tyler Moore Show*, Sue Ann Nivens – TV station WJM's 'Happy Homemaker' – acted cloyingly sweet while in front of the camera despite being sardonic and man-hungry behind it. In *The Golden Girls*, Rose Nylund was genuinely sweet, but markedly naïve, innocently misunderstanding conversations about sex and popular culture and unknowingly speaking in double entendre. White's most recent sitcom role arguably synthesises the characters that had made her famous: in *Hot in Cleveland*, landlady Elka Ostrovsky looks like a sweet old woman, but she abuses illegal substances, chases after multiple men, and speaks in brutally frank and colourful language, frequently comparing the other, younger characters to prostitutes. Like the character of Sofia Petrillo in *The Golden Girls,* Elka no longer has an internal censor telling her what is and is not appropriate conversation.[12] Unlike Sofia, however, she has not developed this uninhibited condition from a stroke. Elka is just naturally brassy. She is not just youthful; she is youthfully lewd.

According to Richard Dyer's seminal work on film stardom, a star persona 'consists both of what we normally refer to as his or her "image", made up of screen roles and obviously stage-managed public appearances and also of images of the manufacture of that "image" and of the real person who is the site or occasion of it. Each element is complex and contradictory, and the star is all of it taken together'.[13] The tension at the heart of stardom is the pull between the ordinary and the extraordinary and between the public and the private. White predictably participates in this discourse. She was a star dating back to the early days of television, pioneering the live variety show *Hollywood on Television* (1949–1953), and she has been the recipient of the Life Achievement Award from the Screen Actors Guild as well as seven Emmy Awards. Yet White's frequent guest appearances on talk shows and fervent animal rights activism have earned her the reputation as an approachable person. White attributes this reputation to television, which 'more than any other medium, invites informality...which I think is great. At the market, for example, people go by and say, "Hi, Betty" in passing...as you would to anyone who has been visiting your house for years.'[14] As James Bennett has noted regarding television fame, 'Television's emphasis on intimacy is therefore connected to its domestic viewing situation and the way in which it delivers its performers into the milieu of everyday life via the regularity and repetition of the schedule.'[15] White's first-name basis with fans suggests that perceptions of authenticity are at the heart of her successfully integrated star persona: the person on screen and the person off screen are perceived to be the same.

Yet White's category of celebrity is hard to classify, because she is not just a sitcom star: she is also a comedian, a sketch comedy artist, a variety performer, a chat show host and guest, a film actor, and – as will be discussed in depth in a moment – an Internet phenomenon. Indeed, when casting her role on *The Mary Tyler Moore Show*, the showrunners had reportedly described Sue Ann as a 'Betty White type',[16] demonstrating that White's star persona was already well established by her live sitcom *Life With Elizabeth* (1952–1955) and frequent appearances on the game show *Password* (1961–1975) long before landing the role that brought her fame. Although specifically discussing presenters and personalities, Bennett claims that intertextual circulation of this sort is crucial to the maintenance of stardom: 'In this regard Twitter's and other social media platforms' intertextual circulation of a personality's image, such as blogs, LastFM, MySpace and Facebook, only differs insofar as it promises the revelation of the "authentic" self via a more immediate, intimate connection with audiences than other forms of intertextual coverage, such as the controlled PR interview or even the uncontrolled scandal press story.'[17] White's late-career resurgence – which, unlike her early stardom, occurred during the prevalence of social media – made full use of the Internet to reach diverse audiences, particularly young ones, positioning White as a youthful figure unexpectedly conversant in current slang, tween culture, and the latest technology.

Perhaps the best proof that White reached and was embraced by a multigenerational audience was her appearance on *Saturday Night Live* (hereafter *SNL*). The selection of White as a host was publically credited to a Facebook campaign started by a 29-year-old that went on to gather over half a million people demanding 'Betty White for *SNL* (please?)!'[18] While the campaign may have conceivably begun or gained momentum as a joke or perceived absurdity (because the program had not featured an octogenarian host since Miskel Spillman in 1977),[19] White's guest appearance on *SNL* drew the biggest viewing figures for the program since November 2008 – a full year and a half earlier – when Ben Affleck hosted. White gratefully acknowledged her debt to the Facebook generation in her opening monologue:

> When I first heard about the campaign to get me to host *Saturday Night Live*, I didn't know what Facebook was. And, now that I do know what it is, I have to say it sounds like a huge waste of time. I would never say that people on it are losers, but that's only because I'm polite. People say, 'but, Betty, Facebook is a great way to communicate with old friends.' Well, at my age if I want to connect with old friends, I need an Ouija board. Needless to say, we didn't have Facebook when I was growing up. We had Phonebook, but you wouldn't waste an afternoon on it. Facebook just sounds like a drag. In my day, seeing pictures of people's vacations was considered a punishment. And when we were kids, we didn't say we were single. We were just kids. It was weird if you *weren't* single. Yes, we had 'poking', but it wasn't something you did on a computer. It was something you did on a hayride ... under a blanket.

Although White's monologue claims ignorance regarding Facebook – an ignorance that was likely genuine as she did not own a computer at the time[20] – she demonstrates an awareness of and familiarity with its various features. Her emphasis on social media has an explicit cross-generational address, one which draws comparisons between how things were in 'her day' and 'today': while she expresses concerns about teenage sexuality, she hints that her own teenage years may not have been so different, just less public. White's willingness to playfully mock herself – to go along with appearing on *SNL* in the first place – feeds back in to the perceived 'authenticity' of her affable star persona. Conceding to her possible outdatedness simultaneously speaks to tech-savvy youths *and* older technophobes; White's old-fashionedness paradoxically makes her of the moment.

The cross-generational acceptance of White's cultural icon status is perhaps best exemplified by an endorsement from the ultimate tween icon: then-sixteen-year-old Justin Bieber. The rise of the 'tween' – a marketing demographic comprised of 8- to 12-year-olds – had occurred in tandem with the perceived 'girling' of popular culture and appeared to confirm a cultural focus on and celebration of youth above age.[21] Following the *SNL* broadcast, Bieber sent a tweet reading simply 'BETTY WHITE RULES', which was heavily retweeted by his millions of young followers. White then returned the favour by referencing Bieber in *Hot in Cleveland* ('Good Luck Faking the Goiter', 11 August 2010): Elka and Will, the son of one of her tenants (played by Disney tween heartthrob Joe Jonas), discuss the contents of Elka's iPod. When Will expresses surprise at the heavy volume of Bieber songs, Elka expresses surprise in return: 'Really? I love her!' she exclaims. Will smiles and shakes his head. 'He's a guy', he patiently explains. 'They keep saying that', Elka replies, 'but I'm not buying it.'

Just as in her *SNL* monologue, the joke is that White's character, an old woman, is familiar with current technology: in this case, iPods. She also listens to contemporary pop music – the kind associated with tweens – rather than to music from her own generation. While she calls Bieber female rather than male, the punchline is that she does so intentionally. In fact, her cultural capital is heightened, because the mislabelling fits into a wider youth-oriented discourse of jokes at the expense of Bieber's masculinity and fringed haircut, particularly the viral Tumblr site 'Lesbians Who Look Like Justin Bieber', the subtitle to which asks, 'I mean you get it, right?' and which was featured in major media outlets from *NY Magazine* to *GQ* in March 2010 only months before the *Hot in Cleveland* episode aired.[22] By misidentifying Bieber's sex, White's character is very much 'in' on tween pop culture.

However, it remains important to acknowledge how much of White's star persona is constructed by others: was it White's decision to capitalise on Bieber's fandom and fan base? Or, if left to White, would this scene have ended with the error rather than the knowing follow-up? It was, after all, ostensibly audience demand that prompted White's *SNL* booking. And the writers of *SNL* likely crafted – or assisted in crafting – her jokes about Facebook, just as the writers of *Hot in Cleveland* likely scripted her joke about Bieber. The Bieber joke might never have been included if Bieber had not been so public about admiring White. Which aspects of White's star persona are her decision and which parts are demanded by others is hard to discern. Take, for instance, how White initially resisted filming a promotional video for *The Proposal* in which she blurts (bleeped) profanities and flips the bird at co-actor Ryan Reynolds: 'I said, "I don't want to do that. What does that have to do with our nice little romantic comedy?"'[23] The *Washington Post* speculated that

White relented because 'the sitcom veteran is savvy enough to get the joke.'[24] While her late-career star persona serves the interests of studios and networks – generating publicity, ticket sales, and ratings – it also, ultimately, benefits White, who is able to continue performing at an age when most of her peers have retired.

If White frequently acquiesces to the demands of others, she also regularly capitalises on her late-career fame. She has several lines of officially licensed merchandise, from a pin-up calendar to a comic book documenting her life story. These products appear to be targeted at the younger, technophilic generation. For example, continuing her engagement with discourses of pop music, she released a collection of hooded sweatshirts with built-in headphones in August 2010, the proceeds from which benefited one of White's favourite charities, the Morris Animal Foundation.[25] The sweatshirt designs contained screen prints of her face in pop art style, with slogans ranging from 'White Heat' to 'Long Live the Queen'. Simultaneously self-promoting and self-effacing, White's ventures into merchandising further support the idea that the actress is 'genuinely' down to earth. She even attended the 2010 MTV Movie Awards when she was nominated for 'Best WTF Moment' for her performance in *The Proposal*, and her onstage dancing with Sandra Bullock at the 2010 Teen Choice Awards generated riotous laughter and applause from the audience. Bullock, in response, described her co-star from the podium as 'the eternally youthful, supercool, forever-teen'.

The content of White's comedy – youth focussed, tech savvy, and often rude – is also sexually suggestive. For example, her stock answer to the question 'is there anything you haven't done in your career that you would still like to do?' is 'Robert Redford'.[26] White is often marketed in ironically sexualised terms as a result. In October 2010, she was featured on the cover of *Parade* magazine wearing an orange cardigan, a double string of pearls, and felt tiger ears. The headline ran: 'Who Are You Calling a Cougar?',[27] a statement that could be read both as a denial of her sexual proclivities – White assured readers that she prefers older men – and as a joke, because a woman of White's age is presumably considered sexually unattractive (and inactive). 'I have a suspicion that the definition of "crazy" in show business is a woman who keeps talking even after no one wants to fuck her anymore', joked former *SNL* head writer Tina Fey. 'The only person I can think of that has escaped the "crazy" moniker is Betty White, which, obviously, is because people still want to have sex with her.'[28] Fey's sarcasm implies the opposite: White's sexual undesirability is what makes her an exception to show business' gender bias. Indeed, the terms used to describe White in the popular press – 'adorable', 'cute', 'sweet', and so on[29] – suggest that she is often infantilised rather than sexualised. Not quite falling under the rubric of 'girling', this kind of language undercuts the potential sexualisation of the older person, allowing younger generations to laugh off age-inappropriate comments and behaviour.

Within the context of postfeminist culture, calling White 'America's Grandma' is, consequently, a loaded honorific: one that implies conformity to age-appropriate gender roles. In her personal life, White came to grandmotherhood through non-traditional means: in 1963, she married game show host Allen Ludden, who had three children from his previous marriage, and those children went on to have children of their own. White never gave birth herself: 'Barbara Walters once asked me if I ever had desired to have a child. The answer is, I never did think about it.'[30] Popular culture seems determined, however, to pigeonhole White as a traditional wife, mother, and grandmother. Her appearance on *SNL* fell on Mother's Day, which producer Lorne Michaels deemed appropriate because 'she's the mother of us all in comedy.'[31] It is White's comic lineage – her star persona – that allows her to be embraced (or re-embraced) across generations as a cultural icon.

Boom(er)s and busts: recession-era America and cross-generational comedy

The question remains, however, 'why Betty White, and why then?' As White said when people congratulated her on her comeback, 'Thanks, guys, but I really haven't been away. I've been working steadily for the past sixty-three years.'[32] So why did White's late-career resurgence happen in 2010? What conditions allowed her to rise to prominence so quickly?

One factor is *Golden Girls* nostalgia. Originally scheduled on Saturdays at 9 p.m., the show was touted as family viewing, something that multiple generations could enjoy together. As White writes in *Here We Go Again* (1995), one of her two autobiographies:

> What came as a big surprise to all concerned was the way *Golden Girls* cut across all the demographic lines. Over half of our mail came from kids, but the twenty-, thirty-, and forty-something and beyond were well represented…. How was our show able to reach all the age groups? Perhaps because we weren't specifically aiming at any one of them, but mainly, I think, because we were truly funny.[33]

According to White, *Golden Girls* succeeded as a family show precisely because it was not trying to reach any one demographic. Its humour was universal and, as a result, it was timeless.

Similarly, nostalgia for *Golden Girls* in 2010 was not limited to people who saw the show in its original run from 1985 to 1992. In 1997 *Golden Girls* entered syndication through Buena Vista Television and has been on the air continuously ever since: first on Lifetime, then on Hallmark, We TV, TV Land and Logo.[34] Airing seven times each weekday, the Lifetime reruns boasted an audience of 13 million in 2003; the 11 p.m. timeslot attracted as many women as MTV in the 18–34 age group.[35] By 2005, Lifetime was airing *Golden Girls* only five times a day, but its audience averaged 16 million people.[36] Not only did multiple generations watch *The Golden Girls* when it was originally on the air, but multiple generations have now grown up with White in syndication. *The Golden Girls* remains what White is best known for; when she provided her resume in her *SNL* monologue, the applause began after she referenced *Golden Girls*, not her early television work or *Mary Tyler Moore*. Following the death of Rue McClanahan in June 2010, White became the last surviving member of the core *Golden Girls* cast, meaning that nostalgia for the show in general began to focus on her specifically. *Hot in Cleveland* participates in this nostalgia by drawing on *Golden Girls* as a source text; both shows focus on four women of a certain age who live together and share their hopes and dreams around the kitchen table, but White now plays the foul-mouthed character from an older generation.

It is also possible, however, that White's resurgence of popularity is linked more generally to the changing role of the grandparent within American culture. According to a poll taken by the American Association of Retired People in March 2010 on how the economic recession that followed the semi-collapse of the global financial system in 2007–2008 affected the living conditions of adults aged 50-plus, more than one in ten said they lived with their grandchildren or children.[37] Put another way, 16 per cent of the population was living in a multigenerational household, which was the highest that figure had been in half a century.[38] It also meant that grandparents were taking on an increasingly parental role, filling in as caregivers. While America's youth were metaphorically growing up with White and the other *Golden Girls*, census data indicates that 41 per cent of children living with a grandparent were being raised by that grandparent.[39] Cultural exchanges between the two generations became increasingly possible; the elderly could understand tween humour, and tweens could find humour in the elderly. Cross-generational comedy had greater potential to strike a chord in recession

America than it would have had just five years previously. There was an increased likelihood that all the generations involved would get the joke.

Comedy centring on old people saying dirty things was also on the rise in American society in 2010. For example, Abe Vigoda, White's co-star in the 2010 Super Bowl commercial for Snickers, became the subject of a viral Internet site that tracked whether the octogenarian actor was alive or dead in real time.[40] The Twitter feed @shitmydadsays, in which 29-year-old Justin Halpern broadcast comically frank statements made by his 74-year-old father Samuel, had over two million followers and was in the process of being adapted into the sitcom *$h*! My Dad Says* (2010) starring William Shatner. As Justin told *The Los Angeles Times*, his father 'says the things that [other people] are thinking but they don't say because there are consequences for saying things like that.... You stand the chance of alienating several family members. My dad, he's earned the right to say that.'[41] In other words, frankness becomes acceptable coming from a mature figure. It also implicitly draws upon youthful fantasies: being able to speak your mind no matter the consequences. Older comedians 'hold out the promise that you might grow up to be the granny or gramps the yet-unknown whippersnappers of the future will regard as something better than invisible, not to mention disposable.'[42] Indeed, with the ageing of the baby-boomer generation and their parents, there was and remains growing concern about what end-of-life care in America will entail in years to come. Older cultural icons offered hope that the golden years would indeed be golden. But to what extent was America laughing with these figures, and to what extent was it laughing at them?

Patricia Mellencamp has suggested that 'chronological age...is television and the nation's gendered obsession.'[43] Chronological age signifies the expectation of age-appropriate behaviour: a person in his or her 50s should not seek to relive their childhood, for example. Sadie Wearing notes that the 'girling' of the 'older woman' in *Something's Gotta Give* (Meyers, 2003) implies that 'there is something a little uncomfortable (even uncanny) about the appellation of "girl" – in terms of both gender and generation – to a woman in her fifties.'[44] Transgressing generations and not acting one's age is 'not only inappropriate but dangerous, exposing the female subject, especially, to ridicule, contempt, pity and scorn – the scandal of anachronism.'[45]

The youthful older person does not generally exhibit what American society deems to be age-appropriate behaviour, and that scandal is frequently mitigated with humour. To return to the example of *SNL*, in describing the comedians who created girl characters such as Lily Tomlin's Edith Ann, Gilda Radner's Judy Miller and Molly Shannon's Mary Catherine Gallagher, Kathleen Sweeney argues that 'Women playing loopy little girls allows for an outrageous bacchanal of verbiage and body language not allowed to "ladies" or "women", especially skinny white ones, who must tone themselves down, who cannot easily rant and rave without censure.'[46] In other words, comedy is a safe outlet for experimenting with the transgression of patriarchal constructions of age-appropriate behaviour. The question of who is laughing at whom is therefore complicated. As Brett Mills notes, 'It's problematic to always see the *with* and *at* dichotomy as mutually exclusive, which is how it's normally discussed.'[47] While some audiences are laughing at White, their laughter may have different natures: recognition, disgust, admiration and so on. White may also be simultaneously laughing with and/ or at her audiences.

The generational separation that existed between feminism and post-feminism is superseded by White's cross-generational address, even if White never acknowledges those discourses explicitly. While she concedes that she is part of an older, potentially outdated generation, she makes few attempts at age passing: 'I had my eyes done in 1976 and have let nature take its course ever since. As for my hair, I have no idea what colour it really is, and I never intend to find out.'[48] Her appearance is age appropriate – displaying wrinkles and hair so blonde that it looks white – even if her behaviour is youthful. Indeed, it is through her youthful behaviour that younger generations are invited to identify with her, even if they are not encouraged to aspire to age. White's generation may be outdated, but it is relatable, and White is perceived as making concerted efforts to keep in touch via technology and the music scene. Perhaps these efforts are why, as Vigoda, Shatner, and Halpern receded from the public eye, White's cultural moment continued.

'I'm just luckier than [my father] was, in that there is no retirement age stipulation in my line of work', White says. 'I hope to hang around playing *something* as long as I am able to stand up.'[49] Reflecting on the generation that came before her, White identifies progress and positive change. Looking ahead to the future, her message to the generations that succeed her is that age is what you make of it: 'I don't *feel* eighty-nine years old', she writes in her second autobiography. 'I simply *am* eighty-nine years old.'[50] By ignoring patriarchal constructions of age-appropriate behaviour and by participating in cross-generational conversation, White's late-career star persona offers the hope that all ages are golden.

Notes

1. 'Save Betty White PSA – Grandchildren Speak Out', written and directed by Keith Patterson, Hollywood Bubble (12 September 2010), available at http://www.hollywoodbubble.com/2010/09/save-betty-white-psa-grandchildren-speak-out (Accessed 3 September 2013).
2. See for example Wesley Morris, 'The Proposal,' *Boston Globe* (19 June 2009); Peter Rainer, 'Betty White the Only Good Part of the Movie "The Proposal,"' *Christian Science Monitor* (19 June 2009); Peter Travers, 'The Proposal,' *Rolling Stone* (18 June 2009).
3. Julia Schmalz, Rod Coddington, Christopher Kamsler, David Carrig, Leslie Smith Jr, and Rene Alston, '2010 USA TODAY Ad Meter[SM] Tracks Super Bowl XLIV Ads,' *USA Today* (15 February 2010).
4. See for example Diane Negra, *What a Girl Wants? Fantasizing the Reclamation of Self in Postfeminism* (London and New York: Routledge, 2009), p. 47.
5. Yvonne Tasker and Diane Negra, 'Introduction: Feminist Politics and Postfeminist Culture,' in *Interrogating Postfeminism: Gender and the Politics of Popular Culture*, ed. Yvonne Tasker and Diane Negra (Durham and London: Duke University Press, 2007), p. 10.
6. Tasker and Negra, 'Introduction,' pp. 18 and 12. Sarah Projansky further observes that postfeminism and the cultural obsession with girlhood follow a similar historical trajectory in 'Mass Magazine Cover Girls: Some Reflections on Postfeminist Girls and Postfeminism's Daughters,' in Tasker and Negra, pp. 40–72.
7. Sadie Wearing, 'Subjects of Rejuvenation: Aging in Postfeminist Culture,' in Tasker and Negra, p. 294.
8. Tasker and Negra, 'Introduction,' p. 11.
9. Negra, p. 2.
10. Negra, p. 70.
11. Robert Lloyd, 'Betty White Goes Gently into That "Saturday Night Live,"' *Los Angeles Times* (9 May 2010).
12. For more on *The Golden Girls* and the performance of age, see Rosie White's essay in this volume.
13. Richard Dyer, *Heavenly Bodies: Film Stars and Society* (London: Macmillan, 1986), p. 7. See also Richard Dyer, *Stars*, revised edition (London: BFI Publishing, 1979).
14. Betty White, *In Person* (New York: Doubleday, 1987), p. 13.
15. James Bennett, *Television Personalities: Stardom and the Small Screen* (London and New York: Routledge, 2011), p. 33.
16. Betty White, *Here We Go Again: My Life in Television* (New York: St. Martin's, 1995), p. 197.
17. Bennett, *Television Personalities*, p. 170.
18. The demographics of the Facebook group itself are difficult to confirm, but the *New York Times* assumes that the campaign was primarily youth-driven in Dave Itzkoff, 'Betty White Helps Boost Ratings of SNL' (9 May 2010).
19. Adding to speculations about the tongue-in-cheek nature of the Facebook group, its creator David Matthews confessed that he is not a White 'super fan' or 'even a big *SNL* watcher, but the idea "came up over the holidays" and

took hold' in Gary Levin, 'Live, from New York, It's .. Betty White Hosting "SNL,"' *USA Today* (12 March 2010).

20. Betty White, *If You Ask Me (And of Course You Won't)* (New York: Berkley Books, 2011), p. 243.

21. For more on tweens and popular culture, see Projansky, 'Mass Magazine Cover Girls'; and Melanie Kennedy, *Tweendom: Femininity and Celebrity in Tween Popular Culture* (London: I.B. Tauris, forthcoming).

22. Dannielle Owens-Reid, 'Lesbians Who Look Like Justin Bieber' (2 March 2010), available at http://lesbianswholooklikejustinbieber.tumblr.com (Accessed 3 September 2013); Chris Rovzar, 'Are You a Lesbian Who Looks Like Justin Bieber?,' *New York Magazine* (12 March 2010); Lauren Bans, 'Website of the Day: Lesbians Who Look Like Justin Bieber,' *GQ* (15 March 2010).

23. Jen Chaney, 'Betty White Talks About "The Proposal" and Breaking Out of the "Golden Girls" Mold,' *Washington Post* (19 June 2009). See 'Sandra Bullock and Ryan Reynolds: Behind the Scenes of *The Proposal*,' *Funny or Die* (15 May 2009), available at http://www.funnyordie.com/videos/e8cdc3db45 (Accessed 3 September 2013).

24. Chaney, 'Betty White Talks about "The Proposal"'.

25. 'Made by Betty White,' HoodieBuddie (16 September 2010), available at http://www.hoodiebuddie.com/index.php/2010/09/made-by-betty-white (Accessed 3 September 2013).

26. White, *If You Ask Me*, p. 86.

27. 'Who Are You Calling a Cougar? Betty White Goes Wild,' *Parade* (31 October 2010). The promo for White's *SNL* appearance also questioned her status as a cougar.

28. Tina Fey, *Bossypants* (New York and London: Little, Brown, 2011), p. 271.

29. For example, see Amy Biancolli, 'Cliched "Proposal" Has Pleasant Stars,' *San Francisco Chronicle* (19 June 2009); Hank Stuever, 'The Age of Betty White: From "Mary Tyler Moore" to "SNL", A Timeless Tickler,' *Washington Post* (8 May 2010); Jonathan Storm, 'Betty White, Other Favorites in Funny, Fresh, "Hot in Cleveland,"' *Philadelphia Inquirer* (15 June 2010).

30. White, *If You Ask Me*, p. 247.

31. Levin, 'Live, from New York'.

32. White, *If You Ask Me*, p. 41.

33. White, *Here We Go Again*, p. 201.

34. For analysis of the reruns' contribution to White's resurgence as well as *Golden Girls*'s cult popularity in the LGBT community, see Dan Faltesek, 'Betty's Back? Remembering the Relevance of the Rerun in the Age of Social Media,' *FlowTV* (10 September 2010), available at http://flowtv.org/2010/09/bettys-back (Accessed 3 September 2013). DVD box sets are available for all seven seasons of *The Golden Girls*, and 'The Golden Girls: 25th Anniversary Complete Collection' box set was released in November 2010.

35. Stephen Battaglio, '"Golden Girls" Reruns Are a Hit with Younger Viewers,' *New York Daily News* (26 June 2003).

36. Julie Bosman, 'The Grandchildren of "The Golden Girls",' *New York Times* (8 November 2005).

37. Carole Fleck, 'Multigenerations under One Roof,' *AARP Bulletin* (May 2010).

38. Paul Taylor et al., 'The Return of the Multi-Generational Family Household,' Pew Research Center Report (18 March 2010); Daphne A. Lofquist,

'Multigenerational Households: 2009–2011,' *American Community Survey Briefs* (Washington: U.S. Department of Commerce, October 2012).

39. Gretchen Livingston and Kim Parker, 'Since the Start of the Recession, More Children Raised by Grandparents,' Pew Research Center Report (9 September 2010).
40. 'Abe Vigoda Is,' available at www.abevigoda.com (Accessed 3 September 2013).
41. Tricia Romano, 'Hipster Culture is Having a Senior Moment: Betty White, Samuel Halpern, "Breakfast at Sulimay's" NJ Lady – What's Old Is Cool,' *LA Times* (9 May 2010).
42. Lloyd, 'Betty White Goes Gently'.
43. Patricia Mellencamp, 'From Anxiety to Equanimity: Crisis and Generational Continuity on TV, at the Movies, in Life, in Death,' in *Figuring Age: Women, Bodies, Generations*, ed. Kathleen Woodward (Bloomington: Indiana University Press, 1999), p. 318.
44. Wearing, 'Subjects of Rejuvenation,' p. 277.
45. Mary Russo, 'Aging and the Scandal of Anachronism,' in Woodward p. 21.
46. Kathleen Sweeney, *Maiden USA: Girl Icons Come of Age* (New York: Peter Lang, 2008), p. 184.
47. Brett Mills, *Television Sitcom* (London: Palgrave Macmillan, 2005), p. 107.
48. White, *If You Ask Me*, p. 11.
49. White, *In Person*, p. 67.
50. White, *If You Ask Me*, p. 257.

12
The Older Mother in
One Born Every Minute

Georgina Ellen O'Brien Hill

Mothering and motherhood is the subject of close scrutiny in postfeminist media culture, and this scrutiny encourages women to monitor their performance as mothers against a class-inflected, neoliberal ideal. Discussing the 'powerful resonance' between postfeminism and neoliberalism, Rosalind Gill and Christine Scharff suggest that in this climate mothers are called upon to 'self-manage and self-discipline', to 'work on and transform the self, to regulate every aspect of their conduct, and to represent all their actions as freely chosen.'[1] Mothers are judged by 'type', from the aspirational, middle-class 'yummy mummy', to her opposite, the demonised working-class 'teen Mom' or 'pramface'. Current feminist attention, however, continues to focus upon the younger woman, the 'teen mom', or those women who aspire to youth. Yet, the number of babies born to mothers over 40 in the UK has more than quadrupled in the last three decades, a fact reflected by the intense debate (and often criticism) surrounding older mothers in a wide range of popular media texts.[2] While much important work has focussed upon the pregnant body and the vilification of the young, working-class mother, the older mother and her lived experience of labour and childbirth as explored through popular culture remains neglected. Addressing this omission, this chapter examines the experience of the older woman in the popular television programme *One Born Every Minute* (OBEM) (UK, 2010–).

OBEM is notable on British terrestrial television for exploring the experience of the older mother to an unprecedented extent, and for representing her in a positive light. Unlike the much-maligned figure depicted in the popular tabloid press, here the age of the older mother is a significant benefit when it comes to the physical and emotional challenge of labour and childbirth. Yet, the representation of this group of women is complex; while older women often enjoy a positive experience of labour and childbirth on the programme, a full range of scenarios are explored, suggesting a determination on behalf of the producers to reflect the lived experience of these women. So, we see a nervous 37-year-old first-time mother, confident second- and third-time 40-year-old mothers as well as those who have been traumatised by a previous birthing experience. But what unites all these older mothers and their experiences of childbirth is their evident investment in the 'good mother' myth as well as the ideals championed by the natural childbirth movement.

Part of the entertainment value of *OBEM* stems from the fact that it engages very deliberately with current intense debate surrounding when and how women should give birth. However, this debate is not new; back in 1933, Grantly Dick-Read published his controversial book, *Natural Childbirth*, for which he was largely condemned, but the central tenets of which are now ingrained in western understanding of labour and childbirth.[3] Initially intended to empower women by respecting their choices during labour (Dick-Read wrote that 'a woman's wishes must be considered'[4]), the natural childbirth movement can be interpreted as condemning women's right to choose pharmacological pain relief as a 'poor choice', leaving some women whose experience is medicalised with a sense of failure.[5] As Michelle Kealy and Pranee Liamputtong note, '[t]he ideology of natural childbirth does not adequately consider the needs of women for whom medical interventions such as Caesarean sections are essential. Such women may feel they have failed, or feel excluded and cheated within the natural birth discourse.'[6] In short, asking for pain relief and requiring medical intervention during labour can be deemed within this paradigm as 'a sign of weakness' or of 'giving in' to the pain.[7] Kealy and Llamputtong suggest that the discourse surrounding the natural childbirth movement intersects with the neoliberal ideal of the 'yummy-mummy', arguing that the cultural pressure that surrounds both is largely driven by western, white, privileged women.[8] They argue that these 'women in high-income countries value personal control' and are accustomed to feeling in control of every aspect of their lives, childbirth included.[9] Writing about class and this concept of remaining in control during labour, Ellen Lazarus suggests that 'choices and control are more limited for poor women, who are overwhelmed with social and economic problems'; these women, she notes, are usually young (on average nineteen years old when having their first child) and unmarried. Middle-class women now tend to be older (35 or over) when having their first child.[10] By featuring a significant number of women over 35, *OBEM* reflects the increasing demographic of older mothers in the UK and directly explores issues particularly pertinent to women in this age category (such as concerns over the health of the baby and IVF). But it is the issue of control during labour within the hospital setting that is at the heart of each episode of *OBEM*. Writers such as Sheila Kitzinger have long engaged with this issue, debating how women might remain empowered, caught as they are in the crossfire between the belief that women can be trained to 'work with pain' (the position of the natural childbirth movement) and the lived experience of many women of a painful and traumatic labour that requires medical intervention.[11] Blogs and online forums such as Mumsnet and Netmums host heated exchanges about pain relief, home births and medical intervention, while films such as *Knocked Up* (2007) and *What to Expect When You're Expecting* (2012) and television programmes such as the BBC's *Call the Midwife* (2012–) and *The Midwives* (2012–) all represent childbirth on the screen to an unprecedented extent, often during primetime viewing hours.[12]

As will be explored, the concept of remaining in control by 'coping' or 'working with' the pain intersects with the all-pervasive 'good mother' myth, a myth which, like the natural childbirth movement, is defined by age and class. In other words, older, middle-class women who are not subject to the same socio-economic pressures as their younger, working-class counterparts are more literate in the discourse of childbirth and therefore are heavily invested in the 'good mother' myth.[13] For the older mother, made acutely aware of the potential health risks to her baby engendered by her age, the pressure to be a 'good mother' does not begin when the baby is born; rather, it begins before conception. Pregnancy advice literature such as Annabel Karmel's *Eating for Two* (2012) warns that the time before conception and the first three months of pregnancy are amongst the most important for the foetus: 'Giving your baby the best start in life begins now, whether you are planning to become pregnant, have just found out the happy news, or have a bump well on the way.'[14] Thus, the 'good mother' adopts intensive mothering practices before her child is conceived; she prepares her body for conception, she eats well and exercises during pregnancy, has a 'natural birth' and breastfeeds her child. Looking beyond the early months, the 'good mother' is the one who stays at home to care for her children full time, or fits work commitments around her children (work commitments that also satisfy her intellectual appetite), provides nutritious meals, intellectual stimulation, educational play and consistent discipline. As already noted, both postfeminist and neoliberal sensibilities are marked by an 'emphasis on self-surveillance, monitoring and discipline', and the popularity of reality programmes focussing upon parenting skills such as *Supernanny* (2004–) and *Three Day Nanny* (2013–) demonstrates how closely popular culture judges older mothers against this ideal.[15]

Programmes such as *OBEM* reflect this culture of self-monitoring and self-discipline in relation to current thinking about pain relief, yet few critics have commented upon the link between age and the choices women make during labour. However, as one study has concluded, the 'good mother' ideal as it links to pain relief suggests that 'the experience of pain during childbirth...gives meaning to the transition to motherhood'; so, being prepared to suffer for your child during labour is regarded as a necessary rite of passage into motherhood, and all the older women featured in *OBEM* are seen to be engaging with this ideal.[16] However, before moving on to consider the programme in detail, I want to pause briefly to offer some context on pain relief within the hospital setting as showcased in the programme.

Pain relief during labour

As noted earlier, pain relief during labour is the subject of prolonged and heated debate. The Royal College of Midwives' (RCM) position statement on 'normal childbirth' expresses a deep concern with the 'medicalisation of labour', stating that 'midwives, doctors and childbearing women have become more dependent on technology in labour and birth' and that the 'Royal College of Midwives is concerned about the increasing rise in medical interventions in low risk births.'[17] Their 'Campaign for Normal Birth' addresses the dynamic of cultural expectations and the concept of control during labour, stating that:

> Women...are becoming more and more vocal in demanding what they want. The consumer attitudes that have become common in many areas of our society are spreading to the maternity services. ...This may in time result in a swing...towards undue deference towards what women want. But respecting women's wishes must never involve compromising standards of safety or good practice. What she says she wants may or may not be appropriate, depending on how much information she has and whether she is willing to consider the information given to her. So woman-centred care does not mean that you should subordinate your clinical judgement to her wishes. Instead, it means that she feels you are placing her interests first and that you are hearing her point of view.[18]

The woman described in this statement encapsulates the neoliberal free agent, and the RCM clearly finds this investment in the illusion of choice hugely problematic within the hospital setting. In a model of care which positions the midwife as the expert, the desires and wishes of the pregnant woman – though recognised as important – are not to be privileged. Yet, as *OBEM* reflects, this privileging of her desires and wishes is exactly what the older woman in particular expects and demands when she goes into labour. In her study of the midwifery-led model of care, Sonya Charles discusses the incongruence between consumer culture and the RCM's overemphasis on the importance of 'natural' childbirth, an incongruence which leads to a situation whereby women can be made to feel 'shame, failure, and isolation' should they want or require medical intervention of any kind.[19] Current World Health Organization (WHO) advice on pharmacological pain relief is worth mentioning here in detail for the cultural context that the RCM guidelines elide:

> Epidural and spinal analgesic techniques are the gold standards for pain relief during labour and delivery. However, they may be associated with an increased risk of instrumental vaginal delivery and Caesarean section. Hence, epidurals for labour pain should be provided only in settings that are equipped for instrumental delivery and emergency Caesarean section. Non-pharmacological interventions (e.g. immersion in water, relaxation, acupuncture, massage) appears to be safe and may be effective and applied in under-resourced settings and or at first stage of labour.[20]

In other words, technology in the West is available to help women with their pain, and according to the WHO there is no strong evidence that pharmacological pain relief should not be used in well-equipped hospitals. Women in developing countries simply do not have this option and may have to rely upon the non-pharmacological interventions that are championed by the RCM. *OBEM* reflects, and at times promotes, the RCM's midwifery-led model of a 'normal' birth and older women, who are literate in the discourse of childbirth and are engaged by the neoliberal ideal of choice, are shown to be heavily invested in this narrative. Indeed, they are shown to be able to make informed choices, and this ability helps to make them feel that they remain in control during labour, whether that choice is for a 'natural' birth or for pharmacological pain relief.

One Born Every Minute (UK)

OBEM combines the educational emphasis of the observational documentary with the entertainment value and sensationalism of reality television.[21] In her important study of motherhood and popular television, Rebecca Feasey comments that *OBEM* continues to prove popular with both audiences and critics alike, with viewing figures regularly reaching over three million and the production team (Dragonfly) securing the 'Best Documentary Series' BAFTA in 2010.[22] Channel 4 claims that the programme is 'unique' for being the 'first of its kind in capturing the many different perspectives within a room as labour and birth takes place'.[23] In keeping with the emphasis on the exposed and scrutinised body that we see in programmes such as *Embarrassing Bodies* (2007–) and with current media scrutiny of the pregnant body, the programme makes a spectacle of the female body in pain, and part of that spectacle stems from focussing on how the expectant mother is perceived to be coping (or failing to cope) with that pain.

The climax of each episode is the birth (the 'moneyshot to end all moneyshots', as Benji Wilson puts it) and the candid depiction of extreme pain as the baby is delivered.[24] Wilson's association of seminal ejaculation with the ejection of the baby (through the use of the term 'moneyshot') seems particularly apt; scenes of women in pain during labour are graphic, intimate and almost pornographic for the level of objectification of the body. This graphic nature is nowhere more apparent than the opening sequence (the format of which is the same for each season though the subjects of which change to reflect different hospital settings). The 'siren wail [of a woman screaming] which opens each episode [is] a promise of what's to come' and is accompanied by close up shots of bodies in extreme pain as well as more mundane scenes such as reception staff calmly answering the telephone.[25] As in pornography, the body becomes troublingly objectified; without the identifying feature of a face (which is often just out of shot), we see bodies cut open during Caesarean sections and though vaginas and anuses are largely obscured during the programme itself; in the opening scenes they are directly exposed to the camera at the moment of crowning (albeit during a very fast sequence). The imagery of the opening sequence is oddly similar to that of pornographic iconography; close up shots reveal faces and bodies experiencing intense physical exertion (teeth are gritted, limbs are strained, bodies are sweating and legs and feet are trembling violently); dubbed over these scenes and over the jolly title music are audio clips of women vocalising their experience through screams, grunts, moans and shouts. Yet whereas in mainstream pornography, pleasure is the precursor to the 'moneyshot', in *OBEM*, pain is the necessary precursor to the crowning 'moneyshot'. The use of light-hearted music to accompany these images implies that the pain being depicted on screen is natural and inevitable, and this naturalness and inevitability are nowhere more apparent than in the following case study of two older women who manage to 'laugh' through their labour.

'Laughter is the Best Medicine'

It is significant that the first episode of the first series of *OBEM* focusses upon an older woman, suggesting a determination on behalf of Dragonfly from the outset to reflect the increase of older mothers in the UK. Tracy (37) and Steve (41) already have three children; during an interview while still pregnant, Tracy explains that when her youngest child reached 11 years old, she decided she wanted another baby, and after a year of trying to conceive 'naturally', a round of IVF produced a pregnancy. Tracy's approach to labour is relaxed and calm; she explains that 'I haven't got a birth plan, and I'll do whatever I need to do' (1:1). As Tracy is shown inhaling Entonox, or gas and air, her midwife explains that 'getting the giggles' is often a side effect of the drug, and this sets the tone for the rest of her labour. Although she is, at times, clearly finding the contractions painful (she tells the midwife at one point: 'I'm struggling, sorry, they're becoming really, really painful'), she laughs and jokes with her husband and 18-year-old son throughout the experience (who also keep the tone light by playing a number of practical jokes while Tracy is having contractions, including blowing up a latex glove and tickling her with it). She jokes with her quietly horrified son: 'I'm laughing through it still. Look! Big smile, Liam!' The benefit of her previous experiences of labour, her attitude towards the pain, her technique of using humour to work with it rather than against it and her determination to stay calm are all presented as key to a relaxed labour and positive birth experience.

What is particularly striking about Tracy's story is the level of control that she appears to be enjoying, a concept that is crucial to a positive birth experience as we have already seen and one that is central to the neoliberal narrative of the empowered older mother. Yet as Ellen Lazarus notes, control is a subjective concept: for some women, control during labour means being, 'able to refuse what they consider to be intrusive technology'; for others, it means control of the self, 'not screaming or crying'; and for others still, it is about claiming the right to 'lose control,' to articulate their pain through screams and shouts.[26] Tracy has been warned that the labour ward is extremely busy, the implication being that she must be patient and wait her turn for the time and attention of the midwives on duty. Despite this implication, she instructs both husband and son to contact midwives at various points when she feels she needs assistance, being very clear that she wants an epidural. This is Tracy's fourth labour, and it is clear that this life experience has afforded her the confidence she needs to assert her will and to take command of the situation in a setting which tends to disempower women. When her midwife asks how she is feeling, Tracy politely instructs: 'Put it this way, I'm going to get you to examine me, and if I'm in proper established labour then I want an epidural.' However, when it becomes clear that an epidural is not going to be possible (because Tracy has progressed too far in her labour), she remains calm and in control, philosophising that 'I really don't mind. I thought I'll ask, and if it's there, it's there, but if it's too early or too late then so be it.' For Tracy, it seems to be the *feeling* of having the choice that is important to her sense of empowerment, rather than the choice itself. So, with the assistance of a TENS machine, gas and air and an episiotomy, Tracy's fourth child is delivered, and she immediately expresses a sense of achievement: 'Oh brilliant! Oh I've done it!' It is interesting that even within the context of the ideal 'natural' birth (i.e., no medical intervention at all), Tracy feels elated despite the fact that she gives birth with assistance, suggesting that while she is invested in this ideal, she is also able, to a certain extent, to adapt it.

However, Tracy's sense of achievement is not shared by another older mother who also laughs through the pain. In the seventh episode of Season 2, Hayley (37) is a first-time mother and describes her relationship with her husband (John, 40) as a 'fairytale'. Already step-mother to his two children from a previous relationship, Hayley views this pregnancy as a much longed-for opportunity to experience maternity, albeit later in life than she would have wished. The episode synopsis explains that for Hayley 'laughter is the best medicine' (though it is important to note that this is never a phrase Hayley uses).[27] Like Tracy, Hayley is confident in asserting her wishes regarding pain relief; when first admitted to hospital, she immediately asks about an epidural, and although she is represented as 'coping well' with the pain (because she is not shouting or screaming), her baby is finally delivered with the assistance of an epidural and forceps. Hayley has a more defined plan about pain relief than Tracy; she enters the hospital asserting her right to an epidural, and while she manages to laugh through most of her contractions, by the end of her labour her wishes are respected, and she receives the epidural she requests. For both Hayley and Tracy, the epidural (the 'gold standard' for pain relief as the WHO calls it) seems to symbolise their freedom to choose, despite their midwives' gentle encouragement to resist and to try 'natural' methods of pain relief instead.[28]

Hayley is depicted as 'coping well' with physical pain because she is, like Tracy, largely calm and quiet or laughing. During her cervical examination (a process that many women find excruciatingly painful), Hayley is relaxed, and her midwife jokes: 'You do realise you'll be lulling loads of women into a false sense of security? You're six centimetres and look how happy you are!'[29] This comment implies that Hayley's experience is not the norm in that she is 'coping' better than most women with the pain because she is retaining her sense of humour. However, despite the sense that Hayley is perceived to be 'coping well' with the pain, she focusses on pharmacological pain relief from the outset of her labour and her right to demand it in a system that does not automatically give it. She asks her midwife: 'How soon can I have the epidural?' When the midwife explains 'not yet', Hayley retorts '[s]o you want to see me writhing around in pain before you give me one?' – a comment that raises much laughter from everyone in the delivery room, including Hayley. The birth provides the emotional climax of each episode, and against current RCM guidelines both Hayley and Tracy are shown to be delivering their babies while lying on their backs in bed.[30] Despite securing the labour she desired in terms of pain relief, Hayley does not share Tracy's feeling of elation. For her, there is an immediate sense of dejection, and she apologises to the midwives almost as soon as her son is born, saying: 'God I know I was useless! I never was one for taking pain.' Although Hayley is shown to be responding to the pain appropriately within the discourse of the natural childbirth movement (i.e., calmly and quietly), and although she is able to secure the birth experience she desires (with the assistance of pain relief), her remarks suggest that her choice still leaves her feeling inadequate because she feels she has failed. She has not 'achieved' a natural birth and by implication is already excluded from the ideal – the narrative of the 'good mother'. Juxtaposing the experience of Tracy and Hayley demonstrates that while some older women are able to resist or modify this ideal, others are so heavily invested in it that they are less able to do so. Importantly, however, although Hayley does not have Tracy's previous experience of labour and childbirth, the implication is that their age affords both of them the confidence to articulate and assert their desires in relation to pain relief, leaving them feeling in control of their birth experience (despite the fact that, in Tracy's case, she does not receive the epidural she desires). Yet, while Tracy and Hayley are shown to be feeling in control of their experience, *OBEM* also explores scenarios in which older women are not able to exert control over the situation, and it explores what happens when such women attempt to overcome a traumatic first labour.

'I told you it would be different this time'

Series 3 episode 13 features second-time mother, Canadian-born Diane (43) and her Turkish husband Hussan (33). In an interview at home while still pregnant, Diane jokes that 'it's going to be so easy this time. It's going to be five hours, go in the pool, no drugs...champagne!' As this statement suggests, Diane found her first experience of childbirth traumatic, and she makes clear that she is deliberately learning from this prior experience to ensure that things are different the second time round. She explains:

> [w]ith my first daughter I did end up with an induction, and epidural, and I was on my back in stirrups and everything else and I don't really remember any of it, that part of the birth...ummm...so that wonderful moment when you're told to push and then you push and there's a baby, I didn't really experience any of that, it was all kind of removed from me, so I'd like to have that feeling of being able to feel...to push.'

As for Hayley, there is a sense here that Diane feels robbed of an 'authentic' experience by the medicalisation of her first labour and that the pain and the pushing are an essential part of the process of becoming a mother (the 'difficult rite of passage' mentioned earlier). Her comments suggest that the pain is something that she is actively seeking this time in order to experience a 'natural' labour. Sara (38, Series 2, episode 5) is also focussed upon doing things differently this time as a result of a negative first experience; however, her approach to labour is very different to that of Diane. Sara is unusual for being one of the few working-class, older mothers to be featured across the four series of *OBEM*, and her story is used to explore what happens when a woman is so traumatised by labour that she finds the pain anything but funny (although Sara's partner appears to do so, offering her gas and air and joking: 'Meet Norman the nosel, your new best friend!'). Sara is having her third baby and enters the labour unit already terrified; when her midwife asks her 'What's your plan for pain relief?' she tentatively replies 'See how it goes...push comes to shove, which I think it might cos I don't have a very good pain threshold, I'd want an epidural.' So, unlike Diane, Sara has no explicit plan for this birth. She simply wants to get through it. She explains to her midwife that 'the first time, [the baby] was very distressed and things went really, really wrong...which put me at real tenterhooks for the last one.' In a voiceover, Sara explains further that 'the thought of being in excruciating pain is unbelievable, I'm just terribly frightened of it.' Explaining to her colleagues that Sara is frightened, her midwife jokes: 'She's just really anxious...just really scared...she knows what's coming, you see', and all her colleagues laugh. In this case, experience does not afford the older woman involved additional confidence, and this lack of confidence stems from the fact that Sara is far less literate in the narrative of childbirth than the middle-class Diane; whereas Diane (like Tracy and Hayley) is able to take command of the situation, Sara becomes disempowered and overwhelmed by it.

It becomes apparent very quickly that Sara's fear stems from the fact that she felt out of control during her first labour, and she fears that lack of control again. She is frightened of the pain, but, perhaps more importantly, she is frightened of not being listened to. Like Hayley, she enters the hospital asking for an epidural, but her request is handled very differently to Hayley's request. Whereas Hayley calmly asserts her right to pain relief, and eventually secures it, Sara is described as 'pleading' for an epidural 'and even a Caesarean section' very early on in the labour, telling her midwife: 'I want to have an epidural. I can't do this. I'm so scared.' As the midwife explains that Sara has not progressed enough in her labour for an epidural and encourages her to use other methods of pain relief such as 'walking about' and 'having a bath', Sara simply repeats how frightened she is: 'I'm so frightened...I'm so scared', suggesting that she already feels she is not being listened to, nor her desires respected. The advice of her midwife is in-keeping with the RCM's 'Campaign for Normal Birth' which states, under the rather unfortunate heading of 'hints and tricks', that midwives should '[b]ear in mind that [the patient's] mood will change as the pain increases. ... Review the various forms of distraction that are available to her: rocking, water, massage, counting mobilisation, singing or music.'[31] Yet the treatment that Sara receives confounds the guidelines that state that, in order for the woman to feel in control, she must feel that the midwife is 'placing her interests first and that you are hearing her point of view'.[32] As a new midwife comes on shift, Sara, in tears, once again asks: 'Can I please, please have an epidural?' Neither Tracy nor Hayley are represented as 'pleading' for pain relief in this way; rather, they assert their right to it in a calm and confident manner. When the midwife responds: 'You can, eventually', Sara begins to panic (hyperventilating, throwing her hands in the air and crying), once again exposing her fear that she is not being listened to. It seems that Sara is destined to experience another traumatic labour and with her hysteria rising she is given Pethidine, her midwife explaining to colleagues that 'she's completely zonked', writing on her notes that she is 'sedated' in red pen.

This is the kind of medicalised experience that Diane (Series 3, episode 13) wishes to avoid, and part of Diane's method of achieving this experience is to employ a Doula, who describes herself as 'an ordinary woman who supports another woman during birth'. The Doula acts as a buffer between the labouring woman and the medicalised environment of the hospital, promising to ensure that the woman achieves the birth experience that she desires. The hiring of a Doula is primarily a middle-class privilege, for the service typically costs £500 per birth in the Leeds area where Series 3 was filmed.[33] As Genz and Brabon note, '[i]n today's consumer culture, the notion of freedom is often directly tied to the ability to purchase',[34] and this concept of buying choice is raised directly by Sara (Series 2, episode 5), who is told in no uncertain terms by her midwife that '[t]here's no way you're having that [an epidural]...unless you win the lottery and you [her husband] can offer her a private epidural and pay for it yourself', to which Sara seriously responds: 'How much does that cost?', a question which is left unanswered as both her husband and midwife laugh. Interestingly, the threat of an undisclosed cost is one that simply does not arise in the cases of Tracy, Hayley and Diane. Sara's age and life experience should, like the others, afford her the confidence to do things differently this time; however, Sara is clearly not within the demographic able to afford private health care, nor to hire the services of a Doula. Indeed, the hiring of private help does not seem to have occurred to Sara as an option available to her. Control, in this episode, is represented as something that middle-class women are able to buy through the use of a Doula.

Diane achieves the second birth experience that she desires, taking gas and air (not having time to get into the birthing pool) and resting on all fours on a birthing ball with her Doula and husband at her side. Like Tracy, Diane expresses a deep sense of satisfaction once her baby is born, and her midwife tells her, '[s]ee, I told you it would be different this time', the implication being that Diane's age has proved a distinct advantage as she was able to learn from her past experience in order to effect a change this time. On the other hand, Sara's worst fears appear to be realised as her midwife explains to her that she is now too far progressed in her labour for an epidural, joking with her husband that she is going to have to do this '*au naturale*'. As we have seen, Tracy remains calm upon learning that it is too late for an epidural, still feeling in control of the situation because she feels that her desires were respected from the outset of her labour; Sara, however, responds to this news with panic, a response heightened by the fact that her husband and midwife then forcibly remove the gas and air from her, the midwife curtly instructing: 'Come on, we can do this without.' Yet, despite clearly feeling out of control for the duration of her labour and despite her requests for an epidural and Caesarean section being actively ignored, the sense of achievement that Sara feels about giving birth 'naturally' is very clear. Despite class differences, Sara, like all the older women featured in this chapter, is clearly invested in the narrative of a natural childbirth. Once her baby is born, she exclaims: 'I did it!' to which her midwife responds: 'Yeah you did. Without an epidural. See. Told you, you didn't need it.' Sara even tentatively asks: 'Am I allowed to say I'm proud of myself?...I never thought I could do that without any assistance' and in a later interview direct to camera, she reflects: 'It was just euphoric, it was such an amazing feeling...I was so proud that I managed to do that ...I gave birth to her naturally, wow!' Like Tracy, Sara takes pain relief yet feels she has achieved a 'natural' birth because she avoided an epidural, and the elation she expresses exposes that investment in the natural childbirth movement transgresses class boundaries.

Conclusion

In 2014, the fifth series of *OBEM* will be aired, and it seems that the public appetite for watching graphic depictions of labour and childbirth is as strong as ever. Yet the policing of the birth experience within the postfeminist and neoliberal context is deeply troubling. Older pregnant women, accustomed to enjoying control in most aspects of their lives, are encouraged to invest in the illusion of choice, choice that can often be bought for those who can afford it, as well as the narrative of a birth experience that they can actively control. This pressure to 'achieve' a natural birth intersects with the 'good mother' myth and the myth of remaining in control during labour. *OBEM* is currently unique on British terrestrial television for exploring the lived experience of the most rapidly increasing demographic of mothers, specifically older women, and for representing those women positively. Ageing mothers are seen to be deftly negotiating the complex matrix of midwife, doctor and the hospital setting of the National Health Service; their age is represented as a positive advantage for affording them the confidence and experience to assert their desires within a setting which does not, at times, respect their right to assert their will. In the rare instance in which this is not the case (that of Sara), the mother's lack of confidence is attributable to her class status rather than her age. Yet, even in Sara's case, she is able to achieve the birth experience she desires, and far from feeling traumatised, as she did when she was younger, Sara feels elated by her experience. So *OBEM* demonstrates that whatever their class, older mothers are shown to be heavily invested in both the 'good mother' myth and ideals of the natural childbirth movement, and it explores a range of scenarios in which ageing women are shown to be negotiating both.

Notes

1. Rosalind Gill and Christine Scharff, 'Introduction,' in *New Femininities: Postfeminism, Neoliberalism and Subjectivity*, ed. Rosalind Gill and Christine Scharff (Basingstoke, Hampshire: Palgrave Macmillan, 2013), p.7.
2. Office for National Statistics, 'Statistical bulletin: Births in England and Wales, 2012' (July 2012), available at http://www.ons.gov.uk/ons/rel/vsob1/birth-summary-tables – england-and-wales/2012/stb-births-in-england-and-wales-2012.html. For examples of the vilification of the older mother in popular media, see James Chapman, 'Older Mothers Put Baby at Risk', in 'Health', *Daily Mail* (n.d.), available at http://www.dailymail.co.uk/health/article-5438/Older-mothers-baby-risk.html#ixzz2hWWn6yOf; Daniel Sokol, 'What is Society's Problem with Elderly Mothers?,' *BBC News Magazine* (2010), available at http://news.bbc.co.uk/1/hi/magazine/8480641.stm; NHS Choices, 'Mothers Age Affects Autism Risk', in 'Health News,' *NHS* (9 February 2010), available at http://www.nhs.uk/news/2010/02February/Pages/Mothers-age-affects-autism-risk.aspx.
3. Although published in the 1980s, William Ray Arney and Jane Neill's discussion of Dick-Read's understanding of natural childbirth and the medical perception of pain is worth noting here for it helps to remind us that Dick-Read's original intention was to empower the women, while also emphasising that the understanding of labour pain as a subjective experience was a relatively new concept at that time. See William Ray Arney and Jane Neill, 'The Location of Pain in Childbirth: Natural Childbirth and the Transformation of Obstetrics,'*Sociology of Health and Illness*, 4:1 (1982), pp.1–24.
4. Grantly Dick-Read, 'Letter: Position for Delivery,' *British Medical Journal*, 2 (1955), p. 850.
5. For a recent discussion of this sense of 'failure', see Kirsty Allsopp's blog on the National Childbirth Trust, available at http://kirstiemallsopp.wordpress.com/2013/01/08/140-is-not-enough-for-nct-discussion/.
6. Michelle Kealy and Pranee Liamputtong, 'Contemporary Caesarean Section Theory: Risk, Uncertainty and Fear,' in *Theory for Midwifery Practice*, ed. Rosamund Bryar and Marlene Sinclair (Basingstoke, Hampshire: Palgrave Macmillan, 2011), p.265.
7. Rebecca Feasey, *From Happy Homemaker to Desperate Housewives: Motherhood in Popular Television* (Anthem: London, 2012), p.167.

8. Kealy and Liamputtong, p.264.

9. Ibid.

10. Ellen Lazarus, 'What Do Women Want? Issues of Choice, Control, and Class in American Pregnancy and Childbirth,' in *Childbirth and Authoritative Knowledge: Cross-Cultural Perspectives*, ed. Robbie E. David-Floyd and Carolyn F. Sargent (Berkeley, California: University of California Press, 1997), p.133.

11. See National Childbirth Trust, 'Working with Pain in Labour,' available at http://www.nct.org.uk/birth/working-pain-labour

12. Mumsnet, 'Childbirth' (2013), available at http://www.mumsnet.com/Talk/childbirth; Netmums, 'Labour and Birth' (2013), available at http://www.netmums.com/pregnancy/labour-and-birth.

13. See Susan Douglas and Meredith Michaels, *The Mommy Myth: The Idealization of Motherhood and How It Has Undermined All Women* (London: Free Press, 2005).

14. Annabel Karmel, *Eating for Two: The Complete Guide to Nutrition during Pregnancy and Beyond* (London: Ebury, 2012), p.1.

15. Rosalind Gill, 'Postfeminist Media Culture: Elements of a Sensibility,' *European Journal of Cultural Studies*, 10:2 (2007), p. 149. For a discussion of *Supernanny* in relation to the intensive mothering ideal, see Fiona Green, '*Supernanny*: Disciplining Mothers through a Narrative of Domesticity,' *Storytelling*, 6:2 (2010), pp. 99–109.

16. Ingela Lundgren and Karin Dahlberg, 'Women's Experience of Pain during Childbirth,' *Midwifery*, 14:2 (1998), p. 105.

17. The Royal College of Midwives, 'Normal Childbirth', *Position Statement*, 4 (May 2004), p.1.

18. The Royal College of Midwives, 'Respecting Her Wishes,' *Campaign for Normal Birth*, available at http://www.rcmnormalbirth.org.uk/stories/wheres-the-doctor/respecting-her-wishes/.

19. Sonya Charles, 'Disempowered Women? The Midwifery Model and Medical Intervention,' in *Coming to Life: Philosophies of Pregnancy, Childbirth, and Mothering*, ed. Sarah LaChance Adams and Caroline R. Lundquist (Fordsham University Press, New York, 2013), p. 216.

20. AmedeePeret, FJ, 'Pain Management for Women in Labour: An Overview of Systematic Reviews,' available at http://apps.who.int/rhl/pregnancy_childbirth/childbirth/routine_care/cd009234_amedeeperetf_com/en/index.html.

21. Benji Wilson notes that episodes often cut to an advertisement break 'mid-delivery to ramp up the tension,' in 'One Born Every Minute: Channel 4, Review,' *The Telegraph* (9 Feb 2010), available at http://www.telegraph.co.uk/culture/tvandradio/7198234/One-Born-Every-Minute-Channel-4-review.html.

22. Feasey, *From Happy Homemaker*, p.163.

23. Channel 4, '*One Born Every Minute*: Frequently Asked Questions,' available at http://lifebegins.channel4.com/faq/.

24. Wilson, '*One Born Every Minute*: Channel 4, Review,' http://www.telegraph.co.uk/culture/tvandradio/7198234/One-Born-Every-Minute-Channel-4-review.html.

25. Morwenna Ferrier, '*One Born Every Minute*: Channel 4, Review,' *The Telegraph* (4 January 2012), available at http://www.telegraph.co.uk/culture/tvandradio/8992678/One-Born-Every-Minute-Channel-4-review.html.

26. Lararus, 'What Do Women Want?,' p.143.
27. Channel 4, '*One Born Every Minute*: Season 2, Episode 7,' available at https://lifebegins.channel4.com/episodes/2/7.
28. Peret, 'Pain Management for Women in Labour'.
29. The Royal College of Midwives' Guidelines for assessing progress in labour states that: 'Many Women Find Vaginal Examinations Painful and Distressing,' in *Evidence Based Guidelines for Midwifery-Led Care in Labour: Assessing Progress in Labour* (2012), p. 2.
30. Ibid., p. 1.
31. The Royal College of Midwives, *Campaign for Normal Childbirth*, 'Coping with Pain,' available athttp://www.rcmnormalbirth.org.uk/stories/wheres-the-doctor/coping-with-pain/.
32. The Royal College of Midwives, 'Respecting Her Wishes', *Campaign for Normal Birth* http://www.rcmnormalbirth.org.uk/stories/wheres-the-doctor/respecting-her-wishes/
33. Yorkshire Doula Network, available at http://www.yorkshiredoulanetwork.co.uk/.
34. Stephanie Genz and Benjamin A. Brabon, *Postfeminism: Cultural Texts and Theories* (Edinburgh: Edinburgh University Press, 2009), p. 8.

13
Women, Travelling and Later Life

Sarah Falcus and Katsura Sako

Contemporary culture is saturated with what Kathleen Woodward describes as 'the *youthful structure of the look*'.[1] Women's ageing bodies provoke particularly strong fear and disgust, as their sexual and aesthetic currency is perceived to diminish. Unsurprisingly, this disgust means that older women have been marginalised and have achieved limited visibility in popular film. This situation appears to be changing, however, as Meryl Streep notes:

> I remember when I turned 40, I was offered, within one year, three different witch roles...It was almost like the world was saying or the studios were saying, 'We don't know what to do with you.'...That really has changed, not completely, not for everybody, but for me it has changed.[2]

The proliferation of recent popular films featuring prominent older female characters – such as *Quartet* (Hoffman, 2012), *Song for Marion* (Williams, 2012) and *Hope Springs* (Frankel, 2013) – certainly indicates that older women are achieving greater visibility in cinema. As Sally Chivers explains, the industry has responded to the demographic shift in the market prompted by baby boomers and stars growing older and has been producing more films with older performers and characters.[3] According to the BFI, this shift accounts for their findings that in 2012 the 45+ age groups comprised the highest proportion (36 per cent) of the 15+ audiences.[4] However, ageism is encountered not only by women over 45 but, as Streep notes, by those even younger. This trend bears out Margaret Morganroth Gullette's argument that, in youth-oriented contemporary culture, ageism is moving down the life-course.[5] Ageism therefore extends to female characters and actors in their thirties and early forties, making the issue of ageing significant even in films which do not, on the surface, seem to be about this.

Addressing ageing in film means considering ageing as a movement through the life-course and not just into 'old' age. We must analyse both the new cultural visibility for older women, which does not always successfully challenge the 'fatally flat' decline narrative, and the way in which much younger characters and actors are represented.[6] Significant for these different generations, and what complicates their visibility in film, is the impact of 'new ageing', which signifies a shift in the cultural and gerontological discourses of ageing. Instead of the traditional view of ageing as decline, new ageing envisages 'new' meanings and subjective possibilities for later life, with the ageing body now the subject of intense 'refashioning as well as rejuvenating' in a consumerist and individualistic self-policing: 'No longer viewed as a process through which the subject becomes an object to be managed by others, bodily ageing has emerged as (another) arena for self-care, for lifestyle fashioning.'[7] This self-management results in an emphasis upon leisure, lifestyle and active (hetero)sexuality. According to Chris Gilleard and Paul Higgs, new ageing developed in the eighties as a feature of midlife and by the end of the century had extended to encompass later life. This development creates 'the dilemmas of how to age by not becoming old'.[8] In terms of film new ageing can lead to the 'youthing' of older characters, requiring actors both to act and look young.[9]

The individualist and consumerist character of new ageing also prevails in postfeminism, in which 'youth is fetishized'.[10] Sadie Wearing argues that, out of fear of ageing, postfeminism centralises and simultaneously denies the temporality of women's chronological and biological age, propagating the ideals of 'rejuvenation' and the 'makeover' of the self. Yet, she continues, 'rejuvenation' is both 'necessary and impossible' in postfeminist culture: 'Necessary because in complex ways the aging body is pathologised and disavowed; impossible because…deference to quite rigid demarcations of the appropriate, the decorous, and the "natural" still exerts a profound influence over representations of age and aging.'[11] This paradox makes ageing appropriately a difficult business, with attendant risks of ageing invisibility and age-inappropriate 'anachronism'.[12]

Exploring ageing and ageism for postfeminist women and the generations that precede them, this chapter brings together films which feature characters from their 30s to their 70s: *Sex and the City 2* (King, 2010), *Under the Tuscan Sun* (Wells, 2003), *Eat, Pray, Love* (Murphy, 2010), *Letters to Juliet* (Winick, 2010) and *The Best Exotic Marigold Hotel* (Madden, 2012).

These films represent women ageing towards midlife and into older age, contributing to the increased prominence of older women and their concerns in film.[13] What also links these films is that they all represent women travelling to foreign locations to seek change. On one level, of course, these locations are marketing features in the Hollywood global production system. However, travel also functions as a metaphor for self-seeking, and it is something particularly significant for women who, as Karen R. Lawrence points out, represent the 'symbolic embodiment of home' in the traditional male travel narrative.[14] These older women seek change and freedom, and a different conception of 'home', as they move across the life-course (a temporal movement echoed in the spatiality of travel), developing the exploration of ageing and gender through travel seen in earlier films, most notably *Shirley Valentine* (Gilbert, 1990).

This exploration of the female life-course demands that the films rene-gotiate romance, a normative script for women which has become rein-vigorated in postfeminist culture. Kathrina Glitre argues that 'in recent years, postfeminist film and television narratives (certainly in the US and the UK) have tended to resolve their conflicts by depicting women as "outgrowing" independence and becoming happily co-dependent through heterosexual romance.'[15] These films, however, concern women in the aftermath of romance (divorce, widowhood and marital problems) and ageing into and/or beyond midlife. Romance is thus a less obvious answer, typifying the 'narrative problem' that accompanies the modifi-cation of youth-oriented plots in 'silvering screen' films.[16] Addressing romance also raises the issue of sexuality. Older women's sexuality, like their bodies, is traditionally rendered invisible or, if represented, is often monstrous and inappropriate. However, in new ageing, active later-life sexuality has become part of ageing successfully, just as (hetero)sexu-ality is often a marker of postfeminist success and empowerment.[17]

The five films reveal the complexity and often problematic nature of the new cultural visibility of older women. The new ageing and postfeminist cultures make it difficult to imagine ageing 'successfully' without recourse to youthing and capitalist consumption, and they depoliticise ageing to produce a narrowly optimistic vision of it. The white, middle-class, professionally successful protagonists of *Sex and the City 2*, *Under the Tuscan Sun* and *Eat, Pray, Love*, who exemplify postfemi-nist female subjectivity, are all attempting to negotiate the 'postfeminist life-course',[18] which includes romance, sexuality and family, fore-grounding in particular the postfeminist centralisation of heterosexual coupledom[19] and familial happiness.[20] Featuring protagonists in their (late) 30s, 40s and early 50s, these films represent a range of responses to the pressures of both postfeminist 'youthing' and new ageing. They question romance and the idealised form of marriage and family, and they seek to present alternatives, from childless marriage and the affirmation of space for female independence outside of marriage in *Sex and the City 2*, to an open community of people as an alternative to the nuclear family unit in *Under the Tuscan Sun* and the geographically fluid heterosexual partnership in *Eat, Pray, Love*. Nonetheless, these potentially subversive options are overshadowed by their leanings towards rejuvenation and the 'makeover' of self through consumption. *Letters to Juliet* and *The Best Exotic Marigold Hotel* also confront the conflicting pressures of age-appropriateness and new ageing, producing what are in many ways diametrically opposed narratives of female ageing, from the conservatism of *Letters to Juliet*, to the more challenging older women in *The Best Exotic Marigold Hotel*, for whom travel is an adventure and a time of growth. However, even *The Best Exotic Marigold Hotel* does not escape new ageing's emphasis upon wealth, health and productivity as the requisites for desirable ageing. These five films illustrate the increasing visibility of older women and their lives in film – representing a challenge to the Hollywood obsession with youth – but they also suggest that postfeminist rejuvenation and new ageing cultures overlap to make articulating narratives of ageing that engage with, rather than deny, ageing very difficult.

Sex and the City 2 and *Under the Tuscan Sun*

The TV series (1998–2004) that preceded *Sex and the City 2* challenged the idealisation of marriage and family in postfeminist culture, while it still engaged with the romance narrative as it explored the female lifecourse.[21] *Sex and the City 2*, however, struggles to develop the romance narrative for women in their 40s and 50s in a way that provides a satisfying vision of ageing into midlife. Instead, the film continues, just as the TV series had done, to defy temporality by 'girling' older women and celebrating their rejuvenated bodies and consumerist lifestyles,[22] an approach that represents the ideals of both new ageing and postfeminism. The film retains some of its earlier subversiveness, however, in its questioning of the traditional conception of home as a place of familial love and domestic satisfaction, a conception of home which Carrie (Sarah Jessica Parker) feels does not suit her ideal of (childless) marriage and independent life.

Carrie's journey to UAE with her three friends therefore represents an escape from home and the opportunity to consider her marital situation. However, the trip is not one of life transformation, as it merely transports their usual habit of extravagant consumption into the exoticised foreign location. The travel narrative is full of facile gestures that celebrate 'global' womanhood, as typified by the women singing 'I Am Woman', Helen Reddy's feminist anthem, in a nightclub with fashionable young local women and men, whose power to dress 'freely' is meant to signify their democratic freedom. Another gesture at global consumer sisterhood emerges when the four women meet a group of local women who secretly dress themselves in the latest western designer clothes. Travel here seems to function merely to confirm the value of western glamour, youthfulness and sexuality as the basis of a desirable identity, rather than challenging the youth- and consumer-driven nature of the brand. This insistence on the value of youth is emphasised by Carrie's rekindling of romance with an ex-boyfriend, an episode that offers her a way to reclaim her past and, implicitly, her youth. As Carrie goes to meet him, she wears a tight exotic dress that exposes her toned neck and legs and emphasises her sexual currency. The insistence on rejuvenation and youth is very clear here, with Carrie's sexualised body foregrounded for both the viewer and the ex-boyfriend, playing as much upon the reputation of Parker as the character. This film is undoubtedly challenging the traditional discourse of increasing invisibility for the older woman's body, but it does so in terms which end up 'youthing' both actor and character and promoting individualised, commercialised bodily maintenance as a means for 'ageless' ageing.

Travel in this film, therefore, effects very little change. Carrie returns home and to John, rejecting her affair with her ex and re-appreciating the security of marriage. Her marital crisis is then quickly solved by John's gift of jewellery, a promise of romantic (consumer-based) life for 'just two of them'. At the same time, the film does unsettle the postfeminist conception of home, as Carrie decides to keep her premarital apartment. While undoubtedly motivated by nostalgia for her youthful past, her action symbolically asserts the importance of independence and female friendship for women, even within marriage, challenging the idealisation of home as a privileged site of happiness in a woman's life. Nonetheless, in its stress upon youthfulness, consumption as a means of empowerment and the unchanged romantic resolution, the film offers an uneasy postfeminist compromise to ageing into midlife, a vision of ageing that rejects age.

Under the Tuscan Sun also utilises travel as part of a (more subtle) 'makeover' of the older woman in its treatment of Frances, played by the 38-year-old Diane Lane. Like Carrie, Frances travels as a response to relationship problems, though in her case the problem is the breakdown of her marriage. Travel is, however, life changing as Frances establishes a new community in Italy and the film goes some way to suggesting that a different, equally valid, form of home may be found in non-traditional familial arrangements, where Frances is, significantly, childless. Nevertheless, the film also emphasises sexuality and romance as central parts of Frances' recovery from crisis, making '(emphatically hetero) sexuality...a device of (covert) rejuvenation', as Wearing describes a similar intersection of ageing and gender in the narrative of *Something's Gotta Give* (Meyers, 2003).[23] This yoking of sexuality and rejuvenation leads to a rather uncertain conclusion, where the film seems to desire both the reconfiguration of the meaning of home and midlife happiness for women and conformity to an individualised romance narrative that offers a 'happy ending', perhaps in order to allow the film to be marketed as a romantic comedy.

Home in Italy is traditional, rural and communal, in contrast to urban, modern San Francisco. The story of house restoration then provides the obvious metaphor for Frances' post-divorce recuperation, and this is signalled in the film as the house becomes more homely and is filmed in warmer light.[24] Consumption here may be more muted than in *Sex and the City 2*, but the narrative is still driven by a vision of remaking life that depends upon the ability to pay for the rural idyll. Frances creates an eclectic community – made up of builders, nuns, an estate agent, local farmers and her friend Patti – around her in Tuscany, a family at odds with the nuclear model and with the familial in many postfeminist narratives.[25] This community provides the wedding required at the end of the film, though it is not the wedding of our heroine. The fact that the heroine is not the bride typifies the film's ironic approach to the romantic comedy as a genre, which sees Frances constantly interrogated about her desire for happy heterosexual coupledom. However, as Alexia L. Bowler argues, irony can undermine feminist aims in the romantic comedy: 'the work of the postfeminist romantic comedy disarms and depoliticizes its own feminist critique of sexual negotiations through knowingness, irony and a cosy humour, coupled with discourses surrounding personal choice.'[26] And such undermining is the case here. The film may ironise Frances' search for Mr Right and offer an alternative way to live into midlife, but it nevertheless promotes active heterosexuality in a way that is typical of both postfeminism and new ageing, where the maintenance of sex appeal becomes *the* sign of successful ageing.

The competing desire for and resistance to romantic resolution can be seen in the emphasis upon Frances' rejuvenation throughout the film. Echoing the restoration of the Italian villa, Frances moves from dark clothes and muted hairstyles to a dominance of light clothing and shiny, curled hair. This visual transformation is underpinned by the film's repeated emphasis on her (hetero)sexuality and desirability, from the first scene, where Frances' student jokingly asks if he might French kiss her, to her affair with Marcello in Italy. Frances' relief that she has 'still got it' after this relationship makes clear that active sexuality is key to her rejuvenation, in just the way Wearing describes above. Frances' desire for a family can also be read in this way, in terms of the need to retain youthfulness (symbolised by reproductive ability), but it is also an important representation of the changing life-course for women, as many professional women of the postfeminist generation choose to delay childbearing until their 30s and 40s. The changing life-course is exemplified by Frances' best friend, Patti, giving birth. However, the fact that Patti is lesbian and now single also demonstrates the film's commitment to reimagining the nature of family and community, one of the ways in which it challenges the individualism of new ageing cultures.

Nevertheless, at the wedding at the end of the film, Frances meets a new partner and the film ends with an awkward, epilogue-like scene which positions Frances clearly within a heterosexual, romantic relationship, though at a table of friends. As the final lines suggest, it is not too late for Frances to follow the appropriate life-course model (implying that it just might be): 'Unthinkably good things can happen, even late in the game. It's such a surprise.' The film, therefore, ends up drawing back from the centrality of Frances' eclectic new home, where she is a single woman at the heart of a network of friends, to stress her position as part of a couple.

Transgressive sexuality in *Sex and the City 2* and *Under the Tuscan Sun*

With these compromises, Carrie's and Frances' narratives are representations of age which rely heavily upon the reclamation of youthful heterosexual romance, despite the ways in which the films offer alternatives to this reclamation in the forms of extra-marital, female independence and fluid, intimate community. In contrast, there are in the films unruly older women who challenge what is 'appropriate' and 'decorous'[27] in more excessive ways and whose treatment suggests the continued existence of a deep-seated ageism. 52-year-old, menopausal Samantha (Kim Cattrall) in *Sex and the City 2* has abundant sexual appetite and opportunity. The representation of her menopausal state is unusual in popular film, but it is not entirely positive. Her age-resistance, represented by pills and anti-ageing books, is associated not only with the postfeminist discourse of 'self as a project',[28] but also with the culture of new ageing. Without denying the benefit of treatments such as hormone replacement therapy, it is important to recognise that, as Stephen Katz and Barbara Marshall explain, such 'remedies for sexual dysfunction rest on a recent cultural-scientific conviction that lifelong sexual function is a primary component of achieving successful aging.'[29] After Samantha's pills are confiscated on entry to UAE, her menopausal body is increasingly pathologised, seen particularly in the scene in a local market where she experiences a hot flush and falls down, exposing her body and yelling at a mob of local men. This non-medicalised body is now an example of failed self-management. This scene attaches a strong sense of 'shame' to the older body and establishes a connection between excessive sexuality in older women, madness and the possibility of humiliation for the female body that fails the youthing regime.[30] Similarly, Katherine in *Under the Tuscan Sun*, played by then 53-year-old Lesley Duncan, is a sexually assertive Fellini-esque expat who becomes the object of both pity and ridicule. Her obviously midlife body is dramatically presented during the scene in which she is seen posing almost naked, caressing her semi-naked lover. The challenge to the invisibility of the older female body that this exposure could present, however, is weakened by its comedy and Frances' response to seeing her friend posing naked. As Rose Weitz argues, instead of viewing Katherine's body as an object of desire, the audience is 'position[ed]...to identify with Frances's obvious shock and horror at the sight.'[31] The possibility of humiliation then becomes notable when Katherine acts out the scene in the Trevi fountain from *La Dolce Vita*. This image of independence is undermined by the fact that she is apparently drunk and will not be joined by her lover. The presentation of the character in the subsequent scene as a vulnerable woman lying in bed as Frances tends to her undermines Katherine's assertion that she still wants to continue her life of adventure. The representations of Samantha and Katherine thus reveal the volatility of the postfeminist celebration of female sexuality when yoked to the ageing body, as they walk a fine line between unacceptable excess and successful rejuvenation.

Travel as spiritual makeover in *Eat, Pray, Love*

Like *Sex and the City 2* and *Under the Tuscan Sun*, *Eat, Pray, Love* explores ways of living into midlife for women, as marital problems cause Elizabeth

(Julia Roberts) to leave home and embark on a journey. Like Carrie, she is reluctant to follow the socially prescribed life-course model and have children, but rather than seeking youth-orientated sexual pleasure and romance, she looks for spiritual change and emotional growth. This search suggests a narrative that values ageing as a form of progress, with a promise of romance based upon the satisfaction of (childless) midlife desire. However, despite the film's much less obvious postfeminist and new ageing credentials, the strong sense of 'spiritual tourism' apparent throughout Elizabeth's travels makes clear its commitment to self as project. And the geography of her travels provides a metaphor for the design of her project, with the three countries fairly stereotypically represented: Italy signifies familial tradition; India epitomises spirituality; and Indonesia brings together family, love, friendship and spirituality. This ostensibly non-materialist, cross-cultural travel is in fact a vehicle for self-invention. Drawing on Hilary Radner's notion of neo-feminism, Ana Moya argues that 'neo-feminist cosmopolitanism becomes a new form of empowerment linked to the transnational, where the exposure to different cultural systems gives the female subject the possibility of reshaping herself repeatedly.'[32] Read in this light, though more negatively than Moyer perhaps intends, travel – whilst offering a narrative of ageing that accepts change – can become a solipsistic, consumerist journey that explores difference as a way of achieving lifestyle changes.

The story of spiritual growth into midlife in the film is partly facilitated by the way in which 42-year-old Julia Roberts is aged in the film. The character is seen moving from a tightly fitting, glamorous outfit in New York, revealing Roberts' praised body shape, to plainer and looser clothes once travelling. Roberts' nonsexual appearance, which betrays the star persona that has developed around her sexualised body, helps to fashion the narrative of the film as a story of self-searching rather than one of romantic pursuit. In this context Roberts' physical ageing, which is normally seen as the reduction of the 'visual pleasure' she provides, may even signify her maturity as a female actor, reinforcing the theme of growth in the film. Unlike in the other films, therefore, non-rejuvenation in *Eat, Pray, Love* helps to stress the spiritual dimension of the older woman's change and maturity into early midlife.

Despite this emphasis on spiritual development, the film concludes with a new romantic relationship for Elizabeth and ends in a rather clichéd shot of a motorboat which carries Elizabeth and her new partner Filipe across the sunset-lit ocean to a secluded island. Significantly, however, this resolution does not signal a return to the normative model of the female life-course, as American Elizabeth and Brazilian Felipe (whose son is in Australia) reject the security and stability of the post-feminist domestic in favour of an international 'in-between', as Felipe describes it. Thus, through the fluidity of the geography of home and the rejection of the youthful rejuvenation of the older woman, the film utilises travel as a space for change and the remaking of the narratives of women's lives.

Yet it is undeniable that Elizabeth's travel is a lifestyle choice enabled by the material and social advantages she has as a white, middle-class, professional woman. Elizabeth's 'sisterhood' with a young Indian girl who is forced to marry by her family and with a Balinese single mother who has left an abusive husband provides opportunities for merely complacent self-betterment (by offering her prayer to the former and collecting donations from her western friends for the latter). It is only through leaving home that a different version of midlife can be offered and the place of romance in this part of the female life-course can be reconsidered, but the travel here is a consumerist means that exploits rather than acknowledges difference to achieve a 'spiritual' makeover and a desired self.

Letters to Juliet and *The Best Exotic Marigold Hotel*

Moving beyond midlife, *Letters to Juliet* and The *Best Exotic Marigold Hotel* feature women in their 60s and 70s who also travel in order to find alternative ways to live into the next stages of their lives. *Letters to Juliet* sees the 65-year-old Claire (Vanessa Redgrave) travel from Britain to the Italy of her youth to seek her old love. This is orthodox Hollywood romantic comedy and it deals with ageing in conservative ways that seek to avoid anachronism and reinforce age-appropriate behaviour for women. One significant factor in the film's conservatism is the insistent association of Claire with the past, something Chivers associates with 'silvering screen' films, those which exhibit '[s]ocial anxiety about old age' and 'value and evaluate the present primarily in relation to a distant past, with the intervening years meaning little'.[33] Italy therefore is presented as a place of the past and, as in *Under the Tuscan Sun* and *Eat, Pray, Love*, associated with family value. Unsurprisingly, therefore, Vanessa Redgrave, who plays Claire, is not 'youthed' or rejuvenated in *Letters to Juliet*. Often supported by her grandson, she appears almost too frail for the 65 years of her character and wears generously cut clothes in muted colours matched with plainly arranged hair. Redgrave's typically whimsical acting is exploited to represent Claire as vulnerable, and her reputation, family and acting pedigree magnify her traditional Englishness. Similarly, Claire's rekindled romance is portrayed as entirely age-appropriate, with all intimacy muted, nonsexualised, and placed firmly within a familial context.

Another significant part of the film's conservative representation of ageing is its privileging of youthful romance, as signified by the design of its poster (the young couple foregrounded and the old couple at the back). Ostensibly successful and independent, the young Sophie is a typical postfeminist heroine and her romance narrative is embedded in both the tradition of heterosexual love, back to *Romeo and Juliet*, and the postfeminist return to the familial. This return to the traditional is signalled by her departure from the brash new world of America, which represents Sophie's career and her fiancé's restaurant business: the commercialism and ambition suggest the gains achieved by the second-wave feminist generation at the cost of the familial. Unlike in *Under the Tuscan Sun* and *Eat, Pray, Love*, the traditional meaning of home and family remains unchanged in this film, and the familial emphasis is reinforced by the (grand)mother-daughter relationship between the motherless Sophie and Claire, visualised, for example, when Claire brushes Sophie's hair. This non-confrontational positioning of generations exemplifies the way that the film places ageing to reinforce generational and age hierarchies. The film may end with the marriage of Claire and Lorenzo, but the wedding is overtaken by Charles' declaration of love for Sophie. Claire therefore functions as a wise grandmother figure, suitably visible but age-appropriate and, despite her later-life romance, not a challenge to the normative life-course model or the happiness of the postfeminist heroine.

Offering a more challenging vision of ageing, *The Best Exotic Marigold Hotel* weaves together various narratives of development in later life through a group of characters from different social backgrounds who travel to India to retire. For most of them this trip is a practical necessity rather than a free lifestyle choice. Their prospects for later life in Britain are very limited, hampered by economic circumstance, lack of opportunity and a neoliberal (new ageist), political agenda that designates wellness in later life as an individual responsibility. The film therefore opens with what appears to be a critique of aspects of individualistic, new ageing discourses, and it certainly presents an optimistic narrative of ageing that is not nostalgic but engages with the possibility of change in later life. The backdrop to this presentation is India, both modern and vibrant, and traditional and spiritual, imagined as a chaotic yet life-invigorating space. However, as the film progresses, the exploration of difference and the critique of neoliberal discourses of ageing are played down in favour of an optimism that resonates with new-ageist (and, we could argue, postfeminist) ideals.

The film features two particular types of change. The first of these is paid employment for older women, which is seen as empowering, but it can also be linked to the importance of usefulness and self-reliance in new ageing. In India Evelyn (Judi Dench) gets her first ever paid job as 'cultural consultant' in a call centre, and Muriel (Maggie Smith) uses her accounting skills to save the hotel and becomes assistant manager. These jobs provide not only financial stability, but also psychological and emotional fulfilment, and they place Evelyn and Muriel in new communities of people. Muriel's employment is part of her transformation in India; this change takes her from unpleasant bigot, who reluctantly travels to India to have an affordable hip operation, to efficient, hardworking woman, something symbolised by her movement out of a wheelchair. Her return to able-bodiedness is nevertheless problematic, both in its representation as almost miraculous and in its strong association with her usefulness. Disability is implicitly part of what was keeping Muriel from her full potential, a reading which again links successful ageing with the denial of physical deterioration and supports Chivers' argument that older people with disabilities are faced with 'a separate and damaging normativity' and are expected to '*meet* imposed standards of usefulness'.[34] Similarly, the value placed on work by the two characters does suggest that successful ageing is productive ageing – which demands, as Josephine Dolan argues, the body 'fit for work', one that 'can remain part of the cycle of production and consumption'.[35]

The second type of change represented in the film is one seen in many of the other examples, too: heterosexual romance. One version of this is provided in the intimate relationship between Douglas (Bill Nighy) and Evelyn. 'National treasure' Judi Dench playing Evelyn adds a sense of dignity to this vision of coupledom in later life, which is represented as thoughtful and romantic but nonsexual. Not obsessed with youthful sexuality, this model of later-life romance is both age appropriate and life affirming. While Evelyn remains an age-appropriate, nonsexual heroine of romance, potentially transgressive female sexuality is addressed in the character of Madge. Unlike *Sex and the City 2* and *Under the Tuscan Sun*, however, this film presents older women's sexuality as a source of comedy and optimism rather than as an object of humiliation and pathologisation. Played by Celia Imrie, 59 (at the time), an actor with a reputation for roles as sensual older women, Madge is presented as a woman who has lived off her looks and on a few husbands, and she is now in India to find another. Her readiness to exploit her sexual desirability is treated humorously, such as when she announces herself to be Princess Margaret at an exclusive club and has her lying courteously but firmly acknowledged by the concierge. Such emphasis on sexuality is problematically in tune with a postfeminist culture which sees female sexuality as a source of agency and the culture of new ageing in which older people are expected to be 'forever sexually functional and forever sexually attractive'.[36] At the same time, sexual forwardness in older women carries the risk of age anachronism, and Madge, too, may be punished as she remains 'single by choice' at the end of the film. Yet, the film represents Madge as a confident woman, as seen in her satisfaction with her image in the mirror as she prepares to visit the club. Her characteristically satirical comment that she does not want to be 'the first person they let off the plane in a hostage crisis' also articulates a voice of resistance against the decline ideology. She is thus a source of optimism and, given the age demographic of the film's audience, is more likely to invite sympathy.[37] Nevertheless, the representations of the 'overly' sexual supporting characters in these films – Samantha, Katherine and Madge – suggest that when positioned outside the context of the romance narrative, older women's sexuality can be presented only in a comical way, or else it is subjected to a censorious gaze.

As the final scene with the old and young couples on motorbikes in the sunny, busy street epitomises, *The Best Exotic Marigold Hotel* forges an almost utopian vision of communal home in the chaotic but all-embracing space of India. The old Indian man who lingers in the hotel's courtyard is one figure in the film who projects India's power to bring unity when he prompts Sonny's mother to allow him to marry his 'modern' Indian girlfriend and keep his hotel business, effectively preserving the community at the hotel. This optimistic vision of a later-life community, however, effaces the differences in class, race and culture, which are clearly noted when the film opens. For example, Muriel's class markers and her racial prejudice disappear as she recovers her mobility and gains employment at the hotel. Evelyn's and Douglas's financial difficulties – the reason they came to India – have been solved. Even death is disassociated from suffering and pain, as is evident in the event of Graham's sudden yet peaceful death. Therefore, in order to present an optimistic vision of later life that celebrates health, activity and active sexuality, the film depoliticises ageing just as it effaces difference.

Conclusion

These five films are important in the way they develop the use of the trope of travel as a way to explore gender and ageing and, more crucially still, in the visibility they afford to ageing women. As Imelda Whelehan argues, 'older women in Hollywood offer a path through the maze of postfeminist doublethink simply by enduring and…offering the potential for the values and survival skills of the "mothers" to outlive and vocally contradict the challenges of the daughters.'[38] The films give screen time to the lives and concerns of older women, representing them – largely – as agentic and interesting. Nevertheless, despite their very obvious differences, the films offer a fairly narrow view of progress into midlife and beyond. In their emphasis upon either age-appropriate (in)visibility or consumerist lifestyle fashioning, often allied with youthful self-presentation and active heterosexuality as a central sign of successful ageing, the films illustrate the meeting of new-ageing and postfeminist ideals. Dominated by white, middle-class characters and values, the films elide difference in favour of individualised, consumerist self-management. The self-as-project of postfeminism becomes the self-as-project of new ageing. It is crucial not to undermine the change signalled by the centrality of older women and their concerns in these films, but it is to be hoped that as the visibility of older female actors and characters increases, so too might the variety and challenges offered by the narratives of ageing women.

Acknowledgement

Katsura Sako would like to thank Japan Society for the Promotion of Science for offering her Grants-in-Aid for Scientific Research (Grant Number 25770115), which supported her research towards this co-authored work.

Notes

1. Kathleen Woodward, *Aging and Its Discontents* (Bloomington: Indiana University Press, 1991), p. 155.
2. Meryl Streep and Terry Gross, 'The Fresh Air Interview,' National Public Radio (6 February 2012), available at http://www.npr.org/2012/02/06/146362798/meryl-streep-the-fresh-air-interview.
3. Sally Chivers, *The Silvering Screen: Old Age and Disability in Cinema* (Toronto: University of Toronto Press, 2011), p. xv.
4. British Film Institute Research and Statistics Unit, *BFI Statistical Yearbook 2013* (Online PDF), p. 166, available at http://www.bfi.org.uk/sites/bfi.org.uk/files/downloads/bfi-statistical-yearbook-2013.pdf.
5. Margaret Morganroth Gullette, *Aged by Culture* (Chicago, IL: University of Chicago Press, 2004), p. 13.
6. Ibid., p. 11.
7. Chris Gilleard and Paul Higgs, *Ageing, Corporeality and Embodiment* (London: Anthem Press, 2013), p. xi.
8. Ibid., p.xii.
9. Josephine Dolan, 'Firm and Hard: Old Age, the "Youthful" Body and Essentialist Discourses'. Paper delivered at the 4th International conference of

the Spanish Society for the Literary Study of Popular Culture (2012). available at http://193.147.33.53/selicup/images/stories/actas4/plenarias/DOLAN.pdf.

10. Yvonne Tasker and Diane Negra, *Interrogating Postfeminism: Gender and the Politics of Popular Culture*, ed. Yvonne Tasker and Diane Negra (London: Duke University Press, 2007), p. 10.

11. Sadie Wearing, 'Subjects of Rejuvenation: Aging in Postfeminist Culture,' in *Interrogating Postfeminism: Gender and the Politics of Popular Culture*, ed. Yvonne Tasker and Diane Negra (London: Duke University Press, 2007), p. 278.

12. Mary Russo, 'Ageing and the Scandal of Anachronism,' in *Figuring Age: Women, Bodies, Generations*, ed. Kathleen Woodward (Bloomington: Indiana University Press, 1999).

13. As Toni M. Calasanti and Kathleen F. Slevin note in *Age Matters: Realigning Feminist Thinking* (London: Routledge, 2006), p. 3, 'older' is used by feminists instead of 'old', 'to avoid the negativity of the latter'. We use 'older' intentionally to designate women of varying ages who are, by Hollywood standards, no longer young.

14. Karen R. Lawrence, *Penelope Voyages: Women and Travel in the British Literary Tradition* (Ithaca: Cornell University Press, 1994), p. 1.

15. Kathrina Glitre, 'Nancy Meyers and "Popular Feminism,"' in *Women on Screen: Feminism and Femininity in Visual Culture*, ed. Melanie Waters (Basingstoke: Palgrave Macmillan, 2011), p. 18.

16. Chivers, p. xv.

17. Stephen Katz and Barbara Marshall, 'New Sex for Old: Lifestyle, Consumerism, and the Ethics of Ageing Well,' *Journal of Aging Studies*, 17 (2003), pp. 3–16.

18. Wearing, 'Subjects,' p. 278.

19. Anthea Taylor, *Single Women in Popular Culture: The Limits of Postfeminism* (Basingstoke: Palgrave, 2012).

20. Diane Negra, *What a Girl Wants?: Fantasizing the Reclamation of Self in Postfeminism* (Abingdon: Routledge, 2009).

21. Diane Negra, '"Quality Postfeminism?": Sex and the Single Girl on HBO,' *Genders: Presenting Innovative Work in the Arts, Humanities and Social Theories*, 39 (2004), available at http://www.genders.org/g39/g39_negra.html.

22. Wearing, 'Subjects,' p. 294.

23. Ibid., p. 278.

24. The change in lighting is also noted in the Director's audio commentary.

25. Negra, *What a Girl Wants?*

26. Alexia L. Bowler, 'Towards a New Sexual Conservatism in Postfeminist Romantic Comedy,' in *Postfeminism and Contemporary Hollywood Cinema*, ed. Joel Gwynne and Nadine Muller (London: Palgrave Macmillan, 2013), p. 194.

27. Wearing, 'Subjects,' p. 278.

28. Tasker and Negra, p. 20.

29. Katz and Marshall, p. 12.

30. Sadie Wearing, 'Notes on Some Scandals: The Politics of Shame in *Vers le Sud*,' in *New Femininities: Postfeminism, Neoliberalisim and Subjectivity*, ed. Rosalind Gill and Christina Schariff (Basingstoke: Palgrave, 2001).

31. Rose Weitz, 'Changing the Scripts: Midlife Women's Sexuality in Contemporary U.S. Film,' *Women and Gender Studies*, 14 (2010), p. 25.

32. Ana Moya, 'Neo-Feminism In-Between: Female Cosmopolitan Subjects in Contemporary American Film,' in *Postfeminism and Contemporary Hollywood*

Cinema, ed. Joel Gwynne and Nadine Muller (London: Palgrave Macmillan, 2013), p. 16.

33. Chivers, p. xvi.
34. Ibid., p. 21.
35. Dolan, p. 13.
36. Gilleard and Higgs, p. 113.
37. The data in the *BFI Statistical Yearbook 2013* suggests 45–54 and 55+ age groups together comprised 67 per cent of the audience (p. 169).
38. Imelda Whelehan, 'Ageing Appropriately: Postfeminist Discourses of Ageing in Contemporary Hollywood,' in *Postfeminism and Contemporary Hollywood Cinema*, ed. Joel Gwynne and Nadine Muller (London: Palgrave Macmillan, 2013), p. 94.

14
Kane and Edgar: Playing with Age in Film

Dee Michell, Casey Tonkin and Penelope Eate

'Did you know that Daniel Craig is 44? I thought he was younger. He's pretty old,' said Casey, age 21. 'He may be old to you, but he's young to me,' responded Dee, age 56. 'Well he's twice my age. I'm sure if he were over 100 then you'd think he was pretty old too,' retorted Casey. 'Fair point,' responded Penelope. 'The thing is, though,' Casey went on thoughtfully, 'I was shocked to find out how old Craig is. I mean, when I watch him on film, I don't see him as twice my age'.

In this chapter we explore how perspectives on age and ageing are shaped and revealed through film. Our interest stemmed from the above and other conversations, for example, about recent films which use older actors and celebrate renewal in late middle age (*The Best Exotic Marigold Hotel* (Madden, 2011) and *Hope Springs* (Frankel, 2012)), to the curious phenomenon of Guy Pearce playing an old man in Ridley Scott's *Prometheus* (2012). As one sci-fi fan has written online: 'Why take a young actor (no matter the skill level) and coat him in tons of aging make-up when you could just cast an old dude in the first place?'[1] Why indeed. Our investigation is guided by the following questions: What does it mean that some films use technology in order to convey ageing while others mask age? What are the gendered implications for men and women when ageing is represented in film? And finally, how might the films that utilise these ageing technologies contribute to the ongoing maintenance of harmful cultural notions which posit the elderly as abject?

We begin with a brief summary of classic film *Citizen Kane* (Welles, 1941). Arguably one of the greatest films ever made, and with an innovative use of makeup effects to approximate the gradual ageing of a newspaper tyrant haunted by childhood trauma, it provides an appropriate artistic and thematic touchstone for themes which, we contend, also emerge in the Clint Eastwood directed biopic of the equally tyrannical J Edgar Hoover, aptly entitled *J. Edgar* (2011). Along with 37-year-old Leonardo DiCaprio in the titular role, *J. Edgar* features 78-year-old stellar British actor Judi Dench in the role of Hoover's mother, reprising an overarching theme in *Citizen Kane*, viz. that powerful men are shaped by their mothers. We argue that while both films are critiques of powerful men and the American dream, the narrative focus on overbearing or absent mothers at the expense of a more thorough engagement with the socio-political particularities of the films' respective historical settings plays into the gender politics of the respective times. The focus on mothers aligns both films with the 'expert mother blaming' movements which arose out of national crises in America during WWII and at the beginning of the Cold War. Rather than query dichotomous gender distinctions during periods of domestic unrest in the nation, psychological experts pathologised and blamed mothers for perceived 'masculine failure,'[2] as indeed do both films.

Kane and Hoover are similarly represented as psychologically damaged and ultimately unfulfilled relics ravished by the effects of time. The ageing men are necessarily faced with losing their grip on power – and thus hegemonic masculinity – as they come to the end of their lives, and the sympathetic filmic explorations of their profound loneliness position them as increasingly vulnerable and non-normative, even 'feminine', as they age. Thus, the ageing process is presented to the viewer as concurrently horrific visually and as a negation or transgression of culturally privileged forms of masculinity which insist upon corporeal resilience and emotional indifference. The concept of destiny further informs the examination of these two texts as both men navigate the pitfalls of their vertiginous professional achievements while haunted by the spectre of old age and (either perennially absent or present) monstrous maternal figures.

The characters for whom old age is stimulating reflection and review of the source of their potency and ruthlessness, however, are not played by old men. Instead, both leads are played by young men and ageing technology is employed to simulate ageing and agedness. Although the lead characters are not the only ones for whom ageing technology is used, the only men permitted to appear onscreen as 'naturally' aged, that is, without the aid of ageing technology, are those who present the least cultural or economic threat to the central male lead. We argue, then, that the inconsistent use of ageing technology in the films is another example of embedded ageism whereby few men are allowed to actually have what Martine Beugnet terms the perceived 'disease' of old age: in the context of late capitalistic culture old age renders people of little 'consumer value and [as] low productivity,' and therefore impaired from the perspective of hyperactive cultural norms.[3] Those few men in the films who do have the 'disease' of old age are those in roles where the characters neatly fit stereotypes of older people as incompetent and powerless[4] and are, therefore, more aligned with cultural conceptions of femininity rather than hegemonic masculinity.

This combination of mother blaming and ageism thus combine in both films to reveal the mainstream gender ideals at the core of negative representations of ageing. Rather than critique the limited and troubling concepts of manhood abroad in culture, the narrative embeds as problematic 'masculine' women who supposedly create them and 'feminine' men who do not fit the hardnosed mould of hegemonic masculinity. In doing so, the films reveal profound discomfort about the ageing process and the way it can disturb rigidly held notions of inherent gender differences.

Our discussion commences with a brief overview of Orson Welles' *Citizen Kane* in order to establish a cinematic reference for the themes of mother blaming, ageism, the feminisation of the aged male, narratives of decline and the utilisation of ageing technology which we contend are brought to the fore in Clint Eastwood's *J. Edgar*. Against the backdrop of *Citizen Kane*, we then introduce *J. Edgar* and explore in turn the use of mother blaming and ageing technology. We use 'mother blaming' to describe the common practice of mothers being made accountable for their children's behaviour even well into their adult years and without regard to the social, political, economic and cultural milieu of the family.[5] 'Ageing technology' is a term we are coining to cover the multiple ways in which the age of an actor is manipulated, for example, by the use of prosthetic makeup such as foam latex, silicone, gelatine and strategic lighting.[6] We argue that these synthetic ageing effects, in conjunction with the motif of mother blaming, at once hide and reveal cultural anxieties regarding the spectacle of ageing, motherhood and the inherent vulnerabilities of hegemonic masculinity.

Citizen Kane

Citizen Kane was the first film directed by the then 26-year-old Orson Welles, who also co-wrote and produced it, as well as played the starring role of Charles Foster Kane. Now canonised in western film studies, *Citizen Kane* was inspired by the story of powerful newspaper magnate William Randolph Hearst (1863–1951) who, rather like Rupert Murdoch during the latter part of the twentieth century, consolidated his power through the practice of sensationalist or 'yellow' journalism.[7] The 1941 *film à clef* follows a reporter/investigator, Jerry Thompson (William Alland), who is seen in only the shadows or from behind as he searches for the meaning of Charlie Kane's dying word, 'Rosebud'. During his search Thompson pieces together Kane's life by interviewing the most important people in it: Kane's best friend, Jedediah Leland (Joseph Cotton), another close friend and employee, Mr Bernstein (Everett Sloane), his butler Raymond (Paul Stewart) and Kane's second wife, Susan Alexander Kane (Dorothy Comingore). As part of his investigation Thompson also reads the memoirs of Kane's wealthy childhood benefactor, Walter Parks Thatcher, the man who became Kane's legal guardian and father figure. Told via flashbacks, the film reveals that Charlie Kane was born into a financially inadequate working class family in the western state of Colorado, to parents who both transgress nineteenth-century, middle-class gender ideology. Instead of being the head of the house and returning to the sanctuary of home at the end of each working day, Jim Kane (Harry Shannon) is unemployed and helps out in his wife's boarding house.[8] When gold is discovered on the property, it is Mary Kane (Agnes Moorhead) who makes the decision for the child to be fostered out in the East with the miserly Thatcher who can protect the boy's financial inheritance, provide an Ivy League education, and assimilate Charlie into the upper classes.

Charles Kane, despite his wealth and elevated position in society, is portrayed at the time of his death as spiritually hollow. He ends his life in virtual seclusion within the grounds of Xanadu, the Victorian Gothic mansion Kane had built and which should have, according to the spiritualised separate spheres ideology of the time,[9] housed a wife devoted to him. *Citizen Kane* highlights the plight of rural Americans in the aftermath of the Civil War and reflects Orson Welles' political affiliation to President Roosevelt's ideas of providing for the unemployed and elderly through social security.[10] Separation from his mother, however, gives rise to a lifelong yearning in Charlie Kane to return to her, symbolised in his dying wish to be reunited with his childhood sled, Rosebud, an Oedipus complex of which the powerful, wealthy and reclusive Kane remains unaware.[11]

It is not until the end of *Citizen Kane* that we find out how influential the figure of Mary Kane really is. In the small but powerful boarding house scene, there is a hint that Mary Kane's motivation is to protect her son from his father's potential violence, but she clearly also wants to protect her son more generally from the father's pernicious influence as a failed man. Mary Kane's coldness in the scene, her lack of consultation with her husband and her steely determination to proceed against the father's intensely felt wish to keep his son convey a strong sense that the mother is responsible for the life trajectory of the son. It is implied that Charlie Kane would have been a nicer man had this psychic wound, caused by Mary Kane's questing for her son to be a more successful man than his father, not been inflicted at all. Therefore, despite some foreshadowing of the economic conditions that might be said to have influenced her decision to remove the child from the family home, Mary Kane is nevertheless depicted as monstrous, uncaring and ultimately culpable for her son's fractured emotional state in later life.

There are several themes in *Citizen Kane* which re-emerge 70 years later in Clint Eastwood's *J. Edgar*. The obvious one is that both films review and critique the lives of powerful American men, but in its examination of Hoover, *J. Edgar* also refuses to examine the socio-political circumstances which allowed for the emergence of yet another tyrant and instead engages in the mother blaming rife at the time *Citizen Kane* was made. The use of ageing technology applied to younger actors for the purpose of 'passing' as elderly is another pronounced theme which, we argue, is ageist and unnecessary. As we said at the outset, mother blaming and ageing technology act together in both films to entrench and reveal mainstream notions about appropriate gender roles in representations of the elderly. In the case of *J. Edgar*, this includes the interesting twist that Hoover's mother was to blame for his being a closeted gay man in a homophobic culture.

J. Edgar

J. Edgar is a biographical account of an American man as equally dominant and despicable as William Randolph Hearst, J. Edgar Hoover (1895–1977). Where Hearst was powerful in the private sector, Hoover was influential in the public sector, both men heading up organisations which specialised in the amassing of 'private' information on US citizens which could be then used to expose those citizens. The film was directed and co-produced by 81-year-old Clint Eastwood while the screenplay was written by much younger LGBT activist, Dustin Lance Black. Black wanted to portray Hoover as a complex man rather than as a monster, and he succeeds, but at the expense of Hoover's mother.[12] As in *Citizen Kane*, flashbacks are used to narrate the story, but this time the source is Hoover, played by DiCaprio who is only just on the 'right' side of 40. As the film opens, Hoover is dictating to an FBI agent tasked with the job of writing the boss' autobiography, essentially Hoover's account of his long bureaucratic career as principal founder and director of the reformed law enforcement agency, the Federal Bureau of Intelligence (FBI). Hoover's work at the Bureau of Investigation (renamed the FBI in 1935) commenced in 1919, thus coinciding with the 'Red Scare' and an antiradicalism movement designed to combat the formation of American Communist Parties, strikes by workers and the circulation of 'dozens of new radical periodicals'.[13]

Hoover's talent for storage and retrieval of information is effectively conveyed in *J. Edgar*, but what the film does less well is explore the way in which the social and political structures allowed him to accumulate information on civilians and thus accumulate power. The latter begins with Hoover's initial enthusiasm for developing a library catalogue at the Library of Congress, and it continues with his role as director of the FBI where he authorised FBI field agents to amass private information on US citizens until he had created, 'a system of surveillance and power-knowledge, based on and practised by registration, filing, and records.'[14] The film also acknowledges Hoover's personal 'archival temple' of information on key government officials and civil rights leaders such as Martin Luther King, key figures in Hollywood[15] and members of the nascent women's movement[16] – indeed anyone involved in any activity regarded as 'subversive'.[17] The final scene in the film has his secretary of more than 50 years, Helen Gandy (Naomi Watts), shredding this bastion of Hoover's ongoing power. While Hoover's embracing of scientific methods, as shown through the arrest of Bruno Hauptmann (Damon Herriman) for the murder of famous aviator Charles Lindbergh's (Josh Lucas) son in 1932, is central to the narrative, aspects of Hoover's personal life are also explored. Of particular note is the close relationship he formed with associate director of the FBI, Clyde Tolson (Armand Hammer), and the central place of his mother, Anna Marie (Judi Dench) in shaping his ambitions and ensuring he conformed to heteronormativity.

Mother blaming

At first glance there is no connection between the sexist practice of mother blaming in *J. Edgar* and what we argue below is the ageist practice of ageing technology, beyond both themes being strongly present in the earlier *Citizen Kane* and the later biopic. As we said above, however, it is the interplay between mother blaming and ageing technology that discloses the essentialist conceptions of gender at the heart of ageism. In *J. Edgar*, as in *Citizen Kane*, rather than critique American culture, the films critique transgressive women through mother blaming – and non-normative men through the uneven use of ageing technology.

In *J. Edgar*, Hoover's mother is portrayed as an 'icy matriarch'[18] rather than as a multifaceted woman, and Australian Naomi Watts as Helen Gandy has little acting space beyond occasional appearances as a devoted assistant to Hoover for the full term of his directorship. The women represent the two ends of the spectrum for women during the period under examination: a career woman who rejects marriage and children in order to have that career, albeit in a servile role, and a dominating woman at home who is too large for that limiting one. In reality, however, the situation for women was much more complex.

Anna Marie Hoover is represented in *J. Edgar* as the driving force behind Hoover. She is *the* dominating figure in his childhood and adulthood until she dies. It is Anna Marie, like Mary Kane, who instils a sense of destiny into the child, suggesting he be the one to save the family. In some unexplained way, Dickerson Hoover has brought disgrace upon the family; he has failed in his role as a breadwinner for the family and thus in his role to protect them from social disgrace. The senior Hoover is, therefore, like Jim Kane, 'the weak one' and since Anna Marie was the dominant partner, their marriage betrayed the gender role norm for the time as well.[19] One especially poignant scene shows a sad and enfeebled old man, played by 83-year-old Jack Donner, sitting on the front verandah and looking up eagerly and pleadingly at the approach of the virile young man about to enter the house. Edgar surveys his father with contempt before ignoring him. Shortly after Dickerson shuffles into a room, the door is closed on him by Anna Marie, and he is not seen again. The father obviously has no significant role to play in the family which is dominated by Anna Marie, and her clear intention is to have her youngest son restore the family's position and reputation. In the foreclosure of any role for Hoover senior (or Kane's father), the film assigns him a 'feminine' role, typical of images of old men in popular culture and, therefore, also suffering the associated ambivalence.[20]

By contrast, Anna Marie fits ideas of hegemonic masculinity with her forceful, focussed and ruthless insistence that her youngest son be successful. In relation to her husband she is a male stereotype, an archetypally powerful castrating woman,[21] a peculiar reassertion of 'patriarchal authority in the context of a society in which the order of the phallus [has] been challenged.'[22] This desire to return to 'a simpler time' can be observed in the recent glut of critically acclaimed and commercially successful Hollywood films set in the interwar or postwar years where now outmoded forms of masculinity take centre stage as either agents of change or conflict resolution, and which includes those directed by

Eastwood: for example, *Flags of Our Fathers, Letters From Iwo Jima* (2006) and *Changeling* (2008).[23]

As the film suggests Anna Marie is to blame for her husband's inadequacies, so it simultaneously suggests she is responsible for her son's relentless quest for power. And yet, as Rapoport and Rapoport wrote in the 1970s, 'it is generally accepted that a man must work and men are socialised for this from infancy.'[24] Therefore it can be argued that Anna Marie was socialising her son into a normative gender role, which would need to have included the traditional macho characteristics Hoover displayed so well, that is, 'aggression, dominance and ruthlessness, coupled with a complete lack of compassion for victims.'[25] In order to be a successful man, Hoover was required to reject the caring, nurturing side of himself evident in his devotion to his mother, or he at least needed to contain it to a very few people such as in his homosocial relationship with Clyde Tolson. Rather than representing this as a socio-political problem, the abjection of the feminine[26] evident in both Hoover's and the culture's misogyny,[27] however, Anna Marie is blamed for Edgar's psychopathic personality.

Anna Marie is also blamed for Hoover's lack of freedom to be himself sexually. Given the intransigence of misogyny, it is likely that the domineering Anna Marie would have been implicitly accused of causing her son's homosexuality had the film been written at an earlier time and not by an LGBT activist. In this twenty-first-century film, however, it is Hoover's conflict over his sexuality which is portrayed as resulting from his mother 'who grooms him to be important, famous – and straight.'[28] It is Anna Marie who tells Edgar that she would rather her son die than be a 'daffodil', and it is not until she does die that the 43-year-old man feels free enough to indulge his need for cross-dressing. Because the focus is on the mother seeking to deny or eradicate the homosexuality of her son, to correct a potentially stigmatised identity, the film ignores the state as a heteronormative as well as masculine institution.[29] There is no exploration in the film of the social mores of the time and the illegality of being gay; in other words, Hoover's sexuality is completely depoliticised. Nor is there even a hint of Hoover's own contribution to creating an antidemocratic social environment in which dissent was actively discouraged by the regular and pernicious surveillance and intimidation[30] of citizens, and the programs, such as the Sex Deviates program, designed by him to detect homosexual public servants and promote the expulsion of gays from the military.[31]

Instead of complexities and critique of the socio-political and cultural context, hegemonic masculinity and heteronormativity, all that *J. Edgar* offers is mother blaming. Such a simplistic and sexist portrayal of Anna Marie – a powerful woman – as responsible for both Hoover's success and his suffering, for his will to power and his angst as a 'deeply closeted homosexual'[32] combines with the uneven use of ageing technology, as we discuss below, to reproduce the essentialist gender ideals which inform ageism.

Masking ageism

As we have pointed out above, one of the key similarities between *Citizen Kane* and *J. Edgar* is the use of ageing technology to convey the passage of time and the weight of life on the central characters. Orson Welles in the part of Charles Foster Kane and Leonardo DiCaprio in the part of J Edgar Hoover both occupy a portion of each film's running time portraying the characters at ages more close to their own. As the two stories unfold, Kane and Hoover age accordingly, as do those of their peer group, with the use of what we have termed ageing technology, which is the application of foam latex, silicon, gelatine or harsh, strategic lighting to 'ravish' the actors by emphasising wrinkles, blemishes, and the gradual recession of male hairlines. In *Citizen Kane* the ageing of young actors works reasonably well, particularly in the case of the old Charles Foster Kane played by the young Orson Welles. Welles' ability to change his posture and voice, in addition to the use of ageing technology, convincingly transforms Kane from a young man to an elderly one, a performance which consolidated Welles' reputation as a great actor.[33] As we discuss below, believability is more problematic in *J. Edgar*.

Our primary interest is the uneven use of ageing technology in both movies. It appears the justification for using ageing technology in *Citizen Kane* flows from ageism and Orson Welles' attempt to create opportunities in film for other young radio and stage actors. At the time there were limited chances for young 'unknowns' to break into the industry,[34] and the closing credits for the movie make a statement to this effect. While not denying this motivation, Welles' negative attitude toward older people and men associated with subordinated forms of masculinity is also apparent since ageing technology is not consistently used throughout. Instead of employing young actors and ageing technology for all, those male characters who are the least powerful, the most inadequate and therefore 'unmanly,' he has used older actors – Erskine Sanford for the ineffectual editor, Herbert Carter; Fortunio Bonanova for the only non-Anglo heritage character, Signor Matiste; and Harry Shannon as Jim Kane, the man who has 'failed' in his principal role as family head and breadwinner.

J. Edgar uses a combination of ageing technology and actual older actors in a similarly inconsistent way to *Citizen Kane*. The lead character of Hoover, who varies in age between a young man of 20, a middle-aged one in his 40s and an elderly one well into his 70s, is played exceptionally well by Leonardo DiCaprio whose outstanding acting skills, like those of Welles, in addition to the effective use of ageing technology, creates an entirely believable man. Aging technology is also used for Hoover's powerful allies, Gandy and Tolson, although inexpertly in the case of Tolson.

But when it comes to those characters who transgress their gender roles most vividly – the dominant Anna Marie and the infantilised Dickerson Hoover – old actors are used. The elderly Dench plays the role of the domineering mother, and the equally old Donner plays the mentally incapacitated father, characters who are transgressing normative gender roles and, curiously, played by the only actors who, as in *Citizen Kane*, actually have the perceived ugliness and 'disease' of old age.[35] Nor is there is much attempt to regress Dench's age when she plays in scenes depicting a younger Anna Marie; on the whole her 'witch-marks,' the 'secret marks of age'[36] have not been elided with technology so there has been little requirement for Dench to have 'corrected [the] particular blemish'[37] and thereby 'pass' as younger. There are some plausible reasons for casting the elderly Judi Dench in the role – for example, continuity between actor and character; the fact that Anna Marie was almost 40 when Edgar, the last of the Hoover children, was born; and children believe that parents are always old, anyway. However, the more likely reason for giving 'space to the aging and the old'[38] while simultaneously, and unnecessarily, using ageing technology for the other significant characters of Tolson and Gandy, is ageism. As Barnett points out, when the elderly appear in the media, they are 'generally portrayed as a population that is mentally confused, physically incapacitated, and emotionally isolated,'[39] as Dickerson Hoover was. Anna Marie Hoover was portrayed as the classic battleaxe, a sexist and ageist representation of an older woman.

Another point to be made about the use of ageing technology in *J. Edgar* is that by 2011 the need to create opportunities for young actors had well and truly disappeared and been replaced with a preference for them. Therefore, the use of ageing technology overlooks the many first-rate older actors who could potentially have played at least two of the three significant roles, even if we concede that continuity in playing Hoover throughout gave DiCaprio considerable scope for extending and displaying his acting talent. However, the characters of Tolson and

Gandy could easily have been played by older actors. Naomi Watts' role in the film, as we said above, is a minor one and the prominent actor would not have been missed had an old woman been cast as the aged Gandy. In the case of Clyde Tolson, 27-year-old Armand Douglas is clearly one younger actor 'who feigns older age badly'.[40] Moreover, the ageing technology makes Tolson look inhuman rather than elderly, 'plastic' enough to suggest a person who has undergone too many plastic surgery and Botox procedures in an effort to 'pass' as youthful,[41] rather than an old man who has suffered a stroke. The companionship Hoover and Tolson have shared over the decades is a feature of the film, but in one potentially beautiful scene of closeness and spiritual solace,[42] the moment is lost because Tolson looks unreal rather than realistically ravaged by age.

Not only is ageing technology employed unevenly in the case of *J. Edgar* in terms of whom it is used for, but also the usage is unbalanced. That is, it helps to create a believable old Hoover with DiCaprio, but it is unnecessary with Gandy, and it is appallingly ridiculous with Tolson. Therefore, in contrast to *Citizen Kane*, the use of ageing technology in *J. Edgar* looks more obviously ageist, analogous even to previously discriminatory practices such as applying blackface to white performers in order to represent black people and boys playing the roles of girls and women in Elizabethan England. As one dominant race and/or gender impersonating another can signal racial and gender hegemony, so young actors impersonating the old can be interpreted as an ageist practice.

Conclusion

Citizen Kane and *J. Edgar* are films which can be read as critiques of powerful men, but the way in which they are made reveals prejudicial attitudes towards mothers and older people. As we have shown, both films contain the sexism of mother blaming. Orson Welles may well have been sympathetic to the need for social security, but he effectively blames Mary Kane for her son's psychopathology rather than capitalism and patriarchy. Similarly, in *J. Edgar*, it is Anna Maria who is blamed for her son's distorted personality and raging internal conflict about his sexuality rather than a heteronormative, conservative and paranoid culture. The use of ageing technology, while ostensibly in the service of continuity of characters, also reveals ageism because it is used unevenly. Older actors have been employed, but only in those roles where the characters are clearly transgressing normative gender expectations and in some cases, particularly that of Dickerson Hoover, are stereotypically incapacitated, as well.

J. Edgar is particularly disappointing when it comes to both the sexism and ageism. Clearly in sympathy with the notion of a publically powerful man suffering in private because of a conflicted gender and sexual identity, Dustin Lance Black, who regularly challenges heteronormativity through his LGBT activism, achieves his aim to not represent Hoover as a monster, but he does so only by creating a monstrous mother and failing to critique the homophobic times to which Hoover actively contributed. And rather than employ elderly actors in key 'public sphere' roles, such as Gandy and Tolson, the octogenarian director, Clint Eastwood, engaged them as only 'private sphere' characters who have failed markedly in their prescribed gender roles.

However, what we have demonstrated in this chapter is something even more complex than the agendas of individual men. By juxtaposing the ageism inherent in the practice of ageing technology with the mother blaming in *J. Edgar*, we have shown how the film conveys profound anxieties about the fluidity of gender characteristics in ageing. Old men, even once powerful old men, can become vulnerable, dependent and 'feminine,' but rather than critique essentialist notions of gender, women are blamed. Thus, fear about age disrupting gendered distinctions becomes apparent as the basis for ageism.

Acknowledgement

Thanks go to Nathan Kauschke for his patient assistance with formatting.

Notes

1. *Prometheus – A Film by Ridley Scott*, available at http://www.prometheus-movie.com/community/forums/topic/8177 (Accessed 30 November 2012).
2. Ashley Aidenbau, 'Mother-Blaming and the Rise of the Expert,' available at http://michiganjournalhistory.files.wordpress.com/2014/02/aidenbaum_ashley.pdf (Accessed 19 February 2014).
3. Martine Beugnet, 'Screening the Old: Femininity as Old Age in Contemporary French Cinema,' *Studies in the Literary Imagination*, 39:2 (2006), p. 4.
4. Betty Friedan, *The Fountain of Age*. (New York: Simon & Schuster, 1993), p. 15.
5. Debra Jackson and Judy Mannix, J., 'Giving Voice to the Burden of Blame: A Feminist Study of Mother's Experiences of Mother Blaming,' in *International Journal of Nursing Practice*, 10 (2004), p. 150.
6. Examples of which can be observed in a number of motion picture films spanning the past 60 years. Ageing technology might be utilised for several purposes, for instance to denote the passage of time in both fictional and real life inspired biopics while maintaining continuity as the actor transitions from young adulthood to old age such as in *Giant* (Stevens, 1956), *Little Big Man* (Penn, 1970) *Chaplin* (Attenborough, 1992), *Raging Bull* (Scorsese, 1980),

The Hours and *The Reader* (Daldry, 2002, 2008); to suggest the often humorous pursuit of beauty via medical intervention such as in *Death Becomes Her* (Zemeckis, 1992); to demonstrate an actor's comedic range such as in *Coming To America* (Landis, 1988); magical realism such as in *The Curious Case of Benjamin Button* (Fincher, 2008); or less commonly, in non-narrative experimental absurdism such as in *Trash Humpers* (Korine, 2009).

7. Sarah Street, 'Crises of Masculinity: Homosocial Desire and Homosexual Panic in the Critical Cold War Narratives of Mailer and Hoover,' *Critique*, 48:3 (2007), p. 48.

8. Linda Lichter, 'Home truths,' *Commentary*, 97:6 (1994), p. 49.

9. Lichter, p. 51.

10. Ibid., p. 50

11. Ibid., p. 52

12. Brian Johnson, 'The Gay G-man: FBI Director J. Edgar Hoover is Portrayed as a Deeply Closeted Homosexual in a New Biopic,' *Maclean's*, 124:45 (2011), p. 82.

13. Larry Ceplair, 'The Film Industry's Battle against Left-wing Influences, from the Russian Revolution to the Blacklist,' *Film History*, 20:4 (2008), p. 399.

14. Eric Ketelaar, 'Archival Temple, Archival Prison: Modes of Power and Protection,' *Archival Science*, 2:3–4 (2002), pp. 221. See also: Laura Donohue, 'Anglo-American Privacy and Surveillance,' *Journal of Criminal Law and Criminology*, 96:3 (2006).

15. Andy Meisler, 'How Blacklisting Hurt Hollywood Children,' in *The New York Times* (31 August 1995).

16. Donohue, p. 1068. See also: John Butler, ' Homosexuals and the Military Establishment,' in *Society*, 16 (1993).

17. Ceplair, p. 402.

18. Johnson, p. 82.

19. Michael Snyder, 'Crises of Masculinity: Homosocial Desire and Homosexual Panic in the Critical Cold War Narratives of Mailer and Coover,' *Critique*, 48:3 (2007), p. 252.

20. Toni Calasanti and Neal King, 'Firming the Floppy Penis: Age, Class, and Gender Relations in the Lives of Old Men,' *Men and Masculinities*, 8:1 (2005), pp. 3–23

21. Barbara Bennett, 'Castrating Women,' *Off Our Backs*, 24:1 (1994), p. 16.

22. Simon Hallsworth, 'The Feminization of the Corporation, the Masculinization of the State,' *Social Justices*, 32:1 (2005), p. 38.

23. *Seabiscuit* (Ross, 2003), *The Aviator* (Scorsese, 2004), *Capote* (Miller, 2005) *Cinderella Man* (Howard, 2005), *Good Night, and Good Luck* (Clooney, 2005), *Revolutionary Road* (Mendes, 2008), *Public Enemies* (Mann, 2009), *The Tree of Life* (Malick, 2011), *The Adventures of Tintin* (Spielberg, 2011) and *The Master* (Anderson, 2011) are further examples of the contemporary trend in film towards reclaiming a masculinist past.

24. Rhona Rapoport and Robert Rapoport, 'Further Considerations on the Dual Career Family,' *Human Relations*, 24:6 (1971), p. 519.

25. Hallsworth, p. 35.

26. Anna Claydon, 'The Projected Man: The B-Movie and the Monstrous-Masculine', *Extrapolation*, 48:3 (2007), p. 482.

27. Claire Potter, 'Queer Hoover: Sex, Lies, and Political History,' *Journal of the History of Sexuality*, 15:3 (2006), p. 364.

28. Johnson, p. 82.
29. Raewyn Connell, *Masculinities* (Crows Nest, NSW: Allen & Unwin, 2005), p. 73.
30. Potter, p. 377.
31. Ibid., p. 368. See also: Donohue, p. 1063.
32. Johnson, p. 82.
33. Peter Lehman and William Luhr, 'Citizen Kane: An Analysis of Citizen Kane', Thinking About Movies: Watching, Questioning, Enjoying, ed. by Peter Lehman and William Luhr (Malden, MA: Blackwell Publishing, 2003).
34. Ibid., p. 339.
35. Beugnet, p. 4. See also: Margaret Gullette, *Aged by Culture* (Chicago: The University of Chicago Press, 2004), p. 4.
36. Germaine Greer, *The Change. Women, Aging and the Menopause* (Alfred Knopf: New York, 1991), p. 362. See Also: Barnett, p. 87.
37. Erving Goffman, *Stigma: Notes on the Management of Spoiled Identity* (New Jersey: Prentice-Hall, 1963), p. 9.
38. Beugnet, p. 1.
39. Barbara Barnett, 'Focusing on the Next Picture: Feminist Scholarship as a Foundation for Teaching about Ageism in the Academy,' *NWSA Journal*, 18:1 (2006), pp. 85–98.
40. Gullette, p. 170.
41. Friedan, p. 28.
42. Rand Cooper, 'The Age of Regret: *Trouble with the Curve* & *Hope Springs*,' *Commonweal*, 139:18 (2012), p. 25.

15

Beyond Wicked Witches and Fairy Godparents: Ageing and Gender in Children's Fantasy on Screen

Rebecca-Anne C. Do Rozario and Deb Waterhouse-Watson

In children's fantasy, anything can happen. Castles can rasp and amble across the countryside, houses can float from balloons, a good night's sleep can kill, and an old person can be the hero of their own story. This chapter examines a range of children's fantasy texts in which the elderly are visible. These are texts that particularly centralise elderly embodiment, reimagining the relationship between growing up/ageing and agency, offering alternative ways to imagine femininity and masculinity. Sanna Lehtonen takes the position that '[f]antasy fiction offers writers a field where they can reimagine societal structures, norms and conventions related to gender.'[1] While this potential is not always explored, children's and family-orientated fantasy, especially inspired by fairy tale, provides a particularly imaginative space for negotiating age and its gendered implications, since such fantasy is defined and promoted by age appropriateness. The profusion of witches and older men in addition to youthful heroes and heroines enables explorations of power, agency and marginalisation. It might be expected that representations of ageing in children's fantasy have progressed in recent years, but we show that problematic trends have appeared, particularly regarding ageing women. Older fairy tales prominently feature old women's voices, but although film and television make women's bodies visible, these media often render them marginal, disempowered or pathologised. Nevertheless, representations of old age need not be ageist, and creaking bones and stooped walks can render the ageing body both present and active. By analysing a selection of children's fantasy in film and television, particularly in animation, this chapter highlights the key trends in depicting old bodies, both female and male.

Child/aged agency

The child and the aged adult share an analogous embodied subjectivity, one articulated through physical incapacity and/or restriction. Traditionally, children's fantasies of the golden age, including Lewis Carroll's *Alice's Adventures in Wonderland* (1865) and J.M. Barrie's *Peter Pan and Wendy* (1911), are seen to present an idyllic state of childhood, separate and distinct from the adult world. However, Marah Gubar suggests that such authors 'generally conceive of child characters and child readers as socially saturated beings, profoundly shaped by the culture, manners, and morals of their time, precisely in order to explore the vexed issue of the child's agency: given their status as dependent, acculturated beings.'[2] In essence, the child's agency is a vexed question *because* children are a part of the adult world but deemed incapable of independence; their children's bodies are too undeveloped, uninhibited and inexperienced. The uncertainty of this status manifests in various ways in fantasy: Alice, for instance, cannot even control her size and expands and contracts in an alarming manner, while Peter Pan's refusal to grow up is an unremitting effort to maintain his physical child's body. Childhood itself is a state of slippage, its boundaries constantly renegotiated by texts as social and cultural contexts, laws and mores – including sexual consent, education and labour laws – change. Like childhood, old age is defined by age, but that age varies depending on a wide range of factors including retirement, menopause, physical decline and even the grey hairs on a person's head or wrinkles on their face. Old age, like childhood, is a slippery construct and the agency of the aged is likewise a vexed question since despite adult autonomy, physical infirmity and post-reproductive (even post-sexual) status can render the aged once more dependent or marginalised. Shakespeare succinctly suggests that the old enter a 'second childishness,' which often resonates with the way old age is imagined today.

This application of childishness is used to restrict the embodied subjectivity of the young *and* old by deeming them outside the boundaries of a mature prime. The thorny question of agency is thus linked to the embedding of childishness within young and old bodies, what Teresa Mangum refers to as the 'interplay of past and present.'[3] This chapter examines those old bodies within the bounds of children's fantasy, where issues of agency, and the genre itself, offer empowerment for children that can enable sympathetic representation of old age. The symmetry between the not-yet-independent child and the no-longer-independent old person can promote positive interactions across generations and create space for children to understand the subject position of the aged or reproduce the politics of marginalisation.

Off with her head!: voices, bodies and the storyteller

The bodies of old men and women are frequently visible in children's fantasy, though rarely does an aged figure play a heroic role. The bodies of old women in particular are culturally delineated by a strong fairy tale tradition of key, though not central, roles for aged women. Mangum, for instance, argues that in Victorian fairy tales 'we find more complex qualities attributed to imaginary old women, and more varied and textured alternatives to conventional representations of women in old age.'[4] Conventionally, the sexual objectification of the youthful female body has presented particular problems for the aged female body, subjecting these bodies to the indignity of becoming sexless or even aggressively anti-sexual, marked by decay, with older women doomed to covet a young body. Discourses of sexism and ageism connect, and according to Ruth E. Ray, 'ageism, like sexism and racism, is embedded in the same thought processes, social organizations, and political systems that second- and third- wave feminists have spent the past forty years trying to change.'[5] Ageism becomes a particular area of feminist concern regarding the body. Catriona Mackenzie notes: 'In the case of women's dissatisfaction with ... specific bodily attributes, experiences of alienation from one's bodily perspective are clearly bound up with oppressive social and cultural practices, representations of gender and sexuality, and ideals of beauty.'[6] The dissatisfaction with aged bodily attributes becomes a particularly significant experience of such alienation. The ageism implicit in the imagined female body is largely informed by the maiden/mother/crone construction of femininity, a construction that involves reinscribing the body as it ages, with the subjectivity of youth imagined as distinct and divided from the old body. Old men's bodies, on the other hand, are less frequently reinscribed as they age, with male subjectivity not so tethered to age. Penelope Deutscher affirms that 'norms of feminine subjectivity are more associated with youth than those of male subjectivity.'[7] One result is that there is no popular, masculine equivalent to the desexualised crone figure of fantasy – particularly the crone who wants to occupy a youthful body herself.

While she is an important figure, in fairy tales particularly, the physical body of the crone is generally shifted to the margins of the story or excised, often bundled into an oven and reduced to ashes or melted with a bucket of H_2O. As the crone, she exists as the end point of female subjectivity with a body that is at its terminus, at a point of ruination or expiry, and any attempt to exercise power on her part must be thwarted. Sylvia Henneberg argues:

> Allowing little more than a handful of highly problematic stereotypes such as the wicked witch, the self-effacing good fairy, and the ineffectual crone to take the place of mother figures firmly interlocks ageism and sexism, fuels the continued segregation of the old, particularly the female elder, and further broadens an already deplorably vast gulf between generations within and outside the text.[8]

Yet, in fairy tales, the old woman's *voice* is loud. She claims ownership of the tales that often suppress her, embodied as Mother Goose or as one of her voluble peers. The elderly female voice has evolved over the centuries to become synonymous with that of the tale teller. In early fairy tale collections, such as Giambattista Basile's *Lo cunto de li cunti* (1634–36), storytelling is undertaken by an assembly of crones, all physically articulated; one crone, for instance, '[sucks] her lips at length' before speaking.[9] By the end of the seventeenth century in France, as fairy tale in print became more common, 'commentators connected old women with fantastic tale-telling.'[10] Perrault's 1697 collection ascribes his tales to Mother Goose, and in England she became the dominant figure, frequently embodied in the witch-crone figure with wrinkles and a black pointy hat, riding a broomstick or goose. Yet she remains embodied within the narrative frame and outside the tales of youthful adventure. She rarely tells her own story. The Oscar-nominated short film, *Granny O'Grimm's Sleeping Beauty* (Nicky Phelan, 2008), is one crone's retaliation against such marginalisation, a film that refocuses upon the physical body of the teller and permits her to displace the central, infant heroine and her youthful allies in favour of the crotchety, elderly fairy with whom Granny, as teller, identifies.[11] Old age is affirmed, not rejected or denied.

Betty Friedan argues, '[b]y denying the real infirmities of age, we become its passive victims, forfeiting choice.'[12] Granny O'Grimm is an active proponent of the infirmities of age, refusing to become a passive victim. Her representation in CG animation gives her a three-dimensional, round, squat, postmenopausal body with hair like a bunch of dry, grey twigs. As she moves, the doors, floors and furniture creak in response, echoing her creaking bones. Granny is contemptuous of fairy tale mores, particularly the celebration of youth represented in baby 'Beauty's glamorous godmothers.' Glamour is articulated with animation of blonde-coiffed fairies waving their wands to inflate their perky breasts. The subsequent introduction of 'the elderly fairy' makes explicit the character's marginalisation: 'she was old and decrepit and not one bit useful in the eyes of all the younger, more exciting fairies.' Granny's tone of heavy irony and the young fairies' vacuous expressions subvert more familiar versions of the tale in which the elderly fairy is portrayed as simply a dangerous threat compared with the benevolent younger fairies. For example, Perrault's version introduces 'an aged fairy...who had not been invited, because for more than fifty years she had never left the tower she lived in, so that she was believed to be dead, or under a spell.'[13] Granny elaborates upon Perrault's simple ageism, articulating and making visible the physical decay leading to the elderly fairy's ostracism. She does so by turning her chair deliberately to look at her own aged body in the mirror, repining that youthful fairies do not know 'how it feels to be old and constantly sleeping.' By acknowledging infirmity and drawing attention to the injustice of her exclusion, Granny and by extension, the elderly fairy, cease to be passive victims. Their speech becomes a tool of empowerment, even menace, but maintaining Granny as focaliser ensures that any menace is justified and even treated with empathy.

The elderly fairy finally delivers her curse: the moment everyone falls asleep, they will die. Here Granny ceases her narration on a breathless cackle, the film finishing with her affectionate, but sinister, exhortation for her granddaughter to sleep well. The tale is curtailed at the moment the elderly fairy is usually dismissed from the narrative, refocusing the tale away from the youthful Sleeping Beauty to the prejudice against the elderly fairy. Like Beauty, Granny's granddaughter remains speechless throughout the narrative, thus failing to affect the narrative action. Granny's voice and body are foremost. As Sinead Gillett suggests, 'In many ways Granny is real.'[14] More importantly, her old body is chief protagonist and through acerbic humour she elucidates the prejudices lying behind the stereotype of the mean old crone.

Nevertheless, Granny is exceptional – a critical response to changes in fairy tales influenced by recent Hollywood conventionality. The output of the Disney studios and Hollywood constructions of female glamour, in particular, emphasise youth and sexuality in fairy tale. Marina Warner, taking the long view, observes: 'Prejudices against women, especially old women and their chatter, belong in the history of fairy tale's changing status.'[15] Changes today are caught up in Hollywood discourses on ageing, and fairy tale's old women are viewed as undesirable, not simply as old women, but physically as old bodies. As such, they are frequently expelled from narratives as punishment. Zoe Brennan thus discovers 'a status quo that grounds contemporary Western society – one that is age-sensitive and rewards youth while penalizing old age,' although this status quo mostly applies to older women.[16] Children are certainly not encouraged to sympathise with the aged in these instances.

Even non-Hollywood films today can reinforce the undesirability of old age, sometimes despite deriving from a progressive source text. Diana Wynne Jones' novel *Howl's Moving Castle* (1986) features a youthful heroine transformed into a crone, effectively disrupting the maiden-mother-crone divisions of female subjectivity. On first seeing her elderly reflection, Sophie comments to herself, 'This is much more like you really are.'[17] She articulates no disjunction between her maiden subjectivity and her now old, though healthy, body; in fact, she embraces their synergy. The transformation is the catalyst for her to set off on adventure; it also enables her to speak freely, shriek and yell, actions previously too assertive for her youthful, shy self. Her elderly body is portrayed as the site of power by transgressing feminine behavioural norms. Sanna Lehtonon notes, 'Sophie's transformation highlights how subjectivity is embodied';[18] however, Wynne Jones' portrayal blurs and disrupts the connection between subjectivity and age. Moira Gatens' concept of the 'imaginary body,'[19] whose cultural and historical specificity underpins the capacities and 'normal' functions ascribed to it, is particularly useful here. The imaginary body can help shape individual thought and action; it is also necessarily individual, and Sophie's young imaginary body is very limited. Having access to an old body allows Sophie to broaden the scope of her young body's imagined capabilities. This broadened scope is highlighted when her transformation back into a young woman at the novel's conclusion is unnoticed by the characters and unspecified in the text. Its implied irrelevance suggests that the capabilities her old body enabled will continue, thus disconnecting subjectivity from aged female embodiment. However, the consequent anime adaptation *Howl's Moving Castle* (Hayao Miyazaki, 2004) erases the ambiguity and undermines the novel's progressiveness. While the film begins with a promising representation of the crone's frailty and agency, the visual medium insists on the primacy of youth – although she is not aware of it, whenever 'old' Sophie asserts herself or takes action of any kind, she appears young again, thereby identifying action with youth, not old age. Further, the romance narrative between Sophie and Howl comes to dominate, and in response Sophie progressively appears younger, with silver-grey hair only a token symbol of age. Romantic passion is represented as a youthful concern. Sophie's embodiment in the old body is allowed to fade away unacknowledged, and with it, the space in which the young girl and crone's agencies could co-exist.

The Witch of the Waste, the other old woman figure of *Howl's Moving Castle*, is a more conventional representation of ageing in both novel and anime, although the anime once again provides a more regressive portrayal. This crone has cast a spell on herself to appear youthful, and in the novel this brings about her own destruction and punishment: 'the witch's old heart crumbled into black sand and soot and nothing.'[20] However, in the anime, she is magically returned to an ancient body to reflect her 'real' age, becoming passive and dependent and, like a literal infant, relying on others to feed and move her. Although Elizabeth Parsons argues that the witch's presence '[multiplies] the older women in the frame,' demonstrating that old women 'cannot be simply categorized or stereotyped',[21] the witch's passivity simply reinforces the common lack of power – and, indeed, childishness – ascribed to old bodies. Sophie's increasingly youthful appearance further reinforces this infantile old woman as the 'true' crone.

Striving for youth, punished with age

Crones like the Witch of the Waste are frequently penalised for the magical appropriation of youthful, beautiful bodies, as more adult fantasy films such as *Stardust* (Matthew Vaughn, 2007) and *Into the Woods* (Rob Marshall, 2014) show.[22] In such films, there is little or no explanation of the witch's desire for youth; her desire is simply incorporated into her evil activities, thereby implying that such desire is depraved. Friedan remarks upon a propensity to 'hold on to the illusions and expectations of youth – thinking only in youth's terms of what we wanted and expected of ourselves.'[23] Yet for a witch to do so results in the punishment of oblivion or, perversely, the restoration of her old body – the old body itself is punishment. Old women in film are effectively caught in a double bind not of their own making: youth is celebrated and old age is derided, yet the desire for youth is pathologised.

Such a dynamic is overt in children's fantasy films, too, beyond *Howl's Moving Castle*.[24] In Disney's *Tangled* (Nathan Greno, Byron Howard, 2010), Mother Gothel restores her youth through a secret magical flower. Her motivation appears to be, as Friedan suggests, to hold on to youth, although it is again not made clear why youth is desired. The pregnant queen becomes ill, however, and the flower is discovered and taken to ensure the safe delivery of the baby Rapunzel. The film thus conflates the magic's ability to restore youth with restoring life/health, implying that old age itself is a state of death and infirmity. Mother Gothel kidnaps Rapunzel, whose hair now contains the magic, and although her maternal subjectivity is briefly realised in expressions of love for Rapunzel, her appropriation of youth is punished at the film's climax: when Rapunzel's hair is cut, Mother Gothel begins to age rapidly. Her previously pinkish complexion and smooth skin become grey and wrinkled; her hair turns silver. She reacts in horror, hiding within a cloak as though her old body is repulsive. Quite why she reacts so badly to an old body is never explored, for she conveniently falls from a window, turning to dust. Like many crones before her, Old Mother Gothel is simply done away with. The ageing female body is not fit to be seen and is, in fact, an instrument of death.

Given its prevalence in contemporary fantasy film and television, another fairy tale narrative of particular concern is 'Snow White'. Problematically, despite neither age nor sexual desirability being features of early versions, in retelling, it increasingly pits old and young bodies against each other. Some critics highlight a reading of ageism in the Grimms' fairy tale (1812/1854) of a wicked queen attempting to kill her stepdaughter, with Merry G. Perry arguing, '*Snow White* narrates the story of an aging woman who will stop at nothing to retain her status as the "fairest of them all"'.[25] Although the Grimms' tale never states that the Queen fears ageing, over time, tellers increasingly exploit this culturally situated fear. Its ageism appears to be an effect of the contemporary Hollywood context, often interpreted retrospectively. Perry reads ageism into Disney's *Snow White and the Seven Dwarfs* (David Hand *et al.*, 1937), writing that the queen's 'inability to accept her own aging and loss of beauty reflects an insecurity that the audience might subconsciously understand.'[26] Yet the 1930s Disney Queen is a beauty in her prime, in figure-hugging purple with red lips and eyebrows to rival Joan Crawford's. The Queen is neither old nor losing her looks: she commands the audience's attention.

Only later Hollywood adaptations focus on the queen's age, which resonates with and arguably (re)produces contemporary anxieties about ageing and embodiment. *Snow White and the Huntsman* (Rupert Sanders, 2012) and *Mirror Mirror* (Tarsem Singh, 2012), are explicit that the Queen artificially retains her youth through magic. Both queens are played by established Hollywood leads in their late 30s and 40s, Charlize Theron and Julia Roberts respectively, but both queens are really old women. They are ultimately punished with physical old age – dismissed and destroyed. The films evince Hollywood's own underlying attitudes towards ageing female stars, celebrated in maturity, but threatened with rejection in old age, particularly if they artificially hold on to youth. When the aged female body is thus pathologised, young and old are potentially alienated, and anxieties are promoted in those facing old age.

The *Snow White* narrative is also central to US ABC family series *Once Upon a Time* (Adam Horowitz, Edward Kitsis, 2011–), which does away with the ageing female body in a very different way. Three generations of women are lead protagonists: the evil Queen, her stepdaughter Snow White, and Snow White's daughter, Emma. However, ageing is erased since each generation is embodied as a woman in her late twenties/ early thirties. This disrupts the typical division of female subjectivity according to age, as determined here by familial relationships, but it also erases the elderly body. Cursed by the evil Queen, Regina, the characters remain in a time loop in Storybrooke, Maine. Held in the curse, Snow White remains thirty, while her daughter, Emma, grows up outside the curse and is around her mother's age when first entering Storybrooke. Regina is barely older than her stepdaughter, Snow White, and also does not age. She in fact adopts Henry, Emma's son. The figures of maiden, mother, and crone intersect and merge with all three women embodying the mother role.[27] Elizabeth Bell argues of Disney animated features that women 'are not bifurcated into good and bad, but represent a continuum of cultural representations of women's powers and performances…these constructed performances are rooted in a physical timeline that decrees that these bodies will change.'[28] Ironically, in the live action series the physical timeline is sabotaged and change arrested, effectively effacing the crone. Apart from Granny, notable largely as a figure of sexual repression, the only other old woman given significant screen time is Regina's mother, the glamorous (and murderous) Queen of Hearts. However, she dies in the second season when her daughter returns her heart, mending the maternal relationship. Although the aged body is not portrayed as a punishment, nor is the Queen's death connected to age, once the maternal relationship is resolved, there is no space within the text to explore aged embodiment in positive ways. Maternal priorities marginalise and dismiss the crone.

By contrast, male intergenerational relationships detach subjectivity from age without obscuring it and permit the embodiment of masculine ageing. Regina's villainous rival, Rumplestiltskin, is a visibly ageing man in his 50s. Rumplestiltskin, his son, Bae, and grandson, Henry, embody their generations in contrast to the female leads. In the third season, Rumplestiltskin returns to Neverland to rescue Henry, whom Peter Pan has kidnapped. Pan, the traditional figure of eternal childhood, is revealed as Rumplestiltskin's father, who had to surrender his paternal role and become a physical child again to rule Neverland. Masculine physical embodiment is largely independent of subjectivity and old men and boys can inhabit each other's bodies with apparent alacrity in a way that females cannot. Pan finds agency in the embodiment and space of childhood, even taking over his great grandson's body to remain Neverland's ruler.

Disney's fantastic old men: wise or silly

Elderly male characters in children's fantasy film are not uncommon, although like older women they are mostly secondary characters, if in greater numbers.[29] In Disney animated films the elderly male usually fulfils a paternal role, a number of young heroes having white-haired fathers. Disney's elderly father-figure was ubiquitous in the 1990s and portrayed in two main forms: the tall, wise, muscular father, like King Triton from *The Little Mermaid* (Ron Clements, John Musker, 1989), Powhatan from *Pocahontas* (Mike Gabriel, Eric Goldberg, 1995) and Fa Zhou from *Mulan* (Tony Bancroft, Barry Cook, 1998), and the short, squat and comically childish father, including Maurice from *Beauty and the Beast* (Gary Trousdale, Kirk Wise, 1991), the Sultan from *Aladdin* (Ron Clements, John Musker, 1992) and Professor Porter from *Tarzan* (Chris Buck, Kevin Lima, 1999). Elderly male subjectivity became split between the performance of experience, conforming to the traditional role of guide, and that of 'second childishness,' where a silly old man must be rescued from danger or folly. The physical embodiment of old age is, however, rarely explored in these films, and fathers do not have goals and desires outside their relationships to youthful protagonists. Mulan's father, Fa Zhou, for example, collapses while attempting military manoeuvres, prompting her to discover her own physical agency as a soldier, and Belle's father, Maurice, grows ill, forcing her to discover agency in relationships with the Beast and the townspeople. Their infirmities are explored from the perspectives of their daughters rather than through their own lived experience, becoming motivators to agency rather than examples of agency themselves. The aches and pains of old age are often even erased or ignored as when Professor Porter swings as easily from vines as Jane and Tarzan.

Empowering the elderly male body: *Up*

By contrast, animated feature film *Up* (Pete Docter, Bob Peterson, 2009) not only foregrounds the embodied experience of ageing, it also portrays old age as liberating. The elderly protagonist, Carl, finally gets to live his childhood dream of adventuring in Paradise Falls, a beautiful, remote spot in South America. However, in contrast to most popular fantasy texts, his portrayal acknowledges and works with the ageing male body's limitations. After his wife Ellie's death, Carl resists a property developer's endeavours to convince him to sell the house they lived in together. When Carl attacks a construction worker with his walking stick, the developer forces him to move into a retirement home, Shady Oaks. When two men from Shady Oaks arrive to take him away, their tone is patronising and the hulking size of one implies that they can physically force him into their van. The retirement home is portrayed as a restrictive, infantilising prison. However, rather than comply, Carl breaks free. Turning the house into an airship using thousands of helium balloons, he lifts into the air, heading for Paradise Falls. Significantly, a symbol of childhood is Carl's means of transport, and he finally accesses the freeing, child*like* (not childish) potential he always possessed.

Aged male embodiment in *Up* is used to challenge popular representations of older men's bodies as unaffected by ageing, instead making physical vulnerability visible (and audible). In contrast to the multitude of fantastical representations of older women needing to possess young bodies, the ravages of age for men are routinely denied or subordinated to a younger hero's quest. Although they often bear signs of age, like white hair or wrinkles, representations of older men in fantasy rarely, centrally, engage with the limitations of ageing. Ageing, well-known male actors such as Harrison Ford and Sean Connery frequently play leading action roles where, despite white hair or wrinkles, the ageing body is denied. At 66, Ford reprised his action-hero Indiana Jones role. In an interview, he suggested audiences would not be interested in a protagonist who showed age-related physical limitations: 'No one wants to see a hero have to pick up his cane to hit someone, but I'm still quite fit enough to fake it.'[30] Thus denying male ageing within films implies an anxiety about loss of dominative masculinity, as the audience is presumed to disavow any reduction in masculine prowess that ageing may bring. Indeed, Öberg found that older men were much more likely to feel a loss of masculinity as they aged.[31] It should be acknowledged that Ford and Connery have earlier, youthful performances to live up to; nevertheless, the effect remains that, to be powerful, the older male fantasy hero must not be physically limited. The Red Riding Hood film *Hoodwinked* (Edwards, 2005) arguably also employs this strategy for a female hero, since Granny competes in snowboarding championships and other extreme sports; however, as Elizabeth Parsons argues, she is positioned as the 'exception that proves the rule':[32] 'I'm not like other grannies', she says, playing to stereotypes of old women. The apparent denial of female ageing is a parody reinforcing the physical infirmity of 'typical' old women.

Up parodies denial, too, in the epic battle between Carl and his hero-turned-nemesis, Muntz, but it does so by confronting the anxiety about loss of hypermasculinity represented by the old body and subverting it through humour. Both Carl and Muntz seize up at a crucial moment, unable to wield their weapon of choice. Excessively loud creaks and groans underscore the comic lightness and highlight how ridiculous it is to deny the ageing process. Directly contradicting Ford's quip about canes, Carl's stick becomes his main weapon and the symbol of age-associated weakness transforms into a tool of strength. Significantly, Carl does not defeat Muntz through superior strength or skill, but through chance and help from Russell and Dug the talking dog, thus avoiding the potential to deny the limitations of his age. Muntz's gigantic sword and gun are ultimately irrelevant, and he is somewhat ironically defeated by catching his foot in a bunch of balloons and falling to his death. Since this fate resembles that of many elderly female villains before him, it poses a challenge to hegemonic masculinity itself. Animation thus proves a particularly appropriate means of engaging with the 'realities' of ageing.

In addition, *Up* emphasises the symmetry between old age and childhood, marginalising adulthood in favour of childhood and old age. A montage of Carl's life early in the film actually skims over the years between childhood and old age, whereas childhood and old age are portrayed mimetically. This connection to childhood is anchored by the developing friendship with 8-year-old Russell, a Wilderness Explorer (boy scout) who is accidentally carried along when Carl's house takes off for Paradise Falls. While Russell is close in age to the implied child viewer, Carl's perspective is provided and Carl positioned as the audience surrogate. Elderly characters in children's fiction are generally portrayed as if they were 'always old' and therefore different from the child. Providing the viewer with the mimetic story of Carl's growing up helps to construct him as an empathetic figure for the audience, and it suggests that childhood fantasies can once again be accessed in old age. Rather than marginalising childhood and age, *Up* centralises them, thus inviting a child viewer to perceive elderly people as 'like them', with their own goals and desires and experiences parallel to their own.

Up thematises the symmetry of their struggle for independence. The trajectory of the elderly protagonist's struggle is to transcend old age's limitations and *return* to independence, whereas the child's is to transcend youth's limitations and *attain* independence. The developing relationship between Carl and Russell emphasises the parallels between them, as each learns to recognise the vital knowledge and skills the other brings. Carl ultimately achieves liberation, regaining independence and power through defeating Muntz and helping to protect the female 'snipe', a gigantic, brightly coloured bird Russell has named 'Kevin.' Russell, too, begins to act independently, setting off to save Kevin by himself. After rope climbing failures in school, his plump child's body finally succeeds in climbing up a garden hose to reach the floating house. He receives a surrogate father in Carl, who in the denouement carries out the Wilderness Explorer ritual that Russell and his father once engaged in, eating ice cream and counting cars. While Russell returns to dependence, the parallels between the two characters imply future independence to the child viewer. While the child audience, like Russell, may 'not yet' have their full power and independence, alignment with Carl as protagonist gives hope for future achievement.

Conclusion

Despite the prevalence of marginalised, elderly bodies in children's fantasy, as this chapter demonstrates, some recent texts have capitalised on the genre's subversive reclaiming potential, rejecting ideals of feminine beauty and masculine dominance and affirming the elderly body's value. The link between female subjectivity and age can be disrupted, with the elderly person's perspective privileged and validated. Traditionally, the elderly body is marginalised in children's fantasy and is still often ejected as punishment. There is an increasing drive in Hollywood film to reimagine fairy tales to reflect and (re)produce anxieties about (female) ageing, and even non-Hollywood adaptations of more recent, progressive texts such as *Howl's Moving Castle* (1986) can marginalise and disempower the elderly body. Nevertheless, as this chapter demonstrates, this is not a uniform cultural shift: other texts re-engage with these bodies and maximise the genre's subversive potential to privilege and validate crones and old men. While many recent texts, including Hollywood blockbusters, excise and pathologise the old body, the medium of film can make ageing both audible and visible, providing space for children to sympathise with this embodied experience. Within children's fantasy, there is a kinship between the child and the elderly whereby both seek – and often succeed in obtaining – independence despite their undeveloped or disintegrating bodies.

Notes

1. Sanna Lehtonen, *Girls Transforming: Invisibility and Age-shifting in Children's Fantasy Fiction Since the 1970s* (Jefferson: McFarland, 2013), p. 9.
2. Marah Gubar, *Artful Dodgers: Reconceiving the Golden Age of Children's Literature* (Oxford: Oxford University Press, 2009), pp. 4–5.
3. Teresa Mangum, '*Little Women*: The Aging Female Character in Nineteenth-Century British Children's Literature,' in *Figuring Age: Women, Bodies, Generations*, ed. Kathleen Woodward (Bloomington, Indiana: Indiana University Press, 1999), p. 61.
4. Ibid., pp. 67–68.
5. Ruth E. Ray, 'The Personal as Political: The Legacy of Betty Friedan,' in *Age Matters: Re-Aligning Feminist Thinking*, ed. Toni M. Calasanti and Kathleen F. Slevin (New York: Routledge, 2006), p. 41.
6. Catriona Mackenzie, 'Personal Identity, Narrative Integration, and Embodiment,' in *Embodiment and Agency*, ed. Sue Campbell, Letitia Meynell and Susan Sherwin (Pennsylvania: The Pennsylvania State University Press, 2009), p. 121.
7. Penelope Deutscher 'Three Touches to the Skin and One Look: Sartre and Beauvoir on Desire and Embodiment,' in *Thinking Through the Skin*, ed. Sarah Ahmed and Jackie Stacey (London: Routledge, 2001), p. 154.
8. Sylvia Henneberg, 'Moms Do Badly, but Grandmas Do Worse: The Nexus of Sexism and Ageism in Children's Classics,' *Journal of Aging Studies*, 24 (2010), p. 132.
9. Basile, Giambattista. *Giambattista Basile's The Tale of Tales, or Entertainment for the Little Ones*, translated by Nancy L. Canepa (Detroit: Wayne State University Press, 2007), p. 195.
10. Marina Warner, *From the Beast to the Blonde: On Fairy Tales and Their Tellers* (London: Vintage, 1995), p. 14.
11. The short film's critical success and popular content mean that although not as well-known as other examples in this essay, like the films of Disney or Miyazaki, it nonetheless provides an interesting example of the representation of ageing in popular culture.
12. Betty Friedan, *The Fountain of Age* (New York: Simon & Schuster, 1993), p. 30.
13. Charles Perrault, *The Complete Fairy Tales*, translated by Christopher Betts (Oxford: Oxford University Press, 2009), p. 83.
14. Sinead Gillett, 'Sketching Success: Brown Bag Films go to the Oscars,' *Estudios Irlandeses*, 5 (2010), p. 237.
15. Warner, p. xx.
16. Zoe Brennan, *The Older Woman in Recent Fiction* (Jefferson, NC: McFarland, 2005), p. 17.
17. Diana Wynne Jones, *Howl's Moving Castle* (New York: Harper Collins, 1986), p. 22.
18. Lehtonen, p. 94.
19. Moira Gatens, *Imaginary Bodies* (London: Routledge, 1996), p. 12.
20. Wynne Jones, p. 108.
21. Elizabeth Parsons, 'Animating Grandma: The Indices of Age and Agency in Contemporary Children's Films,' *Journal of Aging, Humanities, and the Arts*, 1 (2007).

22. As adult entertainment, a more in-depth examination of these films falls outside this chapter's remit.

23. Friedan, p. 30.

24. A notable exception is Disney's *The Emperor's New Groove* (Mark Dindal, 2000). The villain is an old woman, Yzma. However, she confidently wears a sexy, slinky dress and, it is implied, has a 'toy-boy.' She does not aim to achieve youth, but considers herself beautiful as an old woman. Rather than being destroyed, she is changed into an adorable kitten. Her exasperation with her new form actually underscores the importance of her embodied subjectivity: her old body is essential to her identity.

25. Merry G. Perry, 'Animated Gerontophobia: Ageism, Sexism, and the Disney Villainess,' in *Aging and Identity: A Humanities Persepctive*, ed. Sara Munson Deats and Lagretta Tallent Lenker (Westport, CT: Praeger, 1999), p. 204.

26. Perry, p. 204.

27. However, the series is highly problematic in privileging biological maternity over adoptive.

28. Elizabeth Bell, 'Somatexts at the Disney Shop: Constructing the Pentimentos of Women's Animated Bodies,' in *From Mouse to Mermaid: The Politics of Film, Gender, and Culture*, ed. Elizabeth Bell, Lynda Haas and Laura Sells (Bloomington: Indiana University Press, 1995), p. 121.

29. Peter Öberg, 'Images versus Experience of the Aging Body,' in *Aging Bodies: Images & Everyday Experience*, ed. Christopher A. Faircloth (Walnut Creek, Cal: AltaMira Press, 2003), p. 116.

30. 'Harrison Ford Biography,' *IMDb*, available at http://www.imdb.com/name/nm0000148/bio. (Accessed 15 December 2013).

31. Öberg, p. 120.

32. Parsons, 'Animating Grandma.'

Index

CPSIA information can be obtained
at www.ICGtesting.com
Printed in the USA
LVOW04*2108180216
475681LV00010B/430/P